D0992501

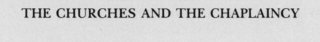

THE CHURCHES AND THE CHAPLAINCY

THE
CHURCHES
AND THE
CHAPLAINCY

Richard G. Hutcheson, Jr.

JOHN KNOX PRESS
ATLANTA

Acknowledgement is made to the following for permission to quote from the sources listed below:

Bureau of Naval Personnel, Chaplains Division, for *Because of You.* Published by the Chaplains Division, Bureau of Naval Personnel.

The Chaplain, for "The Chaplain and the Structures of the Military Society," by R.G. Hutcheson, Jr., *The Chaplain,* November/December, 1966, and "Parish of Transients: Military Ministry and the Chaplain," by R.G. Hutcheson, Jr., *The Chaplain,* June, 1968.

The Christian Century Foundation, for "Should the Military Chaplaincy be Civilianized?" by R.G. Hutcheson, Jr., copyright 1973 Christian Century Foundation. Reprinted by permission from the Oct. 31 issue of *The Christian Century.*

Donald B. Harris, for his pamphlet, "CREDO—The Second Year," and the May, 1974 CREDO newsletter.

U.S. Naval Institute, for "Religious Pluralism and the Navy Chaplaincy," by R.G. Hutcheson, Jr. Reprinted by permission from *Proceedings;* copyright © 1972 U.S. Naval Institute.

Preface

Since the height of the Vietnamese War, the total number of Americans in the armed forces has been reduced by about one-third. The draft has been ended. The military services are smaller than they have been at any time since the brief period between World War II and the Korean War. From one perspective, however, the striking thing is not the reduction of one million, but the two million who remain in the military. For more than thirty years now, a military force in excess of two million has been normal for the United States.

During the Vietnamese War the military chaplaincy came under serious attack in some church circles. But the American churches have probably never really doubted their responsibility to provide religious ministries for young Americans in uniform. Even now, with military forces reduced to what our government regards as the minimum peacetime level, there are more than three thousand chaplains on active duty. For more than thirty years, the number of clergymen in uniform has seldom fallen below that number. Often it has been much higher. By any standard, the military chaplaincy is a significant part of the contemporary ministry of the American churches.

But the churches do not seem to realize it. Strangely enough, no careful and reasonably objective analysis of the nature of this ministry, its military setting, and its relationship to the churches, has ever been made. If an interested churchman were to visit his public library—or even the library of the nearest theological seminary—looking for a basic book describing the military chaplaincy, he would find that there is no such thing. The titles of two recent works might give the impression of such an approach. A 1969 book by sociologist Gordon C. Zahn was called *The Military Chaplaincy,* and a 1972 book edited by theologian Harvey G. Cox was entitled *Military Chaplains.* Both, however, were somewhat partisan books, growing out of the anti-war movement of the Vietnamese War period, and neither made an attempt to be either dispassionate or comprehensively descriptive. Zahn's book reported on a research project conducted with British RAF chaplains, designed to demonstrate role tension in military chaplains and reflecting the author's avowedly pacifist position. The Cox book, sponsored and published by the anti-war organization, Clergy and Laymen Concerned about Vietnam, was equally partisan in its approach. It contained an excellent essay by George H. Williams tracing the history of the military chaplaincy. An essay by Robert McAfee Brown provided an examination of the military chaplaincy as ministry, which was thoughtful and helpful, even if colored by the author's revulsion toward the Vietnamese War and his conviction that the church could not be related to it. Taken as a whole, though, the book was clearly polemical in purpose and anti-chaplaincy in tone. No book designed simply to analyze and describe the chaplaincy and its relationship to the churches has been written.

Another sign of the failure of the churches to take the military chaplaincy seriously is to be found in the fact that it has been ignored until recently by the theological seminaries. Few seminaries offer courses to prepare clergymen for this highly specialized ministry. Yet chaplains are involved, as representatives of the churches, in some of the most delicate and controversial issues now facing the churches—in areas such as church-state relations, civil religion, the relationship of the ecclesiastical and the secular, ministry with young adults, ecumenism, and religious pluralism. *De facto*—by their words and their actions—chaplains are establishing in behalf of the churches a climate of opinion and a number of precedents in some of these areas, in ways of which the churches seem scarcely aware.

There have been several reasons for this failure to take the military chaplaincy seriously as a specialized ministry of the churches. One is historical. Our country had no tradition of a large peacetime military force prior to World War II. Our dominant image was that of the citizen-soldier, mustered in times of national crisis but returning as quickly as possible to civilian pursuits. The churches, like the nation at large, were accustomed to thinking of the chaplaincy as a rare wartime expedient. A second factor lies in the discomfort of the churches with their own military involvement. This traditional discomfort, with its roots in the American pattern of separation of church and state and in the strain of pacifism which has always been present in American Christianity, became particularly strong during the unpopular Vietnamese War. It has now subsided somewhat, but it is likely to—and it should—continue to exist. A third factor is the failure of the chaplaincies themselves to produce a serious body of scholarship. Military ministry is action-oriented, more given to "can-do" than to reflection. For these and other reasons the churches, and often the chaplains themselves, have failed to see the military chaplaincy as a distinctive field of ministry, meriting careful examination and analysis.

It has been my purpose, in preparing this book, to at least begin an attempt at filling the void. This is, I believe, the first book to offer a detailed analysis of the military chaplaincy as a specialized ministry, a unique career field for clergymen. It examines the ways in which it is different from civilian parish ministry and the special kinds of skill and training required for effective military ministry. It is, I believe, the first book to examine the military chaplaincy from a sociological perspective. Utilizing insights from organizational studies, it looks at the place of a chaplaincy within American military institutions. It also looks at the chaplaincy in the light of certain sociological factors in the American culture, including religious pluralism and civil religion. Finally, I believe it is the first book to explore the relationship of the chaplaincy to the American churches, tracing the history of that relationship and the development of denominational chaplaincy structures. It discusses current controversial issues within the churches relating to the chaplaincy, and points to some directions for the future.

Military chaplains are full-fledged clergymen of their churches, and at the same time full-fledged officers of their respective military services. This widely recognized but little understood institutional duality is a key to analyzing and evaluating the military chaplaincy. We shall examine this specialized ministry from both perspectives, military and church. The first half of the book looks at the military side. Armed forces have a character of their own. They are "total institutions," encompassing far more of a soldier's life than his 8-to-5 working hours, and they engender a strong sense of the difference between insiders and outsiders. They are also bureaucracies, and their organizational goals are quite different from the churches' goals of religious ministry. These sociological characteristics of military organizations, their implications for ministry, and the advantages and disadvantages they offer, we will examine in some detail. Against this background some of the unique dimensions of military ministry will be suggested: It is a ministry to the entire institution—to a cross-section of the population, churched and unchurched alike. It is a young adult ministry, eighty percent of the military population being under thirty. It is a ministry characterized by a unique kind of mobility. And it is an ecumenical ministry, bringing together clergymen and churchmen of all denominations, and giving them opportunities to travel all over the world.

The second half of the book examines the chaplaincy in the light of its relationship to the churches. This relationship has developed, and has assumed its own special character, in a climate of religious pluralism. In the early days, chaplains were left entirely to the military; the churches took no interest. Not until the beginning of this century did they even assert their right to examine the qualifications and endorse their clergy-men entering the armed forces. Even today, the problems of a hundred or more autonomous denominations dealing with the armed forces are formidable. The chaplaincy, however, has developed a pattern of cooperative pluralism which has made a significant contribution to American religious life.

The phenomenon of American civil religion has received much recent attention, and chaplains, as living embodiments of both church and state, are a focal point for this attention. We will examine the involvement of chaplains in civil religion. Particularly close attention will be given to the massive military programs of "character education," and to recent involvements of chaplains in a variety of personal growth and human relations programs. The discussion points up the need for the churches to take a more active role in guiding such activities of chaplains.

Controversial issues, such as the replacement of the military chaplaincy with civilian ministries to the armed forces, the holding of rank and wearing of uniforms by chaplains, will be examined in the final chapter. A variety of ways in which the churches of America can assume a larger role in chaplaincy affairs, and ways in which ministry to the armed forces can be strengthened and improved, will be explored.

It was noted above that recent books on the chaplaincy have been polemical in purpose and anti-chaplaincy in tone. It may be charged that my own effort is equally one-sided from a pro-chaplaincy perspective, since I am, at the time of writing, an active duty Navy chaplain completing a thirty-year career, with the rank of rear admiral—a natural-born institution-defender if there ever was one! I can only reply that I have sought to be as objective as I could, examining problem areas as well as strengths of the present chaplaincy system. The reader will note that the main thrust of the book is toward change—in the direction of more active involvement in military ministry on the part of the churches.

I believe I can lay some claim to the perspective of a churchman as well as that of a chaplain. Throughout my ministry as a chaplain I have maintained an active involvement in the affairs of my denomination (the Presbyterian Church in the United States). While on active duty as a chaplain I have twice served as Moderator of my Presbytery, and three times represented it as a Commissioner to General Assembly. I have served on my Synod's Mission Council, and in addition to chairing for several years the General Assembly's Advisory Council on Chaplains, I have participated repeatedly in the denomination's more general activities. I have served on a committee to plan a denomination-wide youth convention, and have taught a class on young adults at a conference of civilian churchmen. From 1969 to 1972 I served on the Ad Interim Committee of the General Assembly which designed the present structure of the denomination's national level boards and agencies. For these opportunities to participate in the life of the whole church I have been deeply grateful, and I mention them here only to suggest that I have at least the potential of being something other than a narrowly pro-chaplaincy institution-defender.

If my readers judge that I have not succeeded in transcending such parochialism, I shall have to settle for the comforting belief that at least the pro-chaplaincy side needed presenting! Several denominations are now engaged in studies of ministries to the military. Other studies will, I trust, be made in the future—in the universities and seminaries as well as the church agencies. It is my hope that this book can contribute to that ongoing process, and thus to a more effective ministry to those millions of young Americans who continue—even in an era of detente and a time of peace—to serve our nation in the armed forces.

Richard G. Hutcheson, Jr.
Norfolk, Virginia
July, 1974

Acknowledgments

This book grows out of thirty years as a Navy chaplain. It is based, to a considerable extent, on personal experience, observation, and reflection. But many, many others have contributed to it. Of special importance has been the help of two chaplains—one in the Air Force and one in the Army—who assisted me in my attempt to ensure that the book is applicable to the chaplaincies of all three services. Chaplain (COL) Richard D. Miller, U. S. Air Force, and Chaplain (LTCOL) John Hoogland, U. S. Army, both read the manuscript. They gave me a number of helpful suggestions and directed me to sources of information. I am deeply indebted to them. All decisions were my own, however, and to whatever extent the policies or practices of their services may be inaccurately represented in this book, the fault is entirely mine, not theirs.

I wish to express my appreciation also to several Navy chaplains who read the manuscript—Chaplains Joseph T. Dimino, John V. Boreczky, Fred R. McAlister, Jr., and Charles L. Greenwood, all of the staff of the U. S. Navy Chaplains School. Chaplain Greenwood was particularly helpful on constitutional issues. I am grateful to several other Navy chaplains, mentioned at various points in the book, whose work I have referred to or whose writings I have quoted, and to all my colleagues in the chaplaincy from whom I have learned through many years of association.

Finally, I want to acknowledge the contribution of my family. My children, Rick, Bill and Libby, have been patient and long-suffering. My deepest gratitude of all goes to my wife, Helen, whose common sense, wisdom, and accurate judgments provided a sounding board and a means of testing my own perceptions throughout my years of Navy ministry. I could not have done it without her.

I would like to emphasize that all statements and opinions are my own, and that they do not in any way represent the position of the Navy Department.

Contents

THE CHURCHES AND THE CHAPLAINCY

Chapter 1
The Chaplain's Two Institutions

Writers on the military chaplaincy frequently begin with the story of St. Martin of Tours, a compassionate fourth century soldier who encountered a shivering beggar on a cold winter night. Having no money in his purse, he took off his cloak and slashed it with his sword to give half to the beggar. Later that night he had a vision in which he saw Christ wearing the half-cloak. As a result of this experience he was baptized as a Christian. Ultimately he left the army to devote his life to the church. In time he became the patron saint of the French kings of the Middle Ages. St. Martin's cloak *(cappella)* was carried into battle by the kings as a banner signifying the presence of God. But since the *cappella* was a sacred relic of the church, a priest went along as custodian. This keeper of the cloak, or *cappellanus,* also tended the king's religious needs, and from his office was derived that of "chaplain." The depository for the cloak became the "chapel," the place of worship.

The story is more than a quaint bit of etymology explaining the origin of the terms "chaplain" and "chapel." It is also a clue which points to the essential nature of the chaplaincy. The *cappellanus* was a member of one institution—a priest of the church—serving in another institution—the king's army. Definitions of the chaplaincy seldom take sufficient account of this fact of institutional duality. Chaplains are unique in the military as the only group of officers whose primary identification is with a non-military institution. But they are also unique in the church, as the only large group of the clergy whose vocational identification is with a non-church social institution. A chaplain has "one foot in heaven" and the other in a combat boot.

An appreciation of the significance of institutional duality—the fact that a chaplain is not just affiliated with, but is fully part of, two major social institutions—is a key to understanding both the problems and the opportunities of the chaplaincy. Part of the difficulty is that it is so obvious. The dual relationship is taken for granted by everyone familiar with the chaplaincy. But the implications have not really been taken seriously by the American churches until quite recently. Only the Roman Catholic church has asserted real control over its chaplains. Within the armed forces even now there are many—including some chaplains—who pay little attention to the fact that military clergymen have a dual set of obligations.

Recently a Navy chaplain introduced his denominational supervisor to his commanding officer with the words, "This is the only man who could get me out of the service quicker than you could." The official was flattered, for this is the way denominations would like to regard their authority. Strictly speaking, however, this is not true. Denominational endorsement is required by law before a chaplain can be commissioned, and it is widely assumed that withdrawal of the endorsement terminates the commission. Generally, this is indeed the result. But there is still no law on the statute books requiring the revocation of the commission under such circumstances. Until recently you could search in vain for any substantial references to church relationship or church authority in the military regulations governing chaplains, and such references are still sketchy.

A serious debate on the chaplaincy has been going on in church circles in recent years. Spearheaded by an organization named Clergy and Laity Concerned about Vietnam, the debate was initially an out-growth of the resurgent pacifism and anti-military feeling prominent within the churches during the Vietnamese War. Published by the organization was the highly critical book, *Military Chaplains,* under the editorship of Harvey Cox.[1] There was much discussion in church journals, particularly the *Christian Century,* of the propriety of clergymen serving in the armed forces in a war which many churchmen regarded as unjust and indefensible. Several denominations (particularly the more liberal Protestant denominations) began studies of the chaplaincy in this context.

As time went on, the end of the Vietnamese War brought a changed perspective. The debate continues within the churches, but it may now fairly be maintained that its thrust is an effort to work out the full implications of institutional duality for chaplains. Much of the debate in church circles has focused on questions now within the military purview—the wearing of uniforms and holding of rank by chaplains, their subjection to military regulations and accountability to military commanders. The churches appear to be seeking to stake out a wider area of responsibility for the ministry of their chaplains in the armed forces and to give greater reality to the chaplain's dual role as member of the church as well as the military.

Few writers about the chaplaincy have until now given serious attention to institutional duality. George H. Williams, author of the excellent brief history of the military chaplaincy included in the Cox volume, saw clearly that the ministry of chaplains is "fundamentally different from that of his pastoral colleagues" because of the chaplain's relationship to the non-religious institution in which he serves. But he noted the difference primarily in terms of the procedures by which the chaplain is chosen and installed in his work.[2] The major aspect of the dual relationship on which he focused was his claim that the Army and Navy have historically taken the place of denominations for chaplains. The implications were not developed beyond this. Few other writers have examined the issue at all.

A full exploration of what it means to be a member of two major social institutions, of the effect of this dual responsibility on the chaplaincy and its potential for creative ministry, will be one of the tasks of this book.

ROLE CONFLICT

Under ordinary circumstances, the vocational identity of a minister is almost completely established by his church. It is the church that controls his professional education in denominational schools. In ordination it confers his credentials. His career unfolds within its institutional structures. His job assignments, his salary scale, his vocational changes and progression, his continuing education opportunities are all determined by institutional regulation or custom. This is no less true in free churches than in those of an episcopal polity. The professional reward and punishment system, the professional expectations and retirement prospects, even the life style, are to a considerable extent church-established. "I am a Baptist minister" or "I am a Catholic priest" is a far more all-encompassing statement than "I am an accountant." It says it all.

To an even greater extent, the professional life of a military officer is governed by his service. Not only are much of his education and training, his commission, his job assignments, his salary and promotions completely under military control, but even the clothes he wears at work and much of his social life are institutionally determined. To say "I am an Air Force officer" says it all.

The chaplain is not just half-military and half-church. He is fully a member of both institutions. Though he leaves the job environment of the church, he retains his full institutional status. He is still subject to the authority of his bishop or his presbytery. He is not only expected but probably required to attend periodically meetings of the annual conference or synod to which he belongs or retreats provided by his church. His function in the armed forces is that of a clergyman, and in reality he cannot continue to function without the ordination and endorsement of his church.

But at the same time he is a commissioned officer and fully a part of his military organization. He wears the same uniform, obeys the same regulations, is paid the same salary, and is assigned to duty by the same kind of orders as any other officer. The chaplain participates fully in both institutions at once.

Students of the chaplaincy have noted that most of the sociological research in the field has focused on role conflict.[3] The first significant research was done by Waldo W. Burchard in the period shortly after World War II.[4] His research instrument consisted of questions designed to "bring the respondent face to face with the proposition that the role of military officer conflicts with that of minister of the gospel."[5] Several other doctoral dissertations and briefer research projects have examined various facets of the role conflict issue.[6] A 1969 book by sociologist Gordon C. Zahn, based on a study of the chaplaincy of the Royal Air Force, focused on "role tension" between the clergyman role and that of military officer.[7] The movement in the American churches for a reexamination of the military chaplaincy, which, as we have noted, began during the Vietnamese War, has made this role conflict issue one of its major concerns. The military officer role was identified with the policies of the government in waging an unpopular war and with incidents, such as the My Lai massacre, which epitomized American revulsion to the war. This role was considered by a substantial number of churchmen to be so incompatible with the clergy role as to necessitate doing away with the chaplaincy.

In a group of persons who are simultaneously full members of two social institutions as disparate as the church and the military, the existence of role conflict is not surprising. The surprising thing would be its absence. But the existence of role conflict is not in itself necessarily a negative factor. The chaplaincy is a profession which deliberately makes role conflict a way of life, and the relevant question is not whether it exists, but how useful the results may be. We will seek to make an assessment of the ministry in which that role conflict is a crucial and—according to some some chaplains—creative element.

Contemporary critics of the chaplaincy have often sought to dramatize the role conflict issue in terms of a choice between Christ or Caesar. On one occasion I was asked by a magazine interviewer, "Do you think it is true, as some claim, that military rank and salaries are operating to make chaplains the servants of Caesar and not of Christ?" It is well to remember that the biblical injunction to "choose this day whom you will serve" did not appear in this context. Rather, Christ's advice was to "render to Caesar the things that are Caesar's, and to God the things that are God's."

Both Burchard and Zahn have claimed that when a chaplain is faced with a situation in which there is a conflict between the expectations of

his clergy role and his military role, he is likely to resolve it in favor of
the military. Zahn noted however, that his conclusion was directly contrary to the chaplains' own verbal assessment of the way in which they
resolve such issues, as given in their responses to a specific question in
this research instrument. Zahn also found that the self-image of the
chaplains whose attitudes he studied almost universally put the clergy
role first and the military officer role second.[8] Some light may be cast on
the differing perceptions of the primacy of the roles by noting the way
in which both institutions are present in the chaplain's perceived world.

   The chaplain's immediate institutional environment is military. His
ministry takes place in the armed forces, and the external characteristics
of his life are militarily determined. He wears the uniform rather than the
clerical collar. Authority resides in a commanding officer rather than a
bishop, a vestry, a session, or a board of deacons. His parishioners are
military people, his church is a military chapel, his laws are military
regulations, and he may be out of direct touch with his own church's
institutional environment for months or even years at a time. It would be
natural to conclude, under these circumstances, that the military influence is dominant, that he has "left the church and entered the military."
A closer examination, however, reveals that the institutional environment
of the church is also immediately present for the chaplain.

   Three elements provide this environment. First, the chapel program in which the work-life of the chaplain is centered, while military in
sponsorship, is thoroughly ecclesiastical in character. Its activities—
church services, choirs, lay councils, religious education programs, community service activities—parallel the activities of the civilian parish. Most
important of all, its goals are religious goals rather than military goals.
While the chapel program is a voluntary, off-duty concern of the military
laymen who participate, it is the primary, on-duty concern of the chaplain.
Its goals are collateral goals for his parishioners, but the central goals of
his work-life. So even in military surroundings, he continues to be vocationally in the church.

   A second environmental element is provided by his chaplain colleagues. The chaplain is part of a military system, but he is also part of
a Chaplain Corps subsystem within it.[9] All his colleagues in the Chaplain
Corps subsystem are, like him, clergymen. To the extent that there is
validity in Williams' hypothesis (not pressed, but repeatedly suggested in
his historical essay) that the Army and Navy have taken the place of
denominations for chaplains, it is probable that it is the Chaplain Corps
of his service, rather than the service itself, which has so operated.

   The Chaplain Corps of each armed service does perform some

functions analogous to those performed by denominational relationships in civilian life. There are corps-wide administrative structures for facilitation of ministry. Provision is made for continuing education, for spiritual retreats, and for professional development. A chaplain's most significant long-term associations are likely to be within his own corps. The group environment thus provided is an important part of his overall environment. Its norms, like those of the chapel program which is the focal point of his work-life, have their source in the church world rather than the military world. In a later chapter we will take a closer look at this Chaplain Corps subsystem within the military system.

A third element which extends the institutional environment of the church into the military world is provided by the denominational structures which oversee the chaplaincy. Each denomination has officials who visit, counsel with, and provide ecclesiastical supervision for chaplains. Each denomination requires reports from its chaplains. Each denomination either encourages or requires periodic attendance at meetings of church courts or conventions. While these denominational relationships are not so pervasive in the everyday life of the chaplain as the chapel program and the Chaplain Corps subsystem, they do serve to keep him continually reminded of the non-military institution which establishes his vocational goals and to which he owes his primary professional allegiance.

Although it is true, then, that a chaplain is a church professional whose ministry takes place in a secular institution outside the church, it is not true that he has "left the church and entered the military." In a real sense he takes the institutional environment of the church with him into the military. A substantial part of the perceived world in which he lives and works is determined by church norms rather than military norms.

HISTORICAL DEVELOPMENT OF INSTITUTIONAL DUALITY

This was not always the case. In the early days of the American military chaplaincy, institutional duality was for all practical purposes non-existent. At that stage of our history, the churches themselves had not, for the most part, assumed the complete institutional form by which they are now characterized. As institutions they had little or nothing to do with the establishment of a chaplaincy. It came about, rather, as a result of the felt need of the citizen-soldiers and sailors of the revolutionary period for the same kind of parochial religious leadership in war to which they were accustomed at peace. The initiative came largely from the militiamen and seamen themselves, and the major institutional loyalty of the early chaplains was to the military congregations they served.

The desirability of a chaplaincy was never really debated in the colonial and revolutionary period when the American armed forces were formed. It was taken for granted. The Continental Army grew out of the local and state militia, and militiamen brought their own parson—usually the town minister—into battle with them as a matter of course. The Diary of President Stiles of Yale indicates that on November 17, 1774, eighty-three armed men of East Guilford marched off with Mr. Todd, their pastor; a hundred men of Haddon with their pastor, Mr. May; and a hundred more from Chatham with their pastor, Mr. Boardman.[10] This pattern was not unusual.

The identification of the interests of the new nation with the interests of Christianity was far more complete during the Revolution than it has been in later periods. In the middle of the last century, J. T. Headley, in one of the early books on the beginnings of American military chaplaincy, commented on their revolutionary ardor. In addition to being "earnest, self-denying ministers of God," many chaplains, he said

> were bold and active patriots besides, stirring up rebellion, encouraging the weak and timid by their example as well as by their teachings, and inspiring the brave and true with confidence by their heroism and lofty trust in the righteousness of the cause they vindicated.[11]

The method of appointing chaplains to the militia units varied from colony to colony. In Virginia, regimental chaplains were appointed by the legislature.[12] In most instances, however, the local initiative principle, with the pastor brought from home or selected by the unit he served, was the norm.

As the militia units were incorporated into the Continental Army, so were their chaplains. In July, 1775, the Continental Congress put the chaplaincy on a legal federal basis by providing that their pay be twenty dollars a month. Within a year after the official authorization of a chaplaincy by the Continental Congress, George Washington issued the following order:

> The honorable Continental Congress having been pleased to allow a Chaplain to each Regiment, the Colonels or commanding officers of each Regiment are directed to procure Chaplains accordingly; persons of good characters and exemplary lives—to see that all inferior officers and soldiers pay them a suitable respect and attend carefully upon religious exercises.[13]

Note that the responsibility was placed on regimental commanders to procure their own chaplains. From the beginning, then, the nation provided chaplains in both the Army and the Navy. There was no thought, however, of common standards, policies, or procurement practices. Not even ordination was a universal requirement. Local initiative and local choice on the part of the militia company, regiment, or ship were the rules for the early period of American military history.[14] The federal government was scarcely involved, and the American religious denominations, as institutions, were not involved at all.

The American churches showed little interest in establishing standards or exercising control over military chaplains throughout the early years of the chaplaincy's existence. The central government gradually assumed responsibility as needs became apparent. Such public debate and legislative action as took place throughout the nineteenth century centered around such matters as pay, uniform, rank, and officer status. The churches as institutions took little or no part in these early debates. The *General Regulations* issued by the Navy Department in 1841 required for the first time that any person appointed a chaplain in the Navy "be a regularly ordained or licensed clergyman,"[15] but a later ruling by the Attorney General determined that the Navy Department did not have the authority to issue such regulations. The first federally-established standards for Army chaplains came with the Act of Congress of 17 July 1872. In addition to ordination or its equivalent, that legislation required a recommendation from the ordaining denomination or from five accredited ministers of that denomination. Similar legislation for Navy chaplains, with the additional requirement of a Bachelor of Arts or Bachelor of Divinity degree and at least one year of pastoral experience, failed to pass the Congress in 1878, but was passed in 1880 with the deletion of the educational requirement.

It should be noted that these developments did not originate in institutional pressure from the churches; major impetus for the establishment of professional standards came from the chaplains themselves. Navy chaplain Joseph Stockbridge, in an 1853 letter to the Secretary of the Navy, complained of the adverse effect on the ministry of chaplains' exclusive accountability to their commanding officers. "Besides these considerations," he added, "there is no ecclesiastical power to which Chaplains are accountable."[16]

As chaplains gradually began to acquire a feeling of identity within their respective services, they sought to establish some measure of control over their professional life. In 1878 six chaplains petitioned the Secretary of the Navy to establish a Board of Chaplains to pass on the credentials and professional qualifications for appointment. In 1906 a group of three chaplains, appointed by the Secretary of the Navy to make a study, presented a similar recommendation, and in 1908 such a board was for the first time established. A Chief of Chaplains was for the first time appointed in the Navy in 1917, and the Army acquired its first Chief of Chaplains in 1920.

Denominational interest in establishing control over the chaplaincy lagged far behind the development of corps identity and organization within the services. The first evidences of interest came during the Civil War. Several southern denominations took an active interest in recruiting chaplains for the Confederate Army, and there was some evidence of similar interest in the North. General awareness of the responsibility of the churches did not become nationally visible, however, until the Spanish-American War. The Protestant Episcopal Church recommended in 1898 that the denomination be consulted before the appointment of any Episcopalian as a chaplain. The government, accepting this principle, established a firm requirement for denominational endorsement for chaplains of both services in congressional acts of 1899 and 1901.[17]

This denominational approval, now known as "ecclesiastical endorsement," has been a firm requirement for appointment since that time. The form and source of such endorsement varied widely for many more years, but the requirement led denominations to begin establishing agencies and procedures for providing it. The Catholic archbishops of the United States in 1905 appointed a representative to deal with the government in the appointment of Catholic chaplains. In 1906 the bishops of the Methodist Espicopal Church, North, asked President Theodore Roosevelt to refer all Methodist candidates for appointment to a board headed by Bishop Cranston of Washington, and this procedure was established.[18] At no time did the government resist participation by the denominations in chaplaincy matters when such participation was offered.

It was at the time of the First World War that institutional concern of the churches for the chaplaincy began to take firm form. In 1914 a number of Protestant churches adopted a unified approach in their dealings with the military services. The Federal Council of Churches in that year established a Washington Committee on Army and Navy Chaplains, consisting of two Methodists, two Presbyterians, and two Episcopalians. After the declaration of war this committee was reorganized to include one member of each of the thirty-two denominations constituting the Federal Council. At that time it was renamed the General Committee on Army and Navy Chaplains.[19]

A significant step in the development of institutional duality came from the Roman Catholic church in 1917, when the pope appointed

Auxiliary Bishop Patrick Hayes of New York as Military Bishop Ordinary. This had the effect of establishing a military diocese, consisting of Catholics in the armed forces under the religious leadership of their chaplains. For the first time a church assumed clear responsibility not just for standards and selection and endorsement of chaplains but also for their ministry to Catholic personnel within the armed forces. There was no inclination whatever on the part of the armed forces to challenge this assumption of ecclesiastical responsibility.

The Second World War brought the final stage in the evolution of the chaplaincy to the present level of institutional duality. With total mobilization for a war supported almost unanimously by the churches of the nation, thousands of civilian pastors became chaplains for the duration, with no sense of loss of denominational identification. The General Commission (formerly Committee) on Army and Navy Chaplains, now independent of the Federal Council, represented an even broader constituency than before. It still spoke for many of the Protestant denominations in dealing with the government, but a number of denominations also formed their own committees or agencies for chaplains. These committees no longer limited themselves solely to endorsement. The churches saw their task as that of extending their ministries to a whole nation at war. They provided equipment for chaplains such as portable altar kits, vestments, books, and Bibles. They published pamphlets and devotional books for military use. They sent their officials all over the world to visit and encourage their chaplains.

In the postwar years the pattern established during the war remained firmly fixed. The General Commission on Army and Navy Chaplains became the General Commission on Chaplains and Armed Forces Personnel, formalizing with the expanded name the Protestant churches' assumption of responsibility not only for the endorsing of chaplains, but for continuing ministry to their personnel in the military services. Wartime committees were replaced by permanent chaplaincy agencies in the administrative structures of the various denominations.

The pattern established by the Roman Catholic Military Ordinariate was highly influential as the model for institutional duality. As diocesan headquarters for all Catholics in the armed forces, the Ordinariate maintains central files for all ecclesiastical records of Catholic chaplains. Baptisms, confirmations, marriages, and other clerical activities are recorded there, and Catholics throughout the military are fully integrated into the institutional life of the church. Other denominations, within the limits of their own polities, have sought to establish similar operations.

PRESENT STATUS OF INSTITUTIONAL DUALITY

In the postwar period churches have demanded, and have been given, authority to participate in the career choices of chaplains entering the regular forces. Most chaplains are commissioned as reservists. When they enter active duty, it is generally for a specified term of years, after which those who so desire may return to civilian life and maintain through affiliation with the military reserve forces their availability for service in national emergencies.

All three services, however, have provisions for accepting into the regular forces those chaplains who apply to remain on active duty permanently. The churches have asserted the right to enter into such career choices by passing on the qualifications of those applying for regular status and re-endorsing prior to permanent appointment in the regular forces.

The churches have also asserted the right to terminate a chaplain's service at any time through withdrawal of ecclesiastical endorsement. That this issue has not yet been fully resolved is an indication that full institutional duality has not yet been achieved. The armed forces have cooperated with the churches to the extent that existing law permits, and without exception they have released reserve chaplains from active duty under such circumstances.

With chaplains of the regular forces, whose permanent tenure is safeguarded by law, the problem is different. The Army and Air Force have had mechanisms (complex, but workable) for releasing regular officers involuntarily (or at least removing them from the chaplaincy) under such circumstances, but the Navy has not. In most instances the combined pressure of church and military has been sufficient to persuade such chaplains to resign. In one instance, however, in the late sixties, a regular Navy chaplain whose endorsement had been withdrawn by his denomination refused to resign. The permanence of his commission, in the absence of officially documented unsatisfactory performance, was protected by law. A compromise was reached, under which he was permitted to remain in the service, still officially a member of the Chaplain Corps but assigned to non-chaplain duties for the two years remaining to enable him to retire with twenty years' service.

Legislation which would make release automatic upon withdrawal of ecclesiastical endorsement has been requested, but not yet enacted. It is interesting to note that even at this late stage of the evolution of church responsibility for chaplains, the request has been made, not by the churches, but by the chaplaincies, through military channels. It is also interesting to observe that the requested legislation does not take note of the unique character of ordination or the uniqueness of the chaplain's institutional duality. It treats ordination as analagous to medical licensure or a lawyer's membership in the bar, and seeks authorization for the release of *any* professional staff corps officer whose professional credentials are lost or withdrawn.

The services have long recognized officially the chaplain's status as a clergyman. The Army Field Manual governing the chaplaincy states:

> The chaplain in the Army represents a recognized religious denomination. His ecclesiastical status obliges him to observe the rules and regulations of his denomination, to maintain an active and continuing membership in his church, and to sustain an effective, continuing relationship to his denomination and its leaders.[20]

A new Navy *Chaplains Manual*, issued as a Chief of Naval Operations Instruction by the Navy Department early in 1974, contains the clearest statement of church responsibility which has thus far been given official standing in any military publication:

> THE CHAPLAIN AS A PROFESSIONAL REPRESENTATIVE OF HIS CHURCH
> 1. The term "professional" as used in this manual refers to those aspects of the chaplain's role which are determined not by the Navy, Marine Corps, or Coast Guard, but by the chaplain's identity as a member of the clergy, whose profession is the ministry of religion.
> 2. The Navy does not generate religious ministry. It receives ministries from the churches and religious bodies of America in accordance with the religiously pluralistic pattern of American society. The United States Code provides that:
> > "An officer of the Chaplain Corps may conduct public worship according to the manner and forms of the church of which he is a member." (10 U.S. Code 6031 [a].)
> The term "church" as used in this manual is used to include denominations and religious bodies of all faiths.
> 3. Since all liturgical, sacramental, and pastoral acts are performed on the basis of ecclesiastical rather than naval credentials, it follows that the ultimate responsibility for the substantive nature of chaplains' religious ministry rests with their churches.
> 4. The maintenance of ecclesiastical credentials (i.e., status as an ordained member of the clergy and valid ecclesiastical endorsement) is the official responsibility of each chaplain.
> 5. The religious context of the Navy, like that of American society at large, is one of religious pluralism, in which independent churches and religious bodies coexist in mutual respect. Because of the impracticality of providing clergy of every faith or denomination in every ship or station, the Navy and the churches of America have

evolved jointly a pattern of cooperative ministry. The principle of cooperative ministry places on every chaplain the obligation to:

    a. Make provision for meeting the religious needs of those in the command who are adherents of other churches.

    b. Cooperate with other chaplains and commands in meeting the religious needs of members of the chaplain's own faith group.[21]

Throughout this manual, official attention is given to the chaplain's relationship to his own church. Explicit recognition is given to all the following aspects of this relationship: (1) the desirability of chaplains preaching, speaking, or otherwise participating in civilian church affairs, (Sec. 1206); (2) the responsibility of the Chief of Chaplains for "liaison with the churches and religious bodies of America, interpreting church policy and positions to the Navy and Navy policy and needs to the churches" (Sec. 2101[4]); (3) encouragement of chaplain participation in local ministeriums, clergy organizations, and Councils of Churches (Sec. 2303[1]); (4) the submission of reports required by churches as an official duty of chaplains (Sec. 2504[5]); (5) the safeguarding of denominational requirements, liturgical and sacramental customs, and church rules in ecumenical services and cooperative ministries (Sec. 5204 and 5205); (6) the desirability of consultation with denominational officials when a chaplain feels that an assignment given by a commanding officer is inappropriate (Sec. 6403); (7) the desirability of close relationships with civilian churches (Sec. 6504); (8) ecclesiastical regulations governing marriage (Sec. 7101); and (9) the church as the sole source of the chaplain's authority to perform liturgical and sacramental functions (Sec. 8101).

This manual represents a far more extensive official recognition of institutional duality than has previously been apparent in any of the armed forces. It might be noted, however, that the initiative for this far-reaching statement came from the chaplaincy, within the Navy. There has been no known instance of church demands, or requests, for more explicit recognition of institutional duality in regulatory publications.

The churches have, however, been making some moves in the direction of assumption of more control and responsibility. In a highly publicized case in 1972, the American Baptist Convention challenged the right of the Navy to try by court martial a chaplain accused of immoral conduct, asserting that the church alone has authority over the conduct of its clergymen in such instances. The jurisdiction of the military over officers accused of violations of the Uniform Code of Military Justice was clearly maintained in this instance. But the Navy did recognize, in its negotiations with denominational officials, that the church has a legitimate interest in the rights and treatment of its clergymen under such circumstances.

DENOMINATIONAL TASK FORCE REPORTS

In 1973 a task force, which had been appointed by the United Church of Christ to "examine the church's ministry to military personnel, particularly as that ministry is embodied in the military chaplaincy,"[22] presented a report to the Ninth General Synod of that church. The report, which was the subject of a good bit of controversy on the floor of the Synod, was approved "in principle," but referred to a special committee for further study and resubmission to the Tenth General Synod. The heart of the report was a call for a sweeping "demilitarization" of the chaplaincy. The specific recommendations included several having a direct bearing on institutional duality:

(1) That standards set by the military regarding the education and age of chaplains be abolished, such standards to be set by each denomination for its own clergymen.[23]

(2) That military screening of candidates for the chaplaincy be abolished. "We recognize only the power of ecclesiastical endorsement exercised by the churches and hold any parallel power on the part of Government to be illegitimate and an unallowable infringement of the church's authority over the qualifications to be set for exercising the ministry."[24]

(3) That the churches negotiate limits on the government security check on chaplaincy candidates.[25]

(4) That chaplains be removed from the control of commanding officers and placed "outside the chain of command and within an independent Chaplain's Corps."[26]

(5) That the Chief of this independent Chaplain's Corps be selected by the churches (final selection to be made by the President from three candidates by the churches).[27]

(6) That chaplains cease to be officers, with removal from the rank and promotion system, and that within the independent Chaplain's Corps they elect their own superiors and they themselves "administer the religious affairs of the military."[28]

The task force either did not examine, or preferred not to dwell on, the probable implication of these recommendations, namely that such an independent Chaplain Corps would become a group of civilian clergymen, serving with, but not part of, the armed forces. Since there were no recommendations for church funding, it must be assumed that the task force expected that the armed forces would continue to pay the salaries, provide the offices and assistance, and support the ministries of the group. The task force apparently assumed that such an independent group could remain part of the military from which it had been demilitarized. This was a somewhat unrealistic assumption. To believe that a military organization would extend full privileges of membership to a group of persons whose selection it has no part in, and over whose conduct and activities within the organization it has no control, reveals a startling naiveté about the military. The effect of the proposal, in reality, would be the complete removal of chaplains from membership in the military services to which they are expected to minister.

The task force recommendations, if adopted, would bring the evolution of institutional duality in a full circle. From an early history in which chaplains owed their sole institutional loyalty to the military, with no official allegiance to or control by the American churches, institutional duality would have been resolved once again, in the opposite direction, with sole institutional loyalty to the churches and no allegiance to or control by the military.

It seems highly improbable that such a step will be taken, either by the churches or by the government. The strong anti-military sentiment of the latter days of the Vietnamese War, which gave rise in some church circles to the conviction that the military role is completely incompatible with the clergyman role, seems clearly on the wane. The examination of the chaplaincy set in motion during that period, however, is likely to lead to a strengthening of church interest, activity, and supervision.

A United Presbyterian study, mandated in 1972, was approved by the General Assembly of that denomination in May, 1975. The background report was far more comprehensive than that of the UCC, and the conclusions were considerably more moderate in tone. The policy statement called unequivocally for a continuation of present arrangements for chaplaincy in the armed forces, as well as for church-sponsored supplementary ministries to military personnel. Its recommendations, however, raised serious questions, called for definitive studies, and proposed changes in a number of areas relating to the chaplaincy. The United Presbyterian report, while far less radical than that of the UCC, appears to point toward a considerably more active involvement of the church in military ministry than has been customary in the past.

Several other denominations, notably the Episcopal church, began studies of the chaplaincy in the early seventies.[29] The end result of the studies is likely to be a further extension of church control over certain aspects of the chaplain's ministry, completing the development of institutional duality which started at the turn of the century and leading to a clearer recognition that the ministry of chaplains is an extension of the ministries of the churches that provide them. The evolution, however, is still far from complete. Many denominational officials still regard themselves primarily as "endorsing officials," screeners of chaplaincy applicants. They are minimally involved in the ministry of chaplains once they are appointed.

Current developments would seem to indicate that this laissez-faire attitude is coming to an end. The United Presbyterian task force report probably points toward the direction for the future: a full recognition on the part of the churches of the implications of institutional duality for them. This means greater church interest, more effective supervision, stronger church-chaplain relationships, and a genuine role for the churches in the shaping of ministry. The churches must recognize the primacy of the military in those matters directly related to the holding of a commission: security, military regulations and laws, integration into the military command structures. But the churches have a clear primacy of interest in the nature of the religious ministry the chaplains provide.

ATTITUDE OF THE MILITARY

The implications of the institutional duality in which the chaplain functions have in the past perhaps been understood even less by military commanders than by civilian churchmen. The superficial aspects of a chaplain's identity as a Protestant, Catholic or Jewish clergyman are clearly recognized. Chaplains are recruited by the armed forces to serve as clergymen, and for no other purpose. A. B. Aronis, in 1972 research for a doctoral dissertation, compared the role perceptions of chaplains with those of their commanding officers. His research indicated that line commanders, even more consistently than chaplains themselves, give the traditional clergy roles of pastor-counselor and liturgist-preacher-priest primary importance in their expectations of chaplains.[30]

Yet the nature of the relationship of chaplains to their churches has not always been clearly perceived. Typical was the attitude of a commanding officer at a military base in the Far East. This commander took a paternal interest in the romance between one of the clerks in his office and an oriental girl of the Buddhist faith. When the young man popped the question and was accepted, the commanding officer volunteered to set up the wedding. He called me in to make the necessary arrangements. I advised him that I could only perform Christian weddings, and that I would not be able to officiate at a ceremony involving a Buddhist girl. The commanding officer exploded. "What do you mean you can't marry them? You're in the Navy, aren't you? You'll marry who I tell you to marry!" It took some tall talking on my part to convince him that I was not only in the Navy, but also in my church, and that my authority to perform marriages was controlled not by the former but by the latter.

Here was a senior military officer of many years' experience, who perceived clearly that a clergyman was required for a certain professional function, but did not understand the institutional duality inherent in the chaplaincy. Because I was also in the military service and a member of his command, he thought of me as his hired professional, available to do his bidding.

The armed services are accustomed to the use of professionals for those functions that come within their professional province. Physicians, dentists, nurses, lawyers—all have held commissioned officer status in the military services, along with chaplains, for many years. These groups of officers make up the "professional staff corps" of the various services. Against this background the military establishment is likely to think of a chaplain's ordination as being comparable to a physician's licensure or a lawyer's admission to the bar. It provides him with professional credentials. Similarly, the chaplain's church membership is thought of as comparable to the physician's membership in the American Medical Association or the lawyer's membership in the state bar.

The comparison is not an entirely a valid one. The medical association and the state bar are professional associations only. While the church operates in some ways as a professional association for its clergymen, its sociological function is far broader, its membership far more inclusive, and the place of clergymen within it is of a different order. The major difference lies at the point of organizational goals. The goals of professional societies are related primarily to the interests of the professionals who make up the membership. Such societies set standards, uphold canons of professional ethics, and promote professional welfare for the professionals who make them up. The goals of churches are related to the good of the entire society, as an institutionalization of the basic human need for religious belief and expression. The function of clergy professionals within them is instrumental in nature; clergymen are agents used by the churches in the realization of larger institutional goals, rather than the focal point of those goals.

All staff professionals incorporated into the military services bring with them professional specialties, standards, and ethical codes. Physicians, dentists, and lawyers, as well as chaplains, provide specialized services, available to the military only from their respective professions. Only chaplains, however, work for goals established by institutions outside the armed forces and are subject to the authority of those outside institutions. We shall look in some detail at the implications of this fact in a later chapter. Chaplains are the only military group who find it necessary to defend themselves against charges that they are "tools of the military establishment." Chaplains are willing to be regarded as tools only of their churches, pursuing their churches' goals within the military establishment.

Few military commanders are deeply aware of this difference between chaplains and other staff corps professionals, as we have noted in connection with proposed legislation on professional credentials. If they think about it at all, they probably regard it as unimportant. This is not to imply that they perceive any conflict between the institutional goals of the churches and their own best interest. They have long regarded provision for religious worship and expression as necessary for the human welfare of those who make up the armed forces. But they have continued to think of chaplains simply as their own professionals in the field of religion, as in the old days. Institutional duality in the Chaplain Corps has simply not been an important issue for them.

Military command is not likely to oppose moves on the part of the churches to take a more active interest in their clergymen and to exercise stronger institutional control over their ministerial functions, so long as there is no serious attempt to remove them from military command and control. As we have seen, a considerable measure of *de facto* recognition of institutional duality has evolved over the years, as the armed forces have reached accomodations with the institutional churches on matters relating to the chaplaincy. The authority over Catholic chaplains exercised by the Roman Catholic church, which has asserted its control over its priests from the beginning of its significant involvement with the armed forces, has long been recognized at every level.

Navy officials raised no objection at all to the statements regarding church relationships and responsibilities in the 1974 *Chaplains Manual.* The ministry of chaplains will be enhanced, however, as military people at every level understand more fully the institutional duality which characterizes all chaplains. The chaplaincy will be most effective when both churches and military services recognize clearly that the chaplain is fully a member of both institutions—a unique kind of officer and a unique kind of clergyman—with clear responsibilities in both directions.

Chapter 2
Setting for Military Ministry:
The Total Institution

The transition from the church environment into the institutional duality of the military environment is a critical step for chaplains.[1] In a graduation ceremony during my assignment as Officer-in-Charge of the Chaplains School, the class speaker described in vivid terms the pangs of transition from civilian parish to chaplaincy. "As a civilian minister," he said, "I was a person of some standing in my community. I had a comfortable church, a secretary, and a competent assistant. People looked up to me and respected me. Then I entered a strange world in which I had to shout, 'Attention on deck!' when someone, perhaps no older than me but clearly identified as an authority figure, entered the room. I learned to stand in a rigid brace at morning inspection while someone with more stripes on his sleeve looked me up and down as if I were a horse. I can only describe the experience as 'culture shock.' "

The graduating chaplains—now old salts of two months' longevity, the gold on their sleeves no longer glaringly new, capable of conversing fluently about bulkheads, billets and dogging the watch—laughed appreciatively if a bit nervously. They had by now survived the initial plunge and had adapted to the outward customs and conventions of the Navy. But the very intensity of their laughter revealed that they were still in that state of culture shock, and likely to remain there for some time to come. Indeed, there are some military chaplains who remain in culture shock for full twenty-year careers. For beneath the superficial level of adaptation to the external symbols and rituals, effective ministry as a military chaplain requires at a deeper level an understanding of the characteristics of the secular institution in which the ministry is to be offered. These characteristics are different from those of the civilian parish church, and unless the difference is understood, the chaplain may go on for years offering a kind of ministry which neither fits nor bears fruit in the institution he has joined.

The basic spiritual qualification can be taken for granted when a clergyman enters the armed forces as a chaplain. He begins with a mature religious faith, tested by time. He has a well-defined system of beliefs, shaped by his own conscience and experience and by the denomination to which he belongs and refined and strengthened by at least three years of high quality post-graduate education. He has acquired the essential skills—homiletical, liturgical, sacramental and pastoral—required by his ministerial or priestly profession. He comes equipped with an appreciation of and commitment to the spiritual dimension of life, and with the motivating force of a divine calling. The churches have rightly maintained that the priests, ministers, and rabbis endorsed by them to the armed forces are fully qualified for religious ministry. When the armed forces have become involved in education for ministry, as in the Navy's World War II V-12 program or the Army's Theological training program, they have left the content of such education entirely to the churches and the seminaries, attempting not even the slightest measure of interference. Ministerial qualification is the province of the church, and ministers enter the armed forces fully qualified in this sense.

But religious ministry never takes place in "spiritual" vacuum. Is is always *in* the world and *for* the world. "As thou didst send me into the world, so I have sent them into the world," said Christ of the apostles in his great prayer for the church, and he was careful to specify that he prayed "not that thou shouldst take them out of the world." The ministry is inevitably in the world, and the form of ministry must be appropriate to the particular "world" in which it takes place. The clergyman's tendency is always to think in terms of the parish church. Its institutional presuppositions have so long been taken for granted that they are often treated as if they were an integral part of every ministry.

The ministry-related courses listed in any seminary catalogue—homiletics, liturgics, worship, counseling, religious education, and pastoral care—all are based on parish church presuppositions. But in the ministry of chaplains, which takes place in a secular institution, it becomes necessary to distinguish the essential from the accidental, to separate the inner spirit from the outward shape. Failure to do so means that the form and style of ministry developed in and adapted to one institution will be carried over unwittingly into another, where they may fail to fit. The key to effective ministry as a military chaplain lies here: the secular institution must be understood; the form of ministry must be made relevant to the institution in which it is offered.

PRESUPPOSITIONS OF MINISTRY WITHIN THE CHURCH

It is useful to note first the presuppositions of ministry within the church, the chaplain's primary institution. Many of these are either not present or present in a radically altered form in the military institution. No claim is made that what follows is an exhaustive or even thorough treatment of those presuppositions. It is offered only as background against which the institutional presuppositions of the military service can be examined.

The Church in the Community

The nature of the community in which the church operates—rural, small town, suburban, inner-city urban, high-rise-apartment urban, poverty-ghetto urban—is in itself of great importance. (It can be argued that the church thus far has not really made its peace with any of these communities except the rural/small town community of its past and the suburban community, which it treats as a modernized version of the small town; but that is another matter.) For immediate purposes, however, the important thing is the place of the church in the community, and with a few exceptions the nature of the relationship is fairly constant regardless of the nature of the community. The church usually stands within the community, clearly recognized as having a significant place in its life, but maintaining a certain apartness. Many churches are deeply involved in social action, but seldom in partnership with other agencies similarly involved. There are exceptions, but generally the church has little direct relationship to the organs of government, commerce, industry, culture, recreation, education (with certain parochial school exceptions), or even social service in the community.

Church members are involved in these various secular institutions but their relationships with the church and the secular organs are parallel rather than integrated. The church expects to be respected by the community. It feels free to seek to influence the secular institutions (on such matters as the sale of alcoholic beverages, the moral tone of literature and movies, and Sabbath observance laws if it is conservatively oriented, and on racial integration, open housing, industrial relations, and welfare policies if it is liberally oriented), but it carefully maintains its independence from any form of influence or control that might be exerted by other community institutions.

Fuller involvement in and cooperation with secular agencies on the part of the church is growing; but in view of the requirements of religious pluralism, and the fear of religious establishment in any form in a period when various community structures are increasingly involved with government, a separation is likely to continue. The church still has some aspects of a "retreat" from the world. Its members, by and large, come apart from their secular pursuits to enter the life of the church. They come out of the world at eleven o'clock on Sunday morning to worship. Even in the church that offers in its parish house a variety of activities seven days a week, those who participate come out of the everyday world to do so. In church the context is different; the language used, the public face presented, the ground rules followed, are all different from everyday life.

The place and status of the minister or priest in society at large has changed significantly since the days when America was a rural/small town nation. But the place of the minister *in that portion of the society in which the church is a significant factor* has not altered materially, and from the standpoint of understanding the ministry, this is what counts. The minister or priest is the universally recognized leader of the church community, with a special "in-but-not-of" status in the community at large, expecting to be respected, free to influence but not to be influenced. His involvement in the secular institutions of the society may be extensive, but it is from the special stance of one who has his own base.

The Minister in the Church Organization

Within his own institution, the minister is the focal point of the organization. Associates and assistants, organist and minister of music, director of religious education, and administrative or clerical employees all report directly to the pastor. Regardless of denominational polity there is generally some form of congregational organization, and usually there is a vestry, session, council, or board of deacons exercising general oversight. The Sunday school, with its own superintendent and administrative staff, is organized into departments and classes. Other family–oriented program activities, for children, youth, and adults, all function through appropriate organizations. Despite denominational or functional differences, all the organizations of the local church tend to look to the minister or priest for leadership, and all of them see themselves as performing in some measure a supportive role for him. The minister is likely to be even more conscious of his leadership role and their supportive roles than are the organizations themselves; he sees them as arms or agencies through which he performs his ministry.

The Church as a Family-Oriented Institution

There is room for debate as to whether the family is still the basic unit in the American society at large. Beyond question, however, the family is still the basic unit of most parish churches. The central Sunday worship service is traditionally for the whole family—even more strongly in the Catholic tradition than in that of Protestants. Ancillary program divisions of the parish follow family lines: nursery for the infants; Sunday school and summer vacation church school for the children; Youth Fellowship and summer camp or conference activities for older children. Leaving the family home is almost universally the signal among youth for leaving these activities. "Women's Work," with its various circles and service activities occupies an ambiguous spot. In theory contemporary churchwomen resent such functional segregation as a manifestation of sexism, but in practice such activities continue to be strongly supported. Parallel "Men's Work" organizations are largely a thing of the past, but the governing structures of the institution—session, vestry, or council— despite the limited opening of such offices to women, continue to be largely an adult male preserve. Every member of the family group is thus provided for.

The normative social event is the Family Night Supper, the family picnic, or the Couples Club. The traditional channel of pastoral activity is the home call by the minister. The pater-familial model on which the pastoral relationship is based is clearly preserved in the term "father," still customary in the Roman Catholic, Orthodox, and Anglican churches. Though Protestants do not use the term and the paternal relationship is less authoritarian, the basic pattern is still the same. So universally is the family the basic unit for the parish church that ruptured families fit in uncomfortably. Whether or not a divorcee should be permitted to teach in Sunday school would still be a hotly debated question in a number of churches.

Institutional Support from the Denomination

Whether the polity of the denomination is episcopal, presbyterian, or congregational, the denominational superstructure offers varieties of institutional support for the local church. The amount of ecclesiastical control coming down from above varies, and, except in the case of Roman Catholicism, the firmest control is by no means identical with an episcopal form of government. But every denomination offers program resources and guidance, especially for religious education and the family-oriented organizations of the church. Every denomination offers channels of cooperation in a larger mission through its national and world mission activities. Every denomination offers publications and media aids. Every denomination offers channels for assignment, calling, or engaging of ministers or priests and channels through which changes may be made.

Similarly, there are liturgical supporting structures, as surely in those denominations that consider themselves non-liturgical and non-sacramental as in those with firmly structured liturgies. A group of like-minded people with a clearly-defined sense of what they expect, worshiping regularly and comfortably in a customary way, provides just as clearcut a structure for the ministry of public worship as does a prayer-book with a prescribed collect for each day of the year. A saintly sister who by proprietary right of long-established custom always bakes the bread for the Lord's Supper, a women's missionary society that lovingly washes the glasses after each quarterly observance, a deacon who in the same phrases offers a free prayer before the breaking of the bread—these are as surely cultic structures as are written rubrics governing the care of sacred vessels and the consecrated host. A plain black suit and the title "Brother" can carry as much meaning as eucharistic vestments and the title "Father." Liturgical structures, whether simple or elaborate, are part of the institutional support. Because of these institutional supports, every local church, no matter how congregational the form of government or how voluntary the associational relationship, feels itself to be a local representative of a larger group. And every minister finds through the supporting structures a relationship with a group of like-minded and similarly oriented fellow clergymen.

The characteristics of the parish church background may be taken for granted rather than explicitly examined or even recognized by the clergyman who performs his ministry in that institution. But they are his presuppositions. In all probability he grew up in the church. Its characteristics were assumed without question by the congregation that nurtured him, the seminary that trained him, the church body that ordained him. So thoroughly are they taken for granted that in all probability he thinks of them as part and parcel of "ministry." It may never occur to him to separate the institutional characteristics from the nucleus of faith, belief, and commitment that works through them.

But institutional duality requires a fresh look. A clergyman who becomes a military chaplain enters a new institution. His commitment to the church remains unchanged, but his ministry for the church must adapt to a new set of presuppositions. Many ineffective and fruitless ministries—and unfortunately they abound in the armed forces—can be explained in terms of a chaplain who does not understand the characteristics of ministry in his new institution, attempting to transfer intact into the military setting a ministry based on civilian parish assumptions. Examples are everywhere: the family-oriented chaplain who devotes all his time to families of a few officers and senior NCO's, ignoring the young adult servicemen and women who make up eighty-five percent of the military population; the chapel-happy chaplain who is lost without a building, who even on a two-week bivouac feels an urgent necessity to "build a chapel"; the office-centered chaplain who keeps himself remote from the military world, expecting his parishioners to leave their everyday pursuits and seek him out. Such chaplains are physically within one institutional environment, but psychologically within another.

The Christian gospel is the same, regardless of the institutional environment. But that gospel will be most effectively communicated by one who understands the institution in which he is working, his place within it, and the kind of ministry which is designed for and appropriate to it. The remainder of this chapter and the next two will be devoted to these issues. This chapter will examine the nature of the military institution, Chapter 3 the chaplain's place within that institution, and Chapter 4 the unique characteristics of military ministry.

CHARACTERISTICS OF TOTAL INSTITUTIONS

There are a number of perspectives from which the nature of a military organization can be examined. From the standpoint of implications for the chaplaincy, none is more illuminating than the concept of the total institution, as developed by sociologist Erving Goffman.

Goffman elaborated his concept in a lengthy essay, "On the Characteristics of Total Institutions," included in his 1961 book, *Asylums*. [2] An institution, in the broad sense, is a social establishment which regularly engages in a particular kind of activity. Some institutions, like railroad stations or airports, are open to everyone. Others, like social clubs or laboratories engaged in secret research, are highly exclusive. Some, like stores or post offices, have a small number of fixed members who provide a service and a continuing flow of others who receive the service. Others, like homes or factories, have a relatively permanent set of participants. Some are concerned with vocational activity; others are devoted to leisure-time activity. Some make serious demands; others are entirely voluntary. Sociology does not have a clearly defined way of classifying institutions, and they cover the entire spectrum of human social activity.

According to Goffman's analysis, total institutions are distinguished from other institutions in society by the fact that they control, to a considerable extent, the total lives of the persons involved. Every institution engages some of the time and interest of its members or users, providing something of a "world" for them. This Goffman calls the "encompassing tendency." Total institutions seek to be totally encompassing. The symbol of this totality is a barrier between the member and the outside world. Sometimes there is a physical barrier—a fence, sentries, barred windows. Always there is a strong sense of the difference between members and the outside world.

A second key feature of the total institution is a breakdown of the barriers which ordinarily separate the different spheres of life. Most people sleep, play, and work in different places, with different companions, under different authorities, and without any overall unifying plan. In a total institution these three spheres of life take place under the same authority, generally with the same co-participants, according to a tightly-scheduled plan designed to fulfill the aims of the institution.

Another feature is the handling of human needs by bureaucratic organization of whole blocks of people. This leads to a divergence between the supervisory group, which does the handling, and the managed group (usually much larger). Another feature has to do with attitude toward work. In a total institution there may be a loss of the direct relationship between work done and money paid. Members are frequently forced to engage in "make work" activities. As a consequence there is a certain incompatibility between the total institution and the basic work structure of our society. There is also an incompatibility in many instances with family life, since the member of the institution is an insider but the members of his family are outsiders.

Such total institutions include sanitariums, hospitals, homes for the blind and aged, jails and penitentiaries, boarding schools, and monastic orders, as well as military organizations. Goffman's analysis was developed during a year at Saint Elizabeth's Hospital in Washington, D. C., and his basic paradigm is closest to a mental hospital. He uses frequent illustrations and insights from other institutions, however, including numerous military applications.

It is clear that the basic characteristics of total institutions, as Goffman describes them, are all applicable to the military situation. It is particularly important for an understanding of the military chaplaincy to recognize that it is a ministry to persons whose lives are encompassed by a total institution, and to understand the effect of the total institution on those lives and that ministry.

There are certain differences, however, between the military service as a total institution and the basic Goffman paradigm, which was developed in a residential hospital. It is helpful to examine those differences at the outset. The only other type of total institution which shares most of the sociological characteristics of the military service is the monastic or religious order. It is probably not accidental that certain religious orders employ military terminology extensively. The Jesuits, for instance, under the command of a vicar-general, have been known as the "army of the Pope." The Salvation Army is explicitly modeled after a military organization in every detail.

The military-monastic type is a single large institution with many small units or branches (bases, squadrons, ships, monasteries). It might be labeled the *extended* type of total institution, as distinguished from the *autonomous* type represented by the single hospital, prison, or asylum. While Goffman did not distinguish between these two types (he used a different typology, and limited himself to examining the single military base or monastery as a total institution), this avenue is worth pursuing for the sake of understanding the military. All the features of total institutions identified by Goffman and summarized above are shared by both the extended and autonomous types of total institutions. Beyond these similarities, there are significant variations:

1. The institutional environment of the autonomous total institution is unique to the local institution. While every hospital or prison has general similarities to all others, the specific regulations, uniforms, and environmental characteristics are locally determined and unique. The particular prison exists as a complete entity, regardless of whether or not there may be any other prisons in the world. The institutional environment of the extended total institution is determined to a considerable extent by the larger organization of which the local unit is a part. It is virtually identical from one unit to another. A sailor, transferred from one ship to another, must establish new interpersonal relationships, but he is automatically at home in the new institutional environment, which is almost a carbon copy of the one he left. He wears the same uniform, uses the same divisional organization and the same titles for his superior officers, follows the same type of published "plan of the day," and has the same working hours and liberty regulations. Even the paint on the bulkhead is likely to be the identical shade of green. After some years in the organization, even the interpersonal relationships may not be completely new. Somewhere in the new unit he is likely to run into an old shipmate from a former assignment. The same transferability of environment would generally apply to the Air Force man, the Benedictine monk, or the Salvation Army officer. In a later chapter we shall look in some detail at the implications for military life and the effect on military ministry of this "total mobile environment."

2. Extended total institutions are characterized by a different kind of relationship between the administrator-leaders and the administered members from their relationship in an autonomous institution. In the latter type, as Goffman points out, the line between staff and inmate/patient is very sharp, and the relationship is one of natural enmity. Goffman recognized that in certain types of institutions (his example was a nunnery), the notion of a staff-inmate division is not fruitful. Instead there can be, he said, a single collegial group, internally stratified in terms of a finely-graded rank order.[3]

In a military service, officers and enlisted men make up the administrator and administered groups. The line between them is sharp (though not so sharp as in an earlier period), and there is a good bit of natural enmity from the perspective of some enlisted men. The major difference, however, is in the relationship of the officer group to the institution. Staff members in an autonomous total institution lack some of the total involvement and subjection to institutional control that the inmate/patients experience. Many are nine-to-five employees whose personal lives are centered elsewhere. Officers in an extended total institution—particularly the military—are as totally involved and as subject to institutional control as enlisted men. Staff in an autonomous total institution may consist of semi-outsiders. An extended total institution is administered by insiders. There is, consequently, a large measure of "we're all in this together" feeling between military officers and enlisted men, which may not exist between staff and members of the autonomous total institution.

Religious orders present a further variation. They are likely to be administered largely by the members themselves, with relatively few superiors, who, though given unquestioned obedience, nevertheless share most of the characteristics of membership. The line between administrators and administered is less sharp than in the military service, but the same sense of common identity, of shared membership as insiders, exists.

3. In most autonomous total institutions, the job of staff consists exclusively of providing some sort of servicing function—healing, rehabilitation, education, custodianship—*for* the inmate/patients. In extended total institutions, members and staff are united in a task exterior to the organization: national defense, fighting wars, converting the heathen, serving society. This sense of commonality of endeavor does much to eliminate the kind of enmity which Goffman found to be characteristic of the autonomous total institutions he examined.

Goffman developed at considerable length a picture of "the inmate world" inside the total institution, with a separate examination of the "staff world." This distinction is not applicable to the armed forces. The "inmate" world—the world inside the total institution—is in many respects the same for both officers and enlisted men. It is the world of the total institution itself, which is contrasted with the outside. A number of the characteristics of this institutional world as described by Goffman contribute to our understanding of military life.

UNDERSTANDING THE MILITARY SERVICE AS A TOTAL INSTITUTION

Goffman devoted a great deal of attention to an analysis of the significance of induction procedures, which mark the transition from the outside world to the insider world of the total institution. A large number of his illustrations came from military recruit training, which is a highly formalized setting for the transition process. He analyzed it in terms of the "mortification of the self"—a process by which the former self is systematically eliminated and replaced by a new institutional self.

The transition takes place in a setting which minimizes or entirely prevents contact with the former world; the new recruit is kept in virtual isolation from the outside world for the first few weeks. Most of his previous bases of self-identification are ignored or denigrated. He is even robbed of his complete name, and is addressed in new ways. The process of photographing, fingerprinting, assigning a number, cutting his hair, issuing him uniforms, instructing him on rules, assigning quarters, all are assaults on the self which prepare the way for a new identity. He suffers the indignity of exposure, both physical and psychological.

Even his informational preserve regarding himself is violated, as he is required to answer questions of a highly personal nature. He suffers forced interpersonal contacts, and forced social relationships. His autonomy is assaulted as he is required to request permission for minor activities that were entirely under his own control on the outside—permission to smoke a cigarette, to use the telephone, to go to the toilet. He is instructed in elaborate deference patterns, of which the salute is the symbol in military life. His life is governed by detailed regulations covering everything.[4]

These elaborate mortifications of the self, Goffman suggested, are justified on different grounds by different total institutions. In monastic orders, such mortification may be eagerly sought by the novice himself because of its perceived intrinsic value. In a prison it may be justified on the grounds of security, or in the belief that the prisoner deserves it. In the military organization it is rationalized because of sanitation or combat capability.[5] But whatever the justification, such induction processes are remarkably similar in every total institution, and the effect in every case is the same—the destruction of the former individualistic self and the creation of a new institutional self which facilitates the bureaucratic management of a large group of people and in other ways serves institutional needs. Its sociological purpose may therefore be described in these terms regardless of the particular reason given.

The effect of the induction procedures is to create the climate which is the central feature of life in a total institution: an "insider" world, single-mindedly dedicated to the activity for which the institution exists, on which the outside world impinges as little as possible. When he leaves recruit training, the soldier, sailor, or airman encounters some relaxation of the high barriers which separate the insider from the outsider. But the whole elaborate process has been designed to make him psychologically an insider no matter how much the physical barriers are relaxed. He is to "think like a Marine, act like a Marine, be a Marine" twenty-four hours a day. The effectiveness of the process is attested to by the durability of the institutional self, vestiges of which remain long after the member has left the military institution. Veterans organizations are evidences of this durability, and "when I was in the service" reminiscences provide continuing conversational material.

There are, of course, aspects of personal and social life which remain always beyond institutional control. The initial intent of the institution, however, is to make that control as total as possible. The extended total institution offers different degrees of totality at different times. Never again is the institution so all-encompassing as in the recruit training period. However, the early assignments of the new member are likely to be situations with a high degree of totality—seagoing ships, infantry training regiments, operational air squadrons, combat divisions—in which his contact with the outside world is limited and his "liberty" (the term itself is characteristic of a total institution, for his free time is a privilege granted by the military authorities rather than a personal right) is severely restricted. In such assignments life is austere, bureaucratically controlled, and highly regimented.

In total institutions the privilege system is such that things assumed as rights on the outside are granted as privileges in return for cooperation with the institution. On this basis, the serviceman will in time "earn" the privilege of an assignment which gives him greater freedom from the institution's total control of his life—shore duty, a choice post in the United States, family quarters, the privilege of having his family accompany him when he is transferred, moving at government expense. The longer he remains in the military, the less total will be the institutional control.

Officers, in general terms, are less rigidly regimented by the total institution than enlisted persons. However, they pass through the same progression from total institutional control at the beginning to lesser control with seniority. Nowhere are the rigid control, the isolation from the former world, the mortification of the self, the psychological exposure, the enforced interpersonal contacts, the elaborate deference patterns, the detailed regulations, and the creation of a new institutional identity more systematically and professionally carried out than in the service academies at Annapolis, West Point, and Colorado Springs. The more seniority the officer acquires, the more freedom from total institutional control he earns.

All military persons, both enlisted and officer, move repeatedly into and out of various degrees of institutional totality, as they rotate from ship duty to shore duty, from deployment to home port, from operational divisions to garrison duty, from isolated overseas bases to administrative assignments. But the desired effect of the system is to create an overall psychological total institution that embraces the whole career. The serviceman can return from an eight-to-five office assignment in Washington to the institutional totality of a ship at sea or an infantry regiment on combat maneuvers with relative ease because he has never left the institutional state of mind. As surely as the newest recruit, the most senior general is still an "insider" in the total institution.

MILITARY CHAPLAINCY IN THE TOTAL INSTITUTION

An understanding from this sociological perspective of the military service as a total institution provides the setting for an examination of several major aspects of the chaplaincy. The first of these has to do with the conditions of ministry. Military chaplains comprise one of the few groups of clergymen—perhaps the only such group—who can minister as "insiders" to a total institution. The hospital chaplain cannot; he belongs to the "staff" group in an institution which follows the classic Goffman paradigm, with the staff world quite distinct from the patient world. (Since, however, the ministrations of the hospital chaplain are for the most part confined to a limited, crisis situation, this is not a serious handicap.) Even less can the prison chaplain, in a total institution marked by bitter enmity from the inmate group toward the staff group. (The disadvantage here is probably a serious one.) But the military chaplain, who wears the same uniform, obeys the same regulations, participates in the same goal-oriented organization, sails the same ships, lives under the same combat conditions, is clearly an insider in the military total institution.

To share insider status with parishioners in a total institution is a condition of ministry of which the importance would be hard to overemphasize. Every chaplain has had the experience, while sitting in uniform waiting for a plane in an airport or a bus in a bus station, of watching a member of his service walk in, look over the crowd, recognize him by his uniform, and join him to strike up a conversation. If the two are the only military people in a waiting room full of civilians it is almost sure to happen, provided the chaplain indicates, by a smile or a word, that officer status is not a barrier and company would be welcome. The serviceman knows by the uniform that they belong to the same club, that they have something in common.

Shared insider status affects ministry in a number of ways. One way
is through the removal of the artificiality, even the elements of hypocrisy,
that sometimes get in the way of relationships between a minister and his
parishioners. The fact that people tend to put on their coats, ties, and best
behavior when they go to church, that they put out tea and the best china
when the pastor comes to call, sometimes stands in the way of direct and
authentic relationships. The military chaplain is probably the only minister in Christendom who habitually sees his parishioners in their skivvy
drawers. He visits with them more often in their dirty utilities than in their
clean dress uniforms. He is accustomed to the earthiness of their everyday language. They may try to clean it up when he is in sight, but they
know as well as he does that before coming around the corner he heard
every profane word. If they get into trouble, he is likely to be standing
by at captain's mast or colonel's office hours.[6] The fact that most Christians are not plaster saints, that like St. Paul they often fail to do things
they would and do things they would not, is out in the open. As a result,
sermons can be more relevant, relationships more direct and honest.

A second advantage of shared insider status in a total institution is
enhanced pastoral ministry through greater awareness of the problems
faced and the life lived by that chaplain's parishioners. A chaplain knows
the boredom of sailors during long periods at sea or airmen at an isolated
radar warning site because he experiences it along with them. He knows
the loneliness of separation from family, because he is separated from his
family too. He shares with them the moral contradiction of participating
in organized killing in the face of the commandment, "Thou shalt not
kill," of fighting wars while loving peace. A ministry of presence and
participation offers a useful stance for counseling and pastoral care.

A third advantage of ministry as an insider in a total institution is
ready-made contact with the unchurched. The young persons in the
armed forces are a cross-section of the people of the United States. They
come from every section, every social stratum, every economic group.
And from the standpoint of the churches, the most striking thing about
them is that most of them are, for all practical purposes, non-Christian.
Churchmen are frequently told that their beliefs and standards are largely
disregarded by Americans today, particularly young adult Americans, but
the knowledge lacks the relevance of immediacy since churchmen tend to
move in circles in which most people are church-related. For a dramatic
demonstration of how far from typical is the church-centered, morally-
oriented society in which they move, one need only put on a sailor suit
and spend a week in the crew's compartment of a ship. Most servicemen
consider themselves in some vague fashion to be "Cat'lic," having been

baptized that way, or Protestant (probably spelled "Prostant" on the preference card), being under the impression that that's what you are if you are neither Catholic nor Jewish. But vast numbers of them have never in their lives spoken meaningfully to a clergyman until they enter the armed forces and meet the chaplain. He is chaplain to the total institution, not just to the explicitly Christian portion of it. He has a recognized place in the institution of which they are part, and recognized functions for which they can turn to him.

One one occasion a group of chaplains of which I was a member joined with several local churches in Newport, Rhode Island, to sponsor an experimental summer ministry—downtown and on the beach—to off-duty sailors. A seminary student, who was by coincidence a member of the Army's chaplaincy training program, was employed for this ministry. He experimented with a number of ways of establishing some measure of rapport and pastoral relationship with the young sailors he encountered. He tried wearing a clerical collar, identifying himself as a representative of the local churches, and other gambits. He discovered that the most effective way of establishing a relationship was to identify himself as one training for the Army chaplaincy. He found that even this degree of military identity was sufficient to give him some measure of acceptance by military men he met.[7]

Every chaplain is aware that his status gives him a ready relationship to the unchurched of the military population. There is probably no ministry of the church that offers a better or more natural opportunity for meaningful encounter with the functionally non-Christian majority of the population.

A fourth advantage, rare for a civilian clergyman, is the opportunity to minister to the secular institution itself. We have learned from social psychology, and particularly from organizational studies, that the lives of individuals are inextricably interwoven with the social groups and organizations of which they are a part. The conditions of life for individuals cannot always be changed without bringing about change in the institutions which establish these conditions. The chaplain has a unique opportunity to act on this insight. As a member of the managerial group of the total institution which establishes the conditions of life under which his parishioners live, with a close relationship to top management, he is in a position to minister to them by ministering to the institution itself.

A chaplain serving in a destroyer tender participated in a Doctor of Ministry degree program offered for Navy chaplains in his home port of Norfolk, Virginia. One degree requirement was the design and completion of a major project in the improvement of ministry. This chaplain, whose shipboard office was located near the mess deck and galley, saw a great deal of the food servicemen—the young enlisted men, new to the Navy and to the ship, who were assigned to three months of mess duty soon after their arrival on shipboard. The chaplain knew that the mess duty assignment was uniformly disliked by the sailors and regarded as an unpleasant obstacle to be endured by all newcomers. He noted that food servicemen were among the most frequent offenders at captain's mast, charged with such offenses as absence without leave, disobedience of orders, and disrespect to seniors. He set out to design a ministry to meet their particular needs. He interviewed each of them at the beginning and end of mess duty. He offered individual and group counseling. He sought to involve them in his congregation for divine services, which were held on the mess deck. He found that they responded readily to his ministry to them as persons. But he also found that much of their unhappiness was the result of correctible conditions relating to the regulations, working hours, and modes of supervision. His ministry led not only to the offering of a more effective and personal pastoral relationship with the group of food servicemen, but also to the proposing of institutional changes which improved their attitudes toward themselves and the persons around them, and to a positive impact by a church representative on the whole command structure.

The chaplain's place in the total institution makes opportunities of this kind possible. An Air Force chaplain in Vietnam was able to talk to his commander about the moral ambiguity of "targets of opportunity." Another Air Force chaplain, stationed at Montgomery, Alabama, was able to eliminate the difficulties experienced by blacks in getting their hair cut.

Shared insider status in a total institution, then, affects ministry in these significant ways. It removes the element of artificiality which sometimes intervenes between the pastor and the parishioner who wants to show only his Sunday self. It enables the chaplain to share fully the conditions under which his parishioners live, and thus prepares him for a more effective pastoral ministry to their needs. It places him in natural and continuing contact with the unchurched as well as the churched. It also makes it possible for him to minister creatively to the institution itself, as well as to the persons who make up the institution.

OBSERVATIONS REGARDING CONTEMPORARY MILITARY TRENDS

An understanding of the military service as a total institution also provides some insights into current trends toward liberalization of the military services as they impinge on ministry to the military. A general anti-institutional and anti-military sentiment became widespread in the United States during the heyday of the youth counterculture in the 1960's. By the beginning of the seventies disillusionment with the Vietnamese War had built up enormous pressure for change in the armed forces. These pressures affected all segments of the society and all those governmental structures that shape the armed forces. The changes that resulted, some by legislation, some by court decision, and some by internal modifications within the services themselves, have been characterized generally as liberalization.

The draft was eliminated in response to pressure from the whole population. Congress vastly increased military pay, thus moving military service out of the category of a duty owed by all young men to their country to be compensated at a subsistence level only, and into the category of labor, bought in the marketplace at competitive wages. A series of court decisions greatly restricted the applicability of military law, eliminating its jurisdiction over the dependents of military personnel in overseas areas and over service persons themselves when in an off-duty status. Use of commanding officer's non-judicial punishment for minor offenders was severely limited. The right to be represented by counsel in all judicial proceedings was greatly expanded.

The services themselves responded in varying degrees to the pressures—the Army making the most extensive changes and the Marine Corps, perhaps, the least—but all of them took some steps in the direction of improving living conditions and public image. Uniforms were modernized. Rules governing the wearing of civilian clothes when off-duty were greatly liberalized. Sailors were allowed to keep civilian clothes on shipboard and wear them on liberty in foreign ports. Standards relating to haircuts and beards were relaxed. Living conditions in barracks (renamed bachelor enlisted quarters) were improved. Ships were home-ported overseas to allow men to be with their families more of the time. Officers were given sensitivity training to improve their relationships with the men they supervise.

While all these changes may accurately be called "liberalization," it should also be noted that from a sociological standpoint their effect was to make a total institution less total. It is quite probable that the real significance of military haircuts—the insistence of young military men that they be allowed to wear their hair long in the style of their contemporaries, and the losing battle of the military establishment to keep it short —lies at this point. Sociologically, the issue for the military was not style but control. The loss of hair in boot camp is a key symbolic act symbolically in the substitution of institutional self for civilian self. The short military haircut emphasizes the separateness of those who make up the total institution. Competition in the wage market for workers, restriction of the scope of the Uniform Code of Military Justice, more time with families, less off-duty identification with the military through the wearing of civilian clothes—each of these steps represents an erosion of the totality of the institution.

The purpose behind the total institution is the total mobilization of resources for the job at hand. A mental hospital operates on the assumption that in order to heal and protect severely disturbed patients, it must control their lives twenty-four hours a day. A monastic order believes that total involvement leads to total commitment to the mission. Similarly, military services have traditionally believed that total mobilization of human resources was required to win wars.

The question the military now faces is how much of its totality can it give up and still accomplish its mission? Can a nine-to-five army win wars? Clearly some liberalization is here to stay, and an emphasis on certain human values enhances rather than detracts from the effectiveness of military organizations. But the armed services are likely to stop considerably short of allowing themselves to become non-total institutions. Reaction has already set in, with a general tightening of discipline and a backtracking on some of the earlier loosening of control. The period ahead is one in which there will be considerable exploration of the proper balance between attention to those human values that enhance the individual and institutional life on the one hand, and attention to institutional control in order to accomplish the mission on the other hand.

The military chaplain has a key role to play in helping the military and the nation find this balance. As a force *within* the total institution standing for human values and the dignity of the individual, he can help the institution avoid the loss of these qualities. He can serve as a bridge figure between those in the institution and the "outside." As one traditionally associated with families and family life, who performs marriages, offers counseling, and frequently serves as a communication channel between families at home and men in deployed and operational forces, he can help military persons live with and overcome the fact that families are inevitably "outsiders" to the total institution. The fact that he represents an outside institution which has made its way inside—the church—is a further bridge to the outside world. His traditional role as ombudsman when distressed military persons "tell it to the chaplain" provides a bridge to the values of the outside world.

In the quest for proper balance between human values and institutional control, the chaplain must recognize that he has obligations to both the individual and the institution. Sometimes the interests of the two may be contradictory, and because his first allegiance is to God as a representative of the church rather than to the military, the chaplain becomes the individual's advocate before the institution in such situations. People come first with him, and full military recognition of the nature of the chaplain's institutional duality will concede this. But a ministry to individuals without full appreciation of the role of the institution in individual welfare, of the inter-relationships between the person and the organization, becomes fruitless and frustrating. The chaplain stands for human values *within* the institution, and he has a key role to play in bringing the interests of the two together.

Chapter 3
Place of the Chaplaincy
in the Military Organization

A primary fact of life for the institutional chaplain, military or otherwise, is that he is a bureaucrat. Any large organization is bureaucratically organized, and the clergyman whose ministry takes place in such an institution must fit into a carefully defined slot in that organization. Generally, his slot is several levels down from the top. This fact alone represents a major adjustment for a clergyman.

PRINCIPLE OF MILITARY COMMAND

For the military chaplain an additional fact of life is that his is an authority-based organization. "I am a man under authority, with soldiers under me," said the Roman army officer to Jesus in St. Matthew's gospel. "I say to one, 'Go,' and he goes, and to another, 'Come,' and he comes." Military organizations have changed little since that day. They operate on the basis of orders, duty, and obedience.

The contemporary social climate is one in which these concepts are unpopular. A study made by the author examined the "humanization values" which set the tone of interpersonal relationships, not only in contemporary "pop" culture but in the behavioral sciences (particularly organizational studies) as well. It was discovered that such terms as authority, orders, duty, and obedience carry a negative connotation for up-to-the-moment managers. The organizational orthodoxy of the day calls for consensus rather than authority; group decision-making rather than orders, self-realization rather than duty, autonomy rather than obedience.[1]

An authority-based organization in a permissive social climate has ready-made problems. The military services, by the extensive employment of managerial and organizational consultants in an attempt to deal with their own problems in these fields, have contributed to their own interior conflict. The humanization values of many of these behavioral scientists have not meshed confortably with the "duty-honor-country" ethic epitomized by the West Point motto. But despite the concessions made to contemporary behavioral doctrine and the uneasy compromise reached with up-to-the-moment managerial expertise, the military services have remained basically authority-based systems. Commanding officers are still in command.

The concept of military command is not nearly so fearful, however, as churchmen with no military experience imagine. At its heart it is not so much a matter of arbitrary and autocratic decisions as of pinpointed responsibility. The military commander is, in fact, probably less likely to make arbitrary, capricious, or poorly-thought-out decisions than is the executive in business, labor, the government bureaucracy, or academe, safeguarded by tenure or operating behind fuzzy lines of responsibility. The military staff system (of which the chaplain is a part) is a precisely designed and long-tested instrument for providing commanders at every level with the best possible professional advice and technical expertise on which to base every decision. The greater authority of the military commander is matched by greater accountability. If the military commander's decision is wrong, he is far less likely to evade the pitiless pinpointing of responsibility than is the non-military bureaucrat.

The power of command in a military institution is, of course, real. Under combat conditions—and it is to be prepared for such conditions that a military organization exists—instant and unquestioning obedience to orders by every person in the command can become a matter of life and death. Military services, therefore, are not likely to surrender this basic institutional characteristic. Every chaplain serves under a military commander, and in theory the authority of that secular commander over his religious ministry can be nearly absolute. In practice, however, the commander is unlikely to interfere in what is recognized as the province of the church. As we shall note in some detail later, the principle of military command and accountability, which operates at subordinate levels as well, is likely to give the average chaplain far more control over and responsibility for his own religious program than is allowed the average civilian clergyman.

THE MILITARY ORGANIZATION AS A BUREAUCRACY

Important as the concept of military command is, a more useful analysis of the chaplain's place in the military organization can be made by recognizing that such an organization is a bureaucracy. The classic description of a bureaucracy was outlined by Max Weber, one of the pioneers in the field of sociology, in the early part of this century. Today the term is frequently understood in a negative sense, as referring to bumbling incompetence, red tape, depersonalization, rigidity, and resistance to change. These characteristics are all too evident in contemporary bureaucracies, and the tendency for them to develop in bureaucracies has been brilliantly satirized in such treatments as *Parkinson's Law*,[2] *The Peter Principle*,[3] and others.

The clergyman as bureaucrat is the *reductio ad absurdum* in such a view. He is likely to be regarded even more scornfully by his fellow-

churchmen than is the secular bureaucrat by society at large. Church
circles place a premium on spirituality, on self-sacrifice, on inspiration,
on prophetic utterance, and on the immediacy of the Holy Spirit. The
picture of clergyman-as-bureaucrat, entangled in his red tape, shuffling
his files, reviewing his "cases," clock-watching through his working
hours, moving papers from the in-basket to the out-basket, and jealously
guarding his pension rights, is at the opposite extreme from these values.
To ask churchmen to examine the place of the chaplain in the military
bureaucracy, then, is to stretch their patience.

Basically, however, and in its original usage, the term "bureaucracy" is a neutral one. Weber used it as almost synonymous with the term
"organization" itself. The function of bureaucracy, as he described it, is
to bring rationality into institutional life. Every organization is in this
sense bureaucratic. In organizational studies today, the existence of so-
called "non-bureaucratic" organizational models is recognized, but they
are non-bureaucratic only in the sense that they depart from the classical
model as described by Weber. All non-bureaucratic models become to
some extent bureaucratized.[4]

The armed forces are bureaucracies not only in the generic sense
of being organized institutions but also in that they follow the classic
model as described by Weber. Indeed, Weber based his analysis in part
on his observations of the Prussian Army of his day. To examine the
implications of the chaplain's membership in a bureaucratic organization,
then, is simply to examine his organizational environment. Negative
stereotypes express a danger, but not an inevitability. Effective ministry
within the organization requires an understanding *of* the organization,
and an examination of the place of the chaplain within the military
bureaucracy is dictated by common sense.

Among the current emphases in theological education on the practice of ministry, one of the most promising of the developing fields is that
of organizational studies. The new Center for the Study of Church Organizational Behavior, established in 1969 at McCormick Theological Seminary of Chicago, has attracted widespread attention. A recent book in the
organizational field is James D. Anderson's *To Come Alive: A New Proposal
for Revitalizing the Local Church*. It attempts to enable church people to
understand the church as an organization—the forces, structures, and
processes that shape the life of the institution—and to apply that understanding in solving the problems faced by churches as institutions.[5]

Chaplains are churchmen ministering in quite a different kind of
organization. The process, however, is identical: that of understanding
the institution for the sake of more effective ministry.

Weber's Bureaucratic Principles

Max Weber described in some detail the main characteristics of bureaucratic organizations.[6] These include the following aspects particularly relevant to the chaplain's place in the organization:

1. A bureaucracy is "a continuing organization of official functions bound by *rules.*" There is an elaborate system of abstract rules, which are applied to particular cases. Such rules save time and make it possible for the business at hand to be handled fairly, without the capriciousness of individual decisions in each individual case. This contributes to the rationality of the organization. As Weber pointed out, these regulations, together with decisions and precedents, must be formulated and recorded in writing. The emphasis on written rules is one of the central characteristics of a bureaucracy.

2. A bureaucracy is characterized by a clear-cut division of labor. There is "a specific sphere of competence" for each official. This involves "(a) a sphere of obligations to perform functions which have been marked off as part of a systematic division of labor; (b) the provision of the incumbent with the necessary authority to carry out these functions; and (c) that the necessary means of compulsion are clearly defined and their use is subject to definite conditions." Here is the heart of the military staff system. Classically, the division of labor has included "line" functions, which are directly concerned with authoritative decisions necessary for the achievement of the organization's goals (hence the term "line officer" for those exercising military command), and "staff" functions, which are technical and advisory in nature, and generally outside the direct chain of the "line" organization.

3. "The organization of offices follows the principle of hierarchy; that is, each lower office is under the control and supervision of a higher one." Each official is accountable to his superior for his subordinates' decisions and actions as well as his own.

4. Incumbency is based on technical qualifications and is safeguarded against arbitrary dismissal. "The rules which regulate the conduct of an office may be technical rules or norms. In both cases, if their application is to be fully rational, specialized training is necessary. It is thus normally true that only a person who has demonstrated an adequate technical training is qualified to be a member of the administrative staff." The bureaucratic system depends on the training and competence of incumbents of positions. This proclivity for training has facilitated the emphasis on continuing education, characteristic of the military chaplaincy, which will be discussed in some detail in a later chapter. A corol-

lary of bureaucracy's emphasis on technical qualification is that promotions within the system are based on seniority, achievement, or both.[7]

The bureaucratic features of a military service constitute its safeguards against arbitrariness and capriciousness in the exercise of military command. Those civilian churchmen who regard the subjection of clergymen to military command as a serious threat to the authenticity of religion, who accuse chaplains of having "traded the freedom of the Christian ministry for bondage to command influence,"[8] need to understand that the threat is balanced by the safeguards of a bureaucratic system. The written word may, as St. Paul suggests, deaden, but it also protects. Bureaucratic written regulations govern every aspect of military life. A bureaucratic division of responsibility recognizes the chaplain's sphere of competence, assigns him responsibility, and gives him authority to carry it out. The hierarchical principle places each commanding officer under the supervision of a higher commander, and places chaplains in staff positions as advisors to senior commanders at every level. The recognition of technical training and competence makes the chaplain the "expert" in his own sphere of responsibility. Though bureaucracy presents dangers to authentic ministry, each of these bureaucratic principles protects the chaplain's ministry from "bondage to command influence."

The Military Staff System

The military staff system brings together the principle of military command and the principle of bureaucratic organization. The military commander bears ultimate responsibility for everything that happens in the command. The captain of a ship may be asleep in his cabin when the ship runs aground. The Board of Investigation may find the cause in a factor over which the captain had no control: human error on the part of the officer of the deck, an inaccurate chart, mechanical failure in the steering mechanism. But blameless though he may be in a direct sense, he is still held responsible as the one in command when it happened, and he is not likely to be chosen for flag rank.

In accordance with this principle of responsibility for everything that happens, the commanding officer is the one who, in an official sense, "causes divine services to be held" in a Navy ship.[9] In the Army, "commanders are responsible for the religious life, morals, and morale of their command, and for the activities of chaplains under their command, with due regard for the limitations imposed by ecclesiastical requirements."[10] Even such routine activities of a chaplain as his contacts with civilian clergymen are done, in a formal sense, "with the consent and permission of his commander."[11] Yet along with this principle of command responsibility goes a staff system in which the commander, who has no technical training whatever in the field of religion and is expected to have none, has been given a staff professional—the chaplain—with a "specific sphere of competence," qualified for the job with "adequate technical training" (the phrases are Weber's) to be his "expert" in the field. Under the staff system the commander is the one who signs his name and accepts public responsibility, but his staff specialist is the one who has full professional responsibility within the organization.

An understanding of the staff system and acceptance of the staff relationship will clarify the place of the chaplain within the military organization. His personal role as a religious leader is at the same time more independently responsible, and less so, than was the equivalent role in the civilian church. It is *more* responsible because the chaplain is a religious professional in a non-religious organization, with fewer professional checks and balances than in a church system. The average commanding officer, who may not be of his brand of Christianity or may not be Christian at all, is far more likely to let the chaplain do whatever he sees fit in his religious work than the average bishop, district superintendent, or board of deacons. If a civilian clergyman should take a notion to re-arrange the mass or rewrite the Apostle's Creed, his bishop or the officers of his congregation would straighten him out quickly. The chaplain's commanding officer may consider him an oddball, but he is likely to let him go right on being an oddball, as long as he confines it to his religious services. As a staff advisor to his commanding officer in administrative matters related to religion, he is an "expert" whose advice and recommendations in his field of competence will, under optimum conditions, be accepted without question by the commander. He stands alone. He has no vestry or session to help him make the decision, and the system is not gentle to "experts" who give bad advice.

But at the same time he is *less* independently responsible because he is not the focal point of the organizational system, as is the pastor of the local church. In a system of military command the commanding officer is the focal point of everything. The chaplain, in his relationship to the religious community he serves, is a sub-focal point, with all religious activities having their place in the larger picture of the command.

The organizational locus of the military chaplain, then, is quite different from that of the civilian pastor. It is determined by the nature of the military command, and, to an even greater extent, by the nature of bureaucratic organizations. But once the organizational principles are understood, it is probably no more restrictive than the church organization. The chaplain will be in a position to minister effectively when he sees

its structures not as bugbears, but simply as the characteristics of a particular kind of institution to be understood and used in ministry.

THE CHAPLAIN SUBSYSTEM WITHIN THE MILITARY COMMAND SYSTEM

Insight into the place of religion in the armed forces can be gained
from looking at the chaplaincy subsystem (devoted to the ministry of
religion) within the larger military command system. It is well at this point
to keep in mind the difference between a formal *organization* and a *system.*
Organizations are social units (or human groupings) deliberately con-
structed to seek specific goals.[12] This deliberate construction provides
formalized ways of fixing responsibility and authority, whether the organization is classically bureaucratic or "non-bureaucratic." A system is a
broader concept, including the non-deliberate as well as the deliberately
structured aspects of human groupings. It is a network of all the relationships, communication channels, and working arrangements related to the
seeking of a specific goal. A military service is a formal organization and
also a system.

The chaplaincy of each service is not an organization except in a
narrowly limited sense. It has some formal corporate identity as a "Chaplain Corps" within the service, but the fixing of authority and responsibility for its task is not done within the Chaplain Corps. Chaplains are
assigned throughout the entire service, integrated into the command
structures. The fixing of authority and responsibility is done through
command structures.

Though not an organization, the chaplaincy is, however, a system
(or subsystem) clearly identifiable within the service, with the goal of
providing religious ministry within the service. The network of interrela-
tionships between the chaplaincy subsystem and the larger military system is extremely complex, but certain aspects can be isolated for examination. A crucially important element in the relationship is derived from
the institutional duality of the chaplaincy, which we have already examined in detail: the fact that the organizational goals of the chaplaincy are
not the same as, nor even derived from, the organizational goals of the
military service itself. It exists as a subsystem with its own independent
goals—an organizational absurdity. Its goals are derived from the other
major institution to which chaplains belong, the churches.

To say that the goals of the chaplaincy subsystem are independently
arrived at is not to say they are in conflict with the organizational goals
of the military service. As pioneer sociologist Emile Durkheim established, religious needs are basic human needs, and no society has ever

existed without provision for meeting those needs.[13] From the beginning military services have recognized the necessity for meeting the religious needs of servicemen and women, and have accepted the religious ministry provided by clergymen as the normal way of meeting those needs in American society. As we have noted before, military commanders have perceived the church-defined goals of religious ministry as fully compatible with their own organizational goals. They have reasoned that a serviceman cannot be a good fighting man unless his basic human needs— for food, clothing, health, recreation, and medical care, as well as spiritual nurture and expression—are met. On this basis, therefore, they have incorporated religious ministry into the general mission of the armed forces. Some have gone beyond this to a positive affirmation of the military value of religion. A book on military chaplains as counselors, dating from the early fifties, quotes a senior Army general as saying, "The work of the chaplain is vital to the success of American arms. We believe that the soldier who prays is a better soldier. . . ." Chaplains themselves have made similar claims. In the same context, this book quotes a Chief of Army Chaplains as pointing out that "the serviceman of disciplined religious character can be trusted to perform his duties in camp or on the battlefield."[14]

But the more the church-determined goal of religious ministry and the service-determined goal of fighting wars are brought together in this fashion, the more uncomfortable chaplains become. For if religion is used to make good fighting men, the chaplain becomes a tool of military organizational goals, rather than a servant of the goals of the church. Some of the most biting criticisms of the present form of military chaplaincy are those that depict the chaplain as "a greased cog in a machine for killing."[15] Not only are the churches unwilling to provide clergymen who might be used as tools in reaching strictly military goals, but chaplains themselves vigorously reject such a role.

However, the more the church-determined goal of religious ministry and the service-determined goal of fighting wars are separated and perceived as unrelated, the less interested the military becomes. Such a chaplaincy defines itself as peripheral to the goals of the military. It is a basic organizational principle that the resources of the organization are directed toward reaching organizational goals. By carefully separating itself from organizational goals and insisting that its own goals are extraneously derived (from outside institutions), the chaplaincy limits its access to military resources and thus its opportunity to be effective within the organization. This is the anomalous position in which the chaplain subsystem finds itself.

The Power-Dependence Paradigm

The organizational context of the chaplain subsystem within the military is illuminated by the power-dependence paradigm, developed by Richard Emerson,[16] and further elaborated by James D. Thompson.[17] Every element in an organization exhibits both dependence and power. Its dependence on other elements in the organizational environment grows out of its need for resources, performances, and other forms of support. Its power within the organization grows out of its ability to produce what is needed by other elements of the organization.

Examined in this light, the chaplaincy subsystem is seen as a highly dependent and relatively powerless organizational element. For fiscal support, personnel assistance, transportation, offices, chapels, and access to people it is completely dependent on the military command structure. But its "product" (call it spiritual well-being) is not nearly so readily identifiable as the products of other professional subsystems. The physicians can point to healthy bodies and recovered casualties; the lawyers to military justice enforced and courts martial completed. Even the dentists can point to toothaches subsided. But chaplains are hard put to point to anything specific which contributes to military goals. And when they do, they are in trouble with the churches and their own consciences!

Thompson cites research by Burton Clark for an illustration of a relatively powerless group within its organizational environment. Clark studied an adult education organization which rested on "precarious values" in the sense that adult education was not a high priority activity for any of the elements within the organizational environment. As a result, it had to scrounge for resources and cater to unstable coalitions based on fleeting interest. It had no ongoing, stable power base, and was unable to plan adequately or function efficiently.[18]

The chaplain subsystem in the military is in an analogous situation. Its church-derived values are "precarious" in the sense that religion is not a high priority activity in relation to military goals. The extent to which its "product" is needed by other organizational elements is subject to widely differing interpretations. So long as institutional duality remains real, and the goals of religious ministry are determined by the churches, the chaplain subsystem is likely to remain relatively powerless within the military organization.

Possibility 1: Increase of Power

Theoretically, there are two possible ways for the chaplaincy to change the equation. One is to increase its power—that is, to increase the ability of the subsystem to produce what is needed by other elements of the organization. This can be done by emphasizing those "products" which have a clear, identifiable pay-off for the military command. Of necessity the pay-offs must be in the area of improved human resources, and chaplains have a long history of developing "programs" to produce such identifiable pay-off. In the early days chaplains doubled as school-masters, producing a clear contribution to organizational goals in the form of literate soldiers and sailors. Through the years they have per-formed a variety of "collateral duties," as recreation officers, public infor-mation officers, tour guides, athletic coaches, and general handymen. Although they have collectively bemoaned such collateral—and non-reli-gious—assignments, individually many chaplains have welcomed them, and have performed admirably in the full knowledge that commanding officers are likely to consider such activities far more closely related to personnel performance (and therefore to watch them more closely) than religious worship and devotion.

In the years following the Second World War, when the chaplaincies were most firmly institutionalized in the greatly expanded armed services, programs developed in all three services known variously as "character guidance," "character education" or "moral leadership." Such a pro-gram, currently known as "Human Self-Development," still exists in the Army. Whatever the name, these programs have involved compulsory classes in which chaplains gave instruction or led discussions on morality, citizenship, and personal growth. We shall examine the character educa-tion movement in considerable detail in a later chapter.

In the heyday of these programs, character education was sold to the military commanders on the strength of studies purporting to show statistically that such classes resulted in fewer AWOL soldiers, fewer disciplinary problems, better conduct on liberty in overseas areas, fewer cases of venereal disease, and better fighting men.

During the Vietnamese War the chaplaincies of both the Army and the Navy (which furnishes chaplains to the Marine Corps) developed a "Personal Response Program" designed to improve relations between American troopers and South Vietnamese nationals. Justified religiously by a theology of reconciliation, it provided once again for compulsory classes, this time in cross-cultural understanding and relationships. Sold to military commanders as a means of "winning the hearts and minds" of the Vietnamese people, it developed an uncomfortably close relation-ship to psychological warfare, and in many instances was clearly so re-garded and so treated organizationally by military command. Chaplains in Vietnam also became heavily involved in "civic action" programs, mustering the humanitarian impulses of soldiers and Marines to build and support innumerable hospitals and orphanages, with a clearly identifiable public relations pay-off for the command.

Command pay-off has been an element even in forms of ministry more central to the church-established goals of the chaplaincy. In recent years the increasing emphasis on personal counseling in the ministry of chaplains has highlighted an activity with clearly identifiable advantages to the command. Large numbers of chaplains have received specialized training as counselors, many of them becoming "specialists" in the field, with full professional accreditation. The professional counseling skills of the entire chaplaincies have been upgraded.

There is no question that pastoral counseling is a legitimate and ecclesiastically recognized aspect of pastoral ministry. It should also be clearly understood that various "programs" of the past have been developed by chaplains of the highest motives, who have considered them soundly based theologically and integrally related to a religious ministry to the whole person. Each of them has been an effort to emphasize human values within the military institution, and as such a legitimate and necessary part of ministry *to* the institution.

It is nevertheless true, however, that each of these programs has also had the effect of bringing church-derived goals of the chaplain subsystem into greater congruence with the militarily-established goals of the organization itself. Each has therefore served the organizational function of increasing the power of the chaplain subsystem through the production of something needed by other elements of the organization. And each has been accompanied by attempts to stake out a more dependable claim to a front-row position at the money trough and a more universally recognized place in the organization.

Paradoxically, however, the more these contributions to military goals have been emphasized, and the better chaplains have become at them, the more trouble chaplains have found themselves in, not only with the church but also with their own internal value systems. The more organizational power chaplains acquire through these methods, the more they lay themselves open to the charge that they are being used by their military commanders as "adjuncts of war."[19]

It is because of their organizational purpose that such activities as character education and human relations programs present a crucial issue in an examination of the chaplaincy. They have been controversial, in terms of whether or not they are appropriate elements in religious ministry, but they are perhaps even more controversial in terms of the place of chaplains in military organizations. The issues involved will be examined in much greater detail in later chapters of this book.

Possibility 2: Decrease of Dependence

A second possible way for the chaplaincy subsystem to change the balance of power-dependence within the military organization would be to *decrease its dependence* on other environmental elements within the organization. Institutional duality decreases dependency in some measure. To the extent that the churches actively support their chaplains, monitor their ministries, and provide concrete forms of assistance, dependence on the military institution is reduced. At the same time the danger of subservience to military commanders is reduced, and authentic religious ministry is facilitated.

In terms of its relationship within the military organization itself, however, the chaplaincy subsystem remains highly dependent. So long as it remains an insider ministry in a total institution—that is, fully part of the military organization—the level of dependence is likely to remain high. Attempts to reduce dependence within the organization have generally taken the form of attempts to establish an independent organizational power base, i.e., to take the chaplaincy out of the category of a sub-system only, and to give it an organizational identity in its own right.

It will be recalled that the United Church of Christ task force, discussed in Chapter 1, recommended that the chaplaincies be removed from the military command structure and placed under an independent Chief of Chaplains. Such a move, were it to take place, would come in this category. We have already noted that the effect of such a move would be to make it a civilian chaplaincy, ministering to military personnel but not part of the military organization. It might be further noted now, in the organizational context, that such a move would seriously limit the ability of a chaplaincy to accomplish any of its church-derived goals within the military. It would increase enormously the power of the Chief of Chaplains *inside* the chaplaincy organization. But the chaplaincy organization itself, severed for all practical purposes from the military organization, would become even more powerless within the military than it now is.

A different kind of effort to establish a more independent organizational power base, this time within the military, is the attempt to enhance the status of the Chiefs of Chaplains. In the past, the significance of the office of Chief of Chaplains within each of the three services has been largely ceremonial and symbolic. It has been his responsibility to make decisions regarding the assignment of chaplains to their duty stations and their continuing professional education. These two functions—moving chaplains and giving them opportunities for professional growth (both of them central in the professional reward and punishment system)—are extremely important to individual chaplains. They add up, therefore, to a potent form of power in relation to chaplains. But the effect is on individuals rather than on the institution.

Each Chief of Chaplains has direct access to the operating head and the secretary of his service, but in each case the ordinary business of the office of the Chief of Chaplains is carried on at a somewhat lower organizational level. The Chief of Army Chaplains, whose organizational placement is the least equivocal of the three, is himself a member of the personal staff of the Chief of Staff. His office is a special staff agency under the Director of the Army Staff, only one echelon lower. The Chief of Air Force Chaplains is also directly under his Chief of Staff, as a special staff agency, but the business of his office is carried on under an Assistant Vice Chief of Staff.

The Chief of Navy Chaplains has the least favorable organizational placement of the three. Although custom and a somewhat equivocal regulation have granted him access to the Chief of Naval Operations and Secretary of the Navy, historically he has always functioned as an Assistant to the Chief of Naval Personnel. At the beginning of the 1970's the Chief of Navy Chaplains instituted the first of what has since become a biennial series of workshops, bringing together all chaplains in each geographical area to discuss their common concerns and to assist in establishing overall priorities for the Chaplain Corps. These have been known as "Pacemaker" workshops, and they have involved approximately ninety percent of the active duty Navy chaplains in each series. When reports of the 1971 workshops were collated the Chief of Chaplains discovered, much to his surprise, that the foremost concern expressed in the various meetings related to his own placement in the Navy Department organization. Almost universally, the chaplains objected to the placement of his office in the Bureau of Naval Personnel (with the implication that religious ministry is a function of personnel administration) and urged him to seek an organizational status directly under the Secretary of the Navy or the Chief of Naval Operations.

An attempt to achieve such an organizational change was initiated, but the issue was still not fully resolved by the time of the 1973 Pacemaker workshop series, and the concern was once again strongly expressed in the various workshops. The final resolution was somewhat ambiguous. The Chief of Chaplains was given a third echelon organizational place in the Office of the Chief of Naval Operations in addition to his placement in the Bureau of Naval Personnel (a "second hat" in military parlance). But since the Deputy Chief of Naval Operations to whom he answered in the new organizational relationship also doubled as the Chief of the Bureau of Naval Personnel, the change was more ostensible than real.

Even if the attempt had been successful to obtain an organizational placement for the Chief of Navy Chaplains directly under the Secretary of the Navy or the Chief of Naval Operations, it is probable that the gain would be not in power, but in influence. Sociologist William Gamson has usefully illuminated the difference between power and influence in social relationships.[20] His concepts are developed in terms of political activity, treating power as the social control exercised by authorities. He uses the term influence to refer to the processes by which partisan groups dedicated to particular objectives affect the decision making of the authorities in larger systems. In this light, the chaplaincy may be seen as an influence subsystem within the military system, but not as a wielder of power. The authorities within the chaplaincy subsystem (Chiefs of Chaplains and supervisory chaplains) have real power in certain areas *within* the subsystem, but in the larger system they have only the ability to influence those who have real power, the military commanders. The significance of a move to a higher organizational level lies in access to and influence on those who make decisions, not in any real increase in power.

A second possible path to a reduction in dependence lies in the direction of increased fiscal control. As in any organization, the power of the purse is real power. In all the armed services, fiscal support of religious program is a function of commanding officers. Funds controlled by the Chiefs of Chaplains are relatively insignificant in amount, and are provided mainly for the operation of their immediate offices.

Some funds are available to the Chiefs of Chaplains for service-wide ministry support, and ministry support from this source does reduce to some extent dependency at the unit level. The amount of support, however, has not been great. Historically, the Army and Air Force have provided more such funds to the Chiefs of Chaplains than has the Navy. As a result, these chiefs have more frequently designed and provided resources for service-wide religious programs. These have included such things as resources for a common topical "emphasis" throughout the service in religious program, mandatory use of a standardized religious education curriculum, standardized topics (standardized lectures) for simultaneous service-wide use in character guidance classes, and a considerable measure of standardization of chapel design and construction. In recent years the Chief of Navy Chaplains, by reprogramming funds previously spent for centrally purchased supplies and equipment (wine, wafers, electronic organs, etc.) has been able to devote additional money to ministry support. The major emphasis has been on the funding of experimental or specialized ministries in specific places and on the providing of "seed money" to assist in starting local projects. Standardized service-wide religious programs have thus far been consciously avoided, and the Navy chaplaincy has tended to encourage pluralism, local initiative, and diversity in ministries. There has been some increase in Chief of Chaplains control over those specific ministries which have been centrally funded but little effort to extend control more generally.

Even in the Army and Air Force, however, the level of control through funding has not been great. Only a major change in the basic fiscal system by which military bases, ships, and units provide religious ministry would significantly alter this. It would be necessary for funding of chapels, chaplains' offices, and religious programs to be taken completely out of the hands of commanding officers and turned over to Chiefs of Chaplains to increase significantly chaplain control over religious program, and thereby decrease the precariousness of such programs at the local level.

Such a change may be possible in some limited situations. Medical facilities have long been funded and controlled through medical channels. In recent years there has been a decided trend in the direction of the establishment of specialized military commands through which professional services of other kinds are centrally dispensed on a regional basis. Regional law centers, public works centers (controlled by Civil Engineer Corps officers), and dental centers as well as medical centers have been established. As yet, no such chaplain-controlled regional center has been initiated. It remains to be seen whether fiscal control of this kind will increase in the future. Even if it should happen, however, it would affect only operational support units. In the operational units themselves—ships, air squadrons, and combat divisions, which make up the backbone of the military establishment—religious programs will necessarily continue to be under the control of commanding officers.

The most productive and immediately available key to less dependence and precariousness is a thorough understanding by each chaplain of the military budgeting system and its efficient use at the unit level. That system provides support for every legitimate part of the organization. It is the task of chaplains—one often poorly accomplished in the past—to assert the legitimacy of their place in the system and take full advantage of the support the system provides.

A real if minor lessening of dependency comes with increasing the prestige of the chaplaincy within the organization. According to Thompson, prestige is the "cheapest" way of acquiring power (Gamson would say influence rather than power), since there is no requirement to give up anything in return.[21] The slight organizational change achieved by the Chief of Navy Chaplains, and any other organizational realignment which might bring about a chaplaincy administration closer to the top level of the military bureaucracies, would result in an increase in prestige. Such an increase could also come from greater interest in and support for the chaplaincies by the churches.

Institutional duality is probably the key factor in evaluating the place of the chaplaincy subsystem in the military organization. It is the source of the subsystem's powerlessness, since the fact that its goals are church-derived rather than service-derived makes its values peripheral for operationally-oriented military commanders. The power-dependence ratio of the subsystem is not likely to change greatly—and properly so, since power for chaplains is not in itself a goal the churches can support. Chaplains are likely to remain a relatively powerless influence group. But institutional duality is at the same time the source of whatever power the subsystem does have. The churches represent values which have considerable importance to the society at large, and the interest of that society in preserving those values, inside as well as outside the armed forces, represents a potent moral force. The churches form an independent moral power base, outside the military institution, of which the chaplaincy subsystem is the continuing representative inside the institution. Even when due allowance is made for religious pluralism, for the organizational fragmentation which denominationalism expresses, and for the historic failure of the churches to deal as a united front with the government, the moral power is still substantial.

The organizational precariousness growing out of their peripheral place in the institution, their dependence, and the absence of power are psychically difficult for chaplains to live with. In a highly structured organization in which everything is focused on the military mission, the chaplain's place is largely unstructured. In a duty-orders-authority oriented organization, he deals with a voluntaristic aspect of life. In a hardware-and-technology oriented organization he deals with intangibles. The danger is always that he will seek to relieve the discomfort by seeking a more central place in the organization (which means giving priority to military rather than church goals). The danger is that he will fall into an authoritarian model of ministry, seeking to provide religious leadership through orders and directives. The danger is that he will accomodate too thoroughly to his environment, in an attempt to escape the sometimes painful tension of institutional duality. The chaplain's major safeguard against these dangers is an understanding of the organization and of his place in it, a conscious recognition and acceptance of the precariousness which institutional duality presupposes.

The individual chaplain participates in both the organizational powerlessness and the moral power of the chaplaincy subsystem. Attempts of the subsystem to acquire power or to lessen dependence within the organization are necessarily limited in effectiveness and will not greatly change his own ministry. He must continue to live with the frustration of working in an organization in which money for bullets, beans, and bulldozers will always have a higher priority than money for church bulletins, in which his own professional goals are always peripheral to organizational goals.

But this does not mean that he must allow himself to be peripheral to the organization itself, a pathetic Chaplain Tappman off in a foggy corner of a *Catch-22* world. Organizational understanding provides a key. The chaplain has a real and legitimate place in the bureaucratic organization. Staff specialists have real and identifiable functions, responsibilities and opportunities. These are positive factors undergirding effective ministry in the organization. Though the priority may be low, the funding system guarantees support to every legitimate part of the organization. The chaplain who thoroughly understands the system can maximize the support that legitimately belongs to his own area of responsibility. The procedures are certainly different from those associated with church relationships and every-member canvasses, but they can provide just as real a foundation for effective ministry for the chaplain who masters them.

Chapter 4

The Shape of Military Ministry

"This is our chaplain," said the young paratrooper at Fort Bragg, North Carolina, as he introduced his unit chaplain to his visiting parents. The chaplain was a Roman Catholic priest. The parents were Methodists. The young soldier practised no religion, and regarded himself as an agnostic. In introducing the chaplain as "our" chaplain, he did not imply that he intended to become a Roman Catholic and thus recognize the priest as his own religious mentor; nor did he intend to return to the Methodism of his parents and look to the priest for Christian leadership in a more general sense. He was not even demonstrating an ecumenical spirit. He was simply recognizing the fact that a chaplain, in the total institutional environment of the military, serves the entire military society rather than those of his own denomination alone. This is perhaps the most important difference between any institutional chaplaincy and the parochial ministry to a congregation of a particular denomination.

All clergymen share a common core of professional responsibilities. As ordained ministers of word and sacrament, they preach, lead worship, and officiate at sacramental observances. As pastors of congregations they nourish the sense of religious community, encourage the sense of moral responsibility to serve others, and provide pastoral care for the faithful. As educators, they teach the young and the newcomers to the faith, and encourage growth in religious maturity on the part of the faithful. These activities make up the inner essence of all ministry. But as we have already noted, the external shape of ministry is greatly affected by the people served, their particular needs, and the conditions of their life. We have been examining the institutional and organizational setting of the military chaplaincy, and now we shall look at some of the distinctive characteristics of ministry within this unique setting.

We shall be emphasizing the differences from parochial ministry, but from the perspective of a recognition of common goals. We shall, for example, be examining first the serving ministry of a chaplain to the entire military society (and in later chapters we shall look in even greater detail at some aspects of this general ministry to the whole institution). The services rendered are unique to the military situation. The impetus to serve the world, however, is by no means unique to this form of ministry. The injunction to serve those outside the Christian fellowship —to visit the sick and imprisoned and receive the stranger, to follow

Christ's own example of unlimited concern for human welfare, to let the divine light shine before all men rather than guarding it under a private bushel—these are central directives for all Christian ministry. The form of outward-looking service to society is shaped by the unique needs of the military society; the dynamic is the same.

Following an initial examination of the chaplain's responsibilities to the entire military institution, the remainder of the chapter will look at specific characteristics of the military environment that affect significantly the shape of ministry—the age of military personnel; the unique kind of mobility characteristic of military life; the requirement for a non-building-centered ministry in much of the military community; the necessarily ecumenical approach to ministry. In all cases, the assumption is that the inner essence is the same as in other religious ministries. The outer shape, however, is unique.

MINISTRY TO THE ENTIRE INSTITUTION

The military minister is chaplain to the entire crew of his ship or station. Beyond the ecclesiastical context which assumes a pastor-congregation relationship, he has long met his larger group of parishioners in the purely human context, as a concerned person in encounter with other persons. It is the connotation of concern for servicemen as human beings of value in their own right—as thinking, feeling, individual persons he is called to serve—which the term "chaplain" chiefly carries in the military society.

In the serving ministry to persons as persons, the particular beliefs and denominational affiliation of the chaplain are assumed on both sides as being *his* context, but they do not make demands on the other uninvited. The paratrooper at Fort Bragg knows his chaplain is a Roman Catholic priest, and does not expect him to be anything else, when he turns to him for help. Nor does the chaplain expect the trooper to become anything other than an agnostic of Methodist background. This dimension of chaplaincy respects but transcends the denominational dimension.

Personal Counseling

Probably the best known and most widely appreciated aspect of the chaplain's ministry to the entire military community, rather than to his denominational constituency alone, is personal counseling. The "tell it to the chaplain" tradition with soldiers and sailors had its origin far back in military history. Long before counseling assumed the specialized connotations it presently has, the chaplain was known as the advisor and confidant to the troops. Chaplain G. W. Smith, in a paper submitted to the Secretary of the Navy in 1871, wrote, "The work done by a Chaplain is not simply the holding of services on Sunday as required by Regulations. That which tells most is the intercourse with individuals one by one."[1]

Prior to and during the Second World War, the "sympathetic advice and counsel" for which servicemen turned to their chaplains was taken for granted, but was not the object of much attention. Navy chaplaincy historian Clifford Drury, in a lengthy (70 page) chapter on "Chaplains at Work" in the Second World War, devoted less than a page to personal counseling. Yet the statistics he quoted (from chaplains' annual reports) were impressive indeed—118,450 interviews, on "all sorts of personal matters and problems" between sailors and chaplains at the Naval Training Station, Great Lakes, Illinois, in 1944.

Drury included a selection of "typical cartoons about chaplains and their work" in that period. Four of the six "typical cartoons" depicted the chaplain's counseling function. In one, a huge bruiser of a Shore Patrolman weeps on the shoulder of a little chaplain, saying, "And nobody loves me."

In another, a sailor says to a weeping chaplain, "But that's only half my story."

In a third, the chaplain leans over his desk to shake a sailor by the shoulders and shout, "Now, for once, you listen to *my* troubles."

In a fourth, a Marine during a monsoon in the tropics complains to a chaplain who is sitting on his desk to stay dry in his waterlogged office, "Chaplain, my tent leaks."[2] In the popular perception, chaplains were clearly personal problem solvers.

The thousands of clergymen who served as wartime chaplains learned at first hand the readiness of military men to turn to their chaplains for counsel and the potential of this form of one-to-one ministry. The millions of Americans who fought in World War II, for their part, learned to think of clergymen as helping persons, willing to assist anyone in need of counsel, whether or not he was a member of a religious congregation. This experience, on the part of both clergy and laymen, undoubtedly contributed significantly to the development of pastoral counseling as a specialized discipline within the ministerial profession.

After the Second World War, as large armed forces became a continuing part of the American experience, involving successive generations of clergy and laymen, the trend continued. Pastors who, while serving as chaplains, learned how vital this ministry could be, returned to their civilian churches and sought to offer it there. Feeling inadequately prepared, they demanded that the seminaries offer more and better courses in pastoral counseling. Former soldiers, sailors, and airmen, having learned from their chaplains the value of personal counseling in applying religious truth to concrete situations in life, began to expect the same thing of their civilian pastors. The influence of the military chaplaincy in establishing pastoral counseling as a major element in the church's ministry has in this fashion been enormous.

Within the military, chaplains in the post-World War II period became increasingly aware of the proportion of their time devoted to counseling and its unique importance in their ministry. In the 1950's a former chaplain described his experience this way:

> "An almost unparalleled opportunity for the chaplain lies in personal counseling. Pacifist critics suggest that by and large such counseling amounts to greasing the sluggish wheels of the military machine. . . . According to another image, the maladjusted serviceman waits his turn in line to cry on the padre's well-worn shoulder and receive his condolence slip. . . . My own experience is quite otherwise. How account for the fact that almost any chaplain who makes himself available is beseiged by more men seeking help with personal problems in a month than most ministers receive in a year? . . . Granted that the strain of military life vastly increases the need for counsel. Granted too that many a man whose unreasonable request has been denied in the chain of command will try the chaplain as another gimmick. This should not blind us to other aspects of the chaplain's role. No symbol of the military system, his uniform notwithstanding, the chaplain is still sought out by servicemen as representative of an abiding order of deeply human and personal values in a life that too often becomes inhuman and impersonal. In the midst of relationships necessarily authoritarian, here is one relationship in which a man can acknowledge his loves and hates, his doubts and fears, his resentments and conflicts of loyalties without being called on the carpet for insubordination or told to keep his personal problems to himself."[3]

Faced with a counseling ministry of these dimensions, chaplains sought to equip themselves to meet the need. As the chaplaincies developed programs of continuing education in the post-war period, counseling training received priority attention. A number of those chaplains selected for postgraduate education in the late forties and early fifties were given specialized training in the field. Since few institutions in that period offered the needed training, special programs were designed. A one-year course for chaplains, developed at the Menninger Clinic in Topeka, Kansas, was one of the early programs of this kind offered in a psychiatric setting for clergymen. Both Army and Navy chaplains participated. As theological seminaries began to develop specialized graduate level courses in pastoral counseling, chaplains selected for postgraduate education began to take advantage of such academically-oriented opportunities. A one-year counseling residency program in the psychiatric service at the Naval Hospital, Oakland, California, began in 1963 to train two Navy chaplains a year.

The number of chaplains who could be assigned for a full year of postgraduate training in civilian institutions was not large enough, however, to provide the level of skill needed in a whole corps for which counseling was increasingly recognized as a major professional responsibility. In the late fifties the Air Force began to provide four weeks of concentrated counseling training for large numbers of chaplains. A course for Protestant chaplains was developed at the Hogg Foundation for Mental Health, University of Texas, and a similar course for Catholic chaplains was provided at Catholic University, Washington, D. C. Approximately one hundred chaplains a year were sent to these two institutions. In the sixties, the Air Force turned to ecumenical training at the Institute of Religion, Texas Medical Center, Houston, Texas.

A survey of the entire Navy Chaplain Corps in the early sixties revealed that specialized counseling training was by far the most widely felt need, with nearly three-fourths of the chaplains expressing a need for such training. As a result, a special four-week course for Navy chaplains was designed. The theme of this course, developed at the Marriage Council of Philadelphia, was "Relationship: the Medium of Help." The basis of the course was a recognition that it is impossible to train a professionally qualified counselor in four weeks, but that some training in the nature of the helping relationship and in basic principles of counseling, coupled with continuing self-study, would make chaplains more effective in the field. By the mid-sixties the course was in operation for Navy chaplains on both east and west coasts, with a total of forty a year attending. Each chaplain agreed to follow up his four-week course with participation for at least six months in a counseling training group in his own area. Chaplains with a full year of postgraduate training were utilized as resource persons for such groups.

In the late sixties another form of counseling training for chaplains was initiated through clinical pastoral education. Such clinical training, standardized and certified by the Association for Clinical Pastoral Education (ACPE), was by that time widely used by theological seminaries as a basic part of counseling training. In 1968, after the qualification of Navy chaplains as ACPE-certified supervisors, an accredited program of Clinical Pastoral Education was initiated in two Naval hospitals, at San Diego,

California, and Bethesda, Maryland. Since that time, each chaplain ordered to duty in a Naval hospital has been given one quarter of Clinical Pastoral Education *en route* to his assignment. The San Diego Naval Hospital program has now been moved to the Marine Corps Base, Camp Pendleton, California, where non-hospital oriented training is being given.

The Army chaplaincy followed the Navy into Clinical Pastoral Education, and its present program is far more extensive than that of the Navy. Six chaplains have been qualified as ACPE-certified supervisors, and others are in training for supervisorship. Five CPE programs are now in operation in Army hospitals, and a sixth, at Fort Knox, Kentucky, follows a community model. Further expansion is planned, with an ultimate goal of community-model CPE programs at ten large installations. The current plan calls for one quarter of training for every incoming Army chaplain, with an ultimate goal of two quarters of training for all chaplains.

The Air Force has initiated one program of Clinical Pastoral Education at the Wilford Hall USAF Medical Facility, Lackland Air Force Base. The Air Force chaplaincy seems to be backing off from ACPE-model training, however, and is likely to depend primarily on other forms of counseling training in the future.

In addition to these various military-sponsored sources of counseling training, numbers of chaplains have on their own initiative enrolled in off-duty courses or degree programs offered by universities and seminaries in the vicinity of military bases. Others have banded together in study groups or entered into individual arrangements for counseling supervision. Counseling clearly occupies a central place in the ministry of most chaplains, and they have responded by making themselves professionally effective in the field. A 1973 Instruction from the Commander in Chief, U. S. Atlantic Fleet, called attention to this fact:

> *Personal counseling.* The provision of adequate means for dealing constructively with personal problems is one of the foundations of a successful human goals and resources program. Chaplains provide the Navy with a large group of professionally trained counselors, and the personal counseling they offer can be a major element in such a program. The following considerations are relevant:
> (1) *Level of counseling training.* The three-year graduate-level seminary course which is a prerequisite for commissioning in the Chaplain Corps includes in most instances training in counseling. A recent survey of a randomly gathered group of 28 Atlantic Fleet chaplains showed an average of 10.7 semester hours of seminary counseling courses. Beyond this, 74% of the chaplains in the group

had additional specialized counseling training. The Navy in recent years has provided a number of counseling training programs, in which a substantial portion of the Chaplain Corps has participated. In most instances, therefore, chaplains can offer the command a high level of expertise in personal counseling. Since this is not universal, the chaplain may appropriately be questioned as to his counseling training to determine the level of professional competence in the field. If additional counseling training is needed, the command may wish to utilize the four-week counseling course for chaplains conducted annually in Philadelphia in the month of January. . . .

(2) *The religious dimensions of the pastoral counseling of chaplains.* In some instances there is a reluctance to utilize fully the counseling skills of chaplains because of denominational affiliation or the expectation that pastoral counseling will deal only with religious problems. The chaplain's own religious context and his utilization of spiritual resources should be taken for granted, but this need not be a limiting factor. A chaplain's counseling ministry is extended to all personnel. It is never appropriate for him to use it as an occasion for proselytizing or forced religious instruction. Every chaplain is fully aware of this, and is trained to make referrals if his own or the counselee's religious orientation is at issue. The confidentiality of the pastoral relationship, which is safeguarded by the Uniform Code of Military Justice, is an asset growing out of the clergyman role.[4]

To a considerable extent the term chaplain means counselor to military men and women. Primarily because of his counseling and helping ministry to the whole community—not just because he makes arrangements for divine services for all—a Roman Catholic or Baptist or Episcopalian chaplain can be known as "the chaplain" of his battalion or ship, rather than as chaplain only to the 30% or 10% or 2% who are adherents of his own denomination.

Concern of Chaplains for the General Welfare of Troops

Service to the whole institution has from the earliest days involved chaplains in educational and humanitarian activities. We have seen that early chaplains, in both the Army and Navy, doubled as schoolmasters. Until the Naval Academy was established at Annapolis in 1845, the main responsibility for preparing junior officers for their future duties rested upon chaplains.[5] As late as the Second World War, official regulations assigned Navy chaplains the duty of instructing the illiterate.

Their interest in the human welfare of soldiers and sailors is of long standing. Outspoken protests from chaplains became a factor in shaping the rising tide of sentiment which led in 1850 to the abolition of flogging as a punishment in the Navy.[6] The influence of chaplains who had long opposed the practice also had much to do with the decision, enacted into law in 1872, to end the daily issue of grog aboard naval vessels. Chaplain George Jones, who procured coffee and sugar at his own expense "for the night drink for the deck watches" and pushed this beverage as a substitute for grog, is credited with having thus originated the tradition of coffee messes on Navy ships.[7] The interest of chaplains in libraries dated from their early days as schoolmasters.[8] One of the first motion picture machines was purchased (at his own expense) by Chaplain B. R. Patrick in 1903 for use aboard U.S.S. *Yankee.*[9] Chaplain C. H. Dickens, serving aboard the U.S.S. *Florida* from 1912 to 1915, replaced the old hand laundry system with modern machinery, an innovation soon copied by other ships of the fleet.[10]

An illustration of the wide-ranging interest of earlier chaplains in the welfare of military men and in general humanitarian endeavors is to be found in the story of Chaplain Walter Colton, who served in the mid-nineteenth century. Early in his career as a chaplain he lobbied for higher Navy pay, published a newspaper which became a platform for his outspoken attempts to put Christian principles into everyday use, campaigned against alcohol, and persuaded the Secretary of the Navy to provide money for reading room periodicals at the Navy Home in Philadelphia. In 1845 he accompanied Commodore R. F. Stockton in the U.S.S. *Congress* as chaplain of the historic Pacific squadron sent to blockade the California coast against a threat from Mexico. He saw to it that the ship left Hampton Roads with a fine library. During his California tour, he was appointed by Commodore Stockton to be Alcalde (governing official) of the Monterey District. While there he started the first newspaper in California, built a town hall, and established a school.

No one, however, would ever have accused this chaplain of allowing his extensive interest in human welfare activities to interfere with his religious ministry. In July 1846 he wrote from Monterey:

> We have had for two or three months past an increased attention in our ship to the subject of religion. It began in my Bible-class but spread beyond that number among the crew. As the interest deepened, I established a prayer-meeting, which has been held three times a week in the store-room, an ample and convenient apartment for that purpose. Here you will find at these meetings some sixty sailors on their knees at prayer; some thirty of them, it is believed, have recently experienced religion; the rest are inquirers, and come to be prayed for. . . . It would affect you to tears to hear these rough, hardy sailors speak in these meetings of their sins, of the compassion of Christ, and their new-born hopes. Almost every evening some new one, the last perhaps expected, comes in, and, kneeling

down, asks to be prayed for. These meetings have no opposition among the officers, and very little, if any, among the men. There has been a great change in the Navy within a few years on this subject. We can now have Bible-classes and prayer-meetings on board our men-of-war, and find among our officers many who will encourage them, and not a few who will give them their efficient aid.[11]

Humanitarian Work

The period following World War II has been marked by a continuing military presence in many overseas areas. The charitable activities of soldiers, sailors, airmen, and marines all over the world have frequently been sparked and led by chaplains. Numerous orphanages have been established and supported by American servicemen, generally with their chaplains providing the inspiration and organization.

Casa Materna in Naples has been the special project of Sixth Fleet chaplains and sailors since the early fifties. For two decades "Operation Handclasp" has made medical supplies, toys, and other American goods, donated by manufacturers and agencies, available to be transported on Navy ships for charitable distribution in the foreign ports they visit. Shipboard chaplains have frequently been the overseers of this program. "Operation Centurion," a continuing effort of the Air Force chaplaincy, has over the years given large amounts of money in support of Union Theological Seminary in Tokyo, Japan.

During the Vietnamese War, with thousands of American soldiers and marines on duty throughout that wartorn and underdeveloped country, volunteer work with orphanages, hospitals, churches and schools so proliferated that it was formalized into a civic action program, largely led by chaplains. G-5 and S-5 sections were added to the classic military staff organization to deal with civil affairs.[12]

Often such humanitarian programs, initiated by chaplains, have been formalized and taken over by others. On every Army post an agency called Army Community Services assists persons with various types of problems. It was started by chaplains in Germany and is now run, Army-wide, by non-chaplain professionals. Throughout the history of the chaplaincies, their extensive involvement in a wide variety of humanitarian endeavors has been a major aspect of their ministry to the total institution.

Collateral Duties

The historic involvement of chaplain in collateral fields other than religion—education from the beginning, and many other activities later —was in time formalized with collateral duty assignments which made chaplains officially responsible for a wide range of activities. In addition to educational responsibilities, these have included libraries, athletics, recreation, movies, unit newspapers, informational services, and a number of other activities generally related to welfare and morale.

The tendency of such collateral duty assignments to get out of hand and to occupy time better devoted to the chaplain's primary religious responsibilities has long been a bone of contention within the chaplaincies, and in some cases chaplains have complained that they were little more than welfare officers. The trend toward increasing specialization, with the development of formalized programs to meet many human needs, has solved the problem in connection with some of these collateral activities. Recreational programs, athletics, motion pictures, information and education services now have their own centrally-administered bureaucracies in the military services. Today their own regulations, in most cases, preclude the assignment of these responsibilities to chaplains. A multitude of jobs remain to be done, however.

When the Air Force became a separate service, in 1949, it solved the problem by outlawing all collateral duties for chaplains. The Army soon followed suit, and this generally has been the line followed by those two services. The recent emphasis on human goals throughout the Department of Defense has led to some limited exceptions to the "religious duties only" policies of the Army and Air Force. Between eighty and ninety Army chaplains are now serving as human relations instructors. At the height of the concern over drug and race-related problems in the early seventies, the Air Force chaplaincy allowed a few chaplains to work full-time in Social Action programs; all have now returned to religious duties. The development of the Chapel Manager career field for enlisted chaplain assistants in the Air Force has permitted chaplains to avoid many administrative duties such as fiscal management. It should be noted, of course, that while regulations protect Army and Air Force chaplains in most cases from assigned collateral duties, they can and do voluntarily undertake activities ranging from Little League officials to United Fund chairmen.

The Navy chaplaincy has consciously resisted pressures to forbid all collateral duties. In the shipboard community (the normative unit for the Navy), numerous extra duties must be divided up among a relatively small number of officers, and chaplains generally have felt that they should assume their fair share of the burden, along with all others. Navy chaplains have tended to feel that to fail to do so would take them out of the mainstream of the life of the shipboard community and isolate them from their parishioners. Their view of ministry has traditionally been one in-

volving the whole person and the whole of life. They have resisted a
definition of the "religious" which isolates it from the total life of the
command and its members. This philosophy was clearly enunciated by
Chaplain John B. Frazier, the first Chief of Navy Chaplains, in the earliest
Chaplains Manual (1918):

> The Navy Regulations very wisely do not specify the duties of a
> Chaplain. The reason for this is that his work is of such a nature that
> to "build a fence" around it would of necessity so handicap him that
> the most important of his duties could not be performed. It is my
> contention that a Chaplain's duties consist of "anything and every-
> thing" that he may do in a wise and tactful way for the social,
> physical, intellectual, moral and spiritual welfare of the ship's com-
> pany.[13]

Collateral duties have continued to be an issue within the Navy
Chaplain Corps, and a number of chaplains feel that they should be
outlawed entirely. Certain duties (such as serving on courts martial and
serving as treasurer of non-chapel-related funds) have long been specifically prohibited. Procedures have been established to prevent the assignment of any duty which violates the conscience of the individual chaplain
or the regulations of his church. Beyond this, guidelines seek to encourage the assignment of collateral duties which are related to the chaplain's
primary duties and appropriate to his professional training. The range
covered by such duties (many voluntarily accepted or solicited by individual chaplains) is still enormous. A study conducted by Chaplain Dennis
C. Kinlaw listed 100 collateral duties being performed by senior Navy
chaplains, ranging from Navy Relief interviewing to writing speeches for
the commanding officer.[14]

The 1974 Navy *Chaplains Manual* spells out current policy regarding
collateral duties for Navy chaplains. It allows considerable flexibility, but
in establishing parameters gives far more detailed guidelines than prior
regulatory publications had provided:

> 1. By virtue of their place in the military organization, Navy chap-
> lains serve the entire command, not just that portion of the com-
> mand which is identified with their particular denomination, or with
> the chapel program as such. Navy chaplains generally consider op-
> portunities for constructive contacts with the total Navy, Marine
> Corps, and Coast Guard community to be part of their religious
> ministry. The assignment of a limited number of appropriate collat-
> eral duties may provide such constructive contacts.
> 2. The centrality of the chaplain's primary duty of religious ministry
> is the basic principle which should determine the place of collateral
> duty assignments. The chaplain is an ordained member of the

clergy, made available to the Navy by the churches for religious ministry, and anything which detracts from the primacy of this identity is prohibited. (See Article 0805, U. S. Navy Regulations)

Appropriate and Inappropriate Collateral Duties

1. The appropriateness of any particular collateral duty is determined by the circumstances.

2. Any collateral duty is inappropriate if it is so time-consuming or the circumstances are such as to interfere with the performance of the chaplain's primary duty of religious ministry.

3. There are certain collateral duty responsibilities to which chaplains may contribute in connection with their religious ministry, but for which they should not be assigned primary responsibility because of the extensiveness of the involvement in non-religious matters. For instance, chaplains contribute substantially to the PAO [Public Affairs Officer] function through their ecclesiastical relations and humanitarian involvement, but they should not be assigned duty as the Public Affairs Officer. They participate in the Casualty Assistance Calls Program, particularly in the early stages, when after the next of kin have been notified of the death the chaplain ministers to the bereaved, assisting in making funeral arrangements and giving religious support. They may assist the CACO [Casualty Assistance Calls Officer], but they shall not be assigned as the CACO. They may be involved in recreational activities, but should not be assigned as Special Services Officer.

4. The most appropriate collateral duties are those most closely related to and supportive of religious ministry, and to the promotion of personal growth and development.[15]

Some churches, as represented by their chaplaincy officials, have preferred the Army and Air Force attitude toward collateral duties. All have raised objections when chaplains have been so heavily burdened with collateral duties as to interfere with the ministry of religion. In general, however, the churches have not objected in principle to such assignments when the duties are appropriate and the number reasonable. The many collateral functions performed by civilian clergymen in their communities are analagous. The Navy chaplaincy, in refusing to outlaw them, has maintained the support of most denominational officials.

Personal counseling, activities meeting human needs and contributing to the general well-being of the troops, humanitarian work, and collateral duties, when appropriate, are all part of the chaplain's ministry to the entire military community. There are other major aspects of the general ministry to the whole military institution which require separate treatment. The involvement of chaplains in character education, and more recently in certain personal growth and human relations activities, has been somewhat controversial. These activities, less closely related to church-oriented religion and directly related to the phenomenon of civil religion, will be examined in detail in Chapters seven and eight.

In the remainder of this chapter we will look at certain other distinctive characteristics of military ministry which set it apart from parish ministry.

YOUNG ADULT MINISTRY

The parish church society is family-centered; the military society decidedly is not. It is made up of young adults. Nearly three-fourths of the men and women in the armed forces are under twenty-five. Eighty to eighty-five percent of them are under thirty. The military chaplaincy is, along with the campus ministry, one of the few places in which the churches are offering a specialized ministry to the young adult generation.

It ought to be noted further that it is, for the most part, a ministry with single young adults, in a setting isolated from family influences. Many servicemen are, of course, married. But in terms of life inside the total institution, the harsh truth is that whether or not these young adults are married is largely irrelevant. This is not to say that families of servicemen are considered unimportant. On the contrary, the military authorities give a tremendous amount of time and attention to families (the term, revealingly, is "family problems") and assume a far more paternalistic responsibility for families than is the case with civilian employers. But the fact remains that from the standpoint of life within the total institution families are peripheral. Separation from family, indeed, is a major factor to be contended with. The parish of the military chaplain is largely made up, then, of single young adults.

When a clergyman leaves the family-oriented ministry of the local parish church and enters a young adult society, one of the major elements in his training, if not the key to his whole transition, is helping him to understand young adults. For this reason, considerable attention has been given in orientation courses at chaplains' schools and various professional training seminars to a study of the young adult age group. The chaplaincies have found the resources of the churches in this field to be somewhat limited. Apart from the campus ministry, churchmen have had little experience with young adults, and most of the available studies and literature in the field are college-oriented. Military young adults represent a cross-section of the population, but their background is predominantly blue-collar, and available resources have not always been relevant. Beginning in the mid-sixties, therefore, the chaplaincies conducted studies of their own. The Navy's Chaplain Corps Planning

Group was especially active in this exploration. A number of consultants from theological seminaries and church agencies were employed, and specialized studies were conducted under government contract. The National Young Adult Project of the Methodist Church (which later became an ecumenical agency) was especially helpful, working with the chaplaincies of all three services.

In developing their understanding of young adults, the chaplains have found the developmental psychology of Robert J. Havighurst[16] and the insights of psychiatrist Erik Erikson, who identified the unique conflicts and developmental tasks of the young adult years,[17] to be especially helpful. Many of the specialized young adult ministries since developed, focusing on identity, value-formation, and relationships, have been informed and shaped by these studies.

At the height of the counterculture movement in the 1960's, there was a tendency to describe the entire young adult generation in terms of the life-style and values of the extremists. The waning of the counterculture has brought a more sober assessment and a recognition that the generation gap is not necessarily so wide as it appeared to be in that period. However, the chaplains have learned a number of useful things from the intensive study of the young adult generation which began then. Young adulthood is now recognized as a unique stage of psycho-social development, a period with its own issues and problems and its own needs, which religious ministry must recognize.

The statement that young adults are the missing generation in the conventional parish church comes as no surprise to any churchman. And this is a fact of crucial importance, for the young adult years are the formative years, the years when value systems are adopted and commitments given. Polls taken during the sixties and seventies have shown a gradual decline in church attendance across the whole population, but a dramatic decline in church attendance by those between 18 and 30. The disenchantment of young adults with the institutional church, which they see as heavily compromised and involved with the status quo, is a truism. These factors must not be underestimated by chaplains providing a young adult ministry.

There are some encouraging and redeeming factors, however. Chaplains find that young adults who talk loudest about the inadequacies and failures of the church are still concerned about it, and in many cases maintaining an active relationship to it. It is often a love-hate relationship. They may reject it intellectually and complain loudly of its irrelevance and hypocrisy. But they are still bound to it with strong ties.

One one occasion a young man looked me up, late one evening, to talk about his problems. He had been arrested for drunkenness the night before, but his sense of failure went far deeper than that. He had flunked out of college before joining the service, and he felt that everything had gone wrong for him. I was impressed by the fact that the attitude toward Christianity he revealed was highly ambivalent. He had come from an active Southern Baptist family, and his thinking and standards had been shaped by his religious background. But he had violently rejected what he considered the narrowness and rigidity and self-centeredness of his own religious heritage. He refused to identify himself as a Christian. He said he had worked out his own standards and beliefs which were quite different from those of the church. Yet in the five weekends since his arrival at that particular Naval base, he had gone to services in three different churches—an Episcopalian, a Roman Catholic, and an Assemblies of God. (The only one he had liked was the Assemblies of God— because the singing reminded him of his home church!) He also complained in some disgust that none of the churches in town had anything going on weekday evenings; they were all locked. Presumably he had found this out first hand. It should never be overlooked that the church still has a strong hold on the very young adults who reject it most vociferously. They have a large reservoir of residual respect for chaplains as representatives of the church, and turn to them readily. Their special problems cry out for religious answers, and they know it.

Many of the specialized young adult ministries developed by the chaplaincies have been experimental. Some have been highly successful; some have failed. But chaplains have learned from all of them.

The LEAD Program

One of the earliest, most ambitious, and (in terms of lessons learned) most productive of the specialized young adult ministries was the LEAD (Lay Enrichment And Development) program, devised by the Navy's Chaplain Corps Planning Group for the Atlantic Fleet Submarine Force during the early sixties.[18] The program was designed for Polaris submarines, the crews of which are far too small to justify the inclusion of a full-time chaplain. On patrol, these crews are submerged and isolated for long periods of time. There was much concern in the sixties, when the Polaris program was new, for the welfare of the young crewmen during these long periods of isolation in close quarters, and considerable attention was given to insuring their physical, emotional, and spiritual health. In this context large amounts of money were made available for the research and development of the LEAD program. Because of the conditions of submarine life, it was based on a major utilization of laymen and a minimum participation of ordained clergymen. It was regarded as a pilot program which might later be applied to small ships, without their own chaplains, throughout the Navy.

Since adequate funding was available, special studies were made and several conferences were convened, with civilian authorities as consultants, to ensure that the program would meet the special needs of the young adults for whom it was designed. Four "issue areas" were identified: (1) the young adult as a social being; (2) the young adult and sexuality; (3) the young adult and his search for life meaning and value; and (4) the young adult and vocation and leisure. Studies of these issue areas became the theoretical base of a carefully designed ministry to the whole person.

The program consisted of two complimentary emphases. The GRADE (Group Religious And Devotional Expression) Phase provided for training of young submarine crewmen to act as religious lay leaders. Special schools were established at New London, Connecticut, and Charleston, South Carolina, the major Polaris submarine bases, and the training was given in an ecumenical context in two-week courses. It was the responsibility of these lay leaders to conduct religious worship, to lead Bible study, and to conduct discussion groups on theological and moral principles and their application to social and personal life. They were carefully limited to non-sacramental religious functions, but the development of the Lay Eucharistic Ministry by the Roman Catholic Church during this period made it possible for the sacrament to be offered at Catholic lay-led services.

The other half of the program, PEP (Personal Enrichment Phase) was the portion which focused most specifically on the young adult issue areas. The heart of the PEP phase was an audio-visual reference system, placed aboard each Polaris submarine for group and personal use. There were three elements in the system. Audio equipment, consisting of a cassette tape playback unit with amplifier and earphones for private listening, provided some discussion and information programs as well as GRADE Phase religious materials (music for worship, devotions, etc.). The second element was a cartridge-loaded sound filmstrip system, providing program material consisting initially of 188 cartridges on twenty-one current subjects, ranging from sex education to current events. The third and most sophisticated element was a versatile cartridge-loaded super 8 mm sound motion picture projector. It provided instant rear-screen projection for up to twenty or thirty persons upon the insertion of a cartridge and the pressing of a button. The reference library accompanying this F-8 projector consisted of 958 films on 86 subjects, ranging over all four young adult issue areas.

The LEAD program was never fully implemented. In the mid-sixties an enormous amount of money was poured into research, and even more into the purchase of the expensive hardware and audio-visual materials. But leadership changes, both in the Submarine Force and the Chaplain Corps, brought declining interest, followed inevitably by declining funds. Chaplain billets were sacrificed by the Submarine Force as priorities were rearranged. Then the Lay Leadership schools were discontinued. By 1972 the GRADE phase was gone, and PEP—Personal *Enrichment* Phase of LEAD—had been turned into PIP—Personal *Information* Program— under line leadership. Despite its failure to win a permanent place, however, it was a germinal program which has influenced many further developments in young adult ministry. The studies of young adult issue areas contributed to the understanding of this age group for all chaplains. Worship materials devised for GRADE lay leaders have been used widely by chaplains and laymen alike. The development of the audio-visual reference library has focused attention on the appeal of well-selected tapes and films to young adults, and a great expansion of their use as ministry resources.

The CREDO Community

One of the most successful of the specialized young adult ministries initiated by chaplains has been the CREDO community, offered to Navy and Marine Corps men and women in the Southern California area. CREDO began as a chaplain-devised response to the drug scare of the late sixties. Its founder, Navy Chaplain Donald B. Harris, had been selected because of successful experience in ministering to drug abusers and had been given a year of clinical training, with emphasis on drug problems, at the Oakland Naval Hospital. He was sent to San Diego to develop a specialized ministry in 1970. The name "CREDO" was originally a somewhat strained acronym, standing for "Chaplains' Relevance to the Emerging Drug Order." A major portion of its funding and support came from the Navy's Human Resources Project, which had responsibility for drug education and rehabilitation programs and which found CREDO to be one of the few efforts that was working.

The CREDO staff has been headed by two chaplains and assisted by one line officer and several enlisted men and women. A number of other chaplains from the San Diego area have worked part-time with the project.

After the first year, the drug focus of CREDO's ministry was deemphasized. The chaplains involved took the position that drug abuse among young adults was a symptom, rather than a cause, of alienation:

For the young, the mutually shared malaise caused by an increasingly depersonalized world may express itself in . . . unconventional ways. That the ways may be anti-social is understandable since the young feel they have little of value to lose. . . . Many people have been overwhelmed with the complexity of the problem and have chosen to drop out. Some of these have found that drugs alleviate the pain and hollowness of their existence. Some feel that drugs enable them to be temporarily freed from societal strictures and thus help them to establish both physical and spiritual contact with something transcendent, authentic, and untied to the utilitarian and the expedient. . . . Certainly the various religious manifestations of the search, be they Eastern meditation, mysticism, introspective disciplines, the Jesus movement, or fundamentalism, reflect a need for roots, for a stability to counterbalance the transitory and temporary character of our age.[19]

It became a ministry, then, to alienated young adults, whether drug abusers or not, and its approach, though non-sectarian, has been thoroughly spiritual in orientation. CREDO functions on two basic levels. One is a 72-hour workshop, conducted from Thursday through Sunday in a lodge high in the mountains east of San Diego. Much use is made in these workshops of youth culture music. The purposes are self-understanding, communication, and relationship. A communion service is the high point. Says the CREDO director:

The workshop is neither intended to be a retreat, sensitivity training, or any other sort of singularly viewed experience. It is hoped that it may open the door to some understanding. No long term attitudinal changes are sought or anticipated from the workshop experience alone, although a growing number of people relate that the workshop has been a turning point in their lives.[20]

The workshop serves as an introductory experience for the other level of CREDO, the community which is centered at CREDO House, located in a converted fire house adjacent to Naval activities in the heart of San Diego. The House is open afternoons and evenings. There is a library with journals ranging from *Rolling Stone* to the *Manchester Guardian;* an audio-visual reference library with cassette projectors, following the LEAD pattern; various crafts—leatherwork, pottery, candle-making; frequent movies (always with discussion); monthly "family" dinners; and an atmosphere of openness and communication. The heart of the program at CREDO House, however, is a wide range of small groups. Any given night finds one or more small groups meeting. Many are religiously oriented. Though the alienated young adults attracted to CREDO are frequently non-religious or even anti-religious, and persons of every religious attitude and orientation are warmly welcomed, the atmosphere of CREDO is forthrightly and unapologetically Christian.

CREDO has succeeded to a remarkable degree in establishing a genuine sense of community—a family feeling—among the thousands of young adults to whom it has ministered. A monthly newsletter, much of it devoted to letters from "family members" who have moved on to other areas, is distributed. The May, 1974 address roster mailed out to "family members" listed 912 names. 432 were active duty military men and women, representing a total of 43 shore activities, covering an area from Long Beach, California, to Yuma, Arizona. 192 were shipboard sailors, serving on 72 ships of the Pacific Fleet. The remaining 286 had civilian addresses, some of them military people with homes in the civilian community, others former military men and women who have since been discharged but have continued the CREDO relationship. A satellite group meets regularly at the Marine Corps Base, Yuma, Arizona. Groups of members who happen to be together maintain their relationship and identity as "family members" in such places as Okinawa and aboard ships deployed in the western Pacific. The sense of community which has been developed is quite remarkable.

A letter from a recently discharged Navy man, published in the May, 1974 CREDO Newsletter, gives something of the feel of the community:

> Dear Friends,
> . . . I was baptized with [my wife] on 19 April. I realized that I have been a Christian basically all my life and am glad that I finally took steps to recognize it. Being a Christian used to have a different meaning to me, it used to mean going to church every Sunday and conforming to a bunch of rules that I didn't agree with, etc. I felt that a great deal of the traditions were not real and that if I were to be baptized as a Christian that it would mean that I could not be myself, that I would have to put on a phony mask and go through a lot of rituals that were meaningless to me. I realize now that it does not need to be that way, that I can be a Christian and be myself at the same time. . . . I know that no matter how bad I act and no matter how many times I fail there is always someone who loves me and will look out for me. And He will love me for what I am, I don't have to put on an act for Him. It feels really neat. . . . I still will be down at CREDO and plan on starting school in June. I feel happier than last month, I guess it is because I had a real neat workshop at the end of March that set things off right for this month. I feel that I have gotten closer to some people that I have known for awhile and have made a lot of new friends. Having people around that I love and care about makes it hard for me to have time to get depressed. . . .[21]

Special Need Ministries

Because young adulthood is a period of searching and transition, and because soldiers, sailors, and airmen are young adults in an unrooted and crisis-prone environment, many young adult ministries developed by the chaplaincies have been designed to fill special needs. One of the greatest of these needs centers around what Erik Erikson called the "intimacy crisis" of the young adult period—the search for permanent relationships, particularly in marriage, problems of sex and singleness, marriage and divorce.

To meet this special need, the Army chaplaincy has established Family Life Centers at a number of major bases. Staffed by chaplains and in some instances by Civil Service sociologists, psychologists, or social workers as well, these centers offer a broad range of pre-marriage and family life educational services as well as counseling services. Group counseling is often a major emphasis.

A number of shipboard Navy chaplains have conducted marriage and pre-marriage workshops or seminars on the return trip to the United States after extended deployments, finding interest high at such a time. A wide range of coffee houses, contact centers, and after hours drop-in ministries have been provided by chaplains on Army, Navy, and Air Force bases, particularly in the late afternoon and evening hours.

Chapel-Centered Activities

Most of the work of chaplains with young adults takes place, of course, as part of the regular chapel program. Both traditional and non-traditional approaches are used. One of the most striking of the non-traditional chapel programs is that of the Recruit Chapel at the Naval Training Center, Orlando, Florida. Sunday services, both Protestant and Roman Catholic, are planned and largely conducted by the recruits themselves. The services are free-wheeling, loosely structured, and highly contemporary. They generally feature a rock band, much hand-clapping and a great deal of recruit participation. A song, composed by the chapel organist, called "Five (or Four, Three, Two) Sundays to Go," is a fixture at these services.

A visiting chaplain who attended one such service recently described the dramatization of the temptation of Jesus, which was the "sermon" that day. A black recruit, clad in black leotards, played the role of the devil. The top of the altar was the mountaintop, and the altar rail was the pinnacle of the temple. In a staged interruption, two black recruits strode up the aisle challenging the use of a black man as the devil, and raising questions about racial concerns, whereupon the group turned to the chaplain for some explanations and comments. The entire service had been planned and rehearsed by the participants in their brief Saturday morning free time.

The visiting chaplain professed himself to have been somewhat shocked by the irregularity of it all, but greatly impressed by the impact, as compared with a traditional service. The Orlando chapel does offer traditional services as well, but the recruit-conducted services are much better-attended, with a packed chapel despite the voluntary attendance which is now the rule in recruit centers.

Despite difficulties, frustrations, and failures, there are many hopeful signs for chaplains ministering to young adults. The early seventies have been marked by an upsurge of spiritual interest on the part of young adults, including those in the military. The politically-oriented radicalism which military authorities so feared in the sixties has largely dissipated. The underground anti-military newspapers, the "GI Unions," and the court challenges to military authority have for the most part evaporated along with the anti-Vietnamese War movement.

Some military commanders have been disturbed to discover that the radicalism of the sixties has been replaced by a number of non-conventional, spiritually-oriented movements among the troops. With military personnel who have served or have been home-ported in Japan, groups of members of the Soka Gokkai Buddhist sect have proliferated. Throughout the services there are a number of followers of various eastern gurus, swamis, and divine light movements. Transcendental meditation and various "pop" therapies have many military adherents. Some commanding officers, learning of the existence of such groups of believers in their commands, have viewed it as a threat to "good order and discipline," and some chaplains have seen it as a threat to established religions.

Many chaplains, however, see this resurgence of spiritual interest as good news. A search for spiritual answers to human problems, no matter what the form of spirituality, is a hopeful starting point. The spiritual answers to young adult needs which are available through the Christian gospel can surely compete with those offered by pop therapies and gurus.

This optimistic assessment is borne out by the fact that by far the most pervasive and vigorous manifestation of spiritual resurgence in the armed forces is taking place within Christianity. The small lay groups of evangelical Christians, earlier known as the Jesus movement and still proliferating without organization or central direction, is a young adult phenomenon. Such groups, some of which are charismatic in character and others of which are not, are to be found throughout the armed forces. For the most part they are lay-led, and whether or not the chaplain is even aware of their existence in a particular unit is likely to depend largely on his attitude. If the "official" chapel program is viewed as irrelevant or hostile to their kind of Christian fellowship and witness, their existence is likely to be "underground"; not secret, but out of communication with the chaplain. For the most part, however, they are not anti-church or anti-chaplain. They eagerly welcome the help and support of a cooperative chaplain, and when so encouraged are likely to become the backbone of his congregation.

In 1973 and 1974, while I was serving as Fleet Chaplain of the U. S. Atlantic Fleet, I was impressed by the extent and potential of this almost entirely unorganized lay movement among sailors and marines. Established lay movements, including the Navigators (a well-organized evangelical Christian movement among military enlisted men, with a number of staff persons and Christian Servicemen's Centers) and the Campus Crusade for Christ (which has in recent years been active among the military, also employing a number of staff persons), have sought to give leadership. To a considerable extent, however, the small groups have remained spontaneous and unaffiliated. In my visits to ships and stations, as I began to ask questions, I discovered that such groups were present in almost every command. Some were quite small, and some chaplains were unaware of their existence. But on the whole, chaplains related to them extremely well, and the result was mutual reinforcement. These dedicated young adults represent an enormous potential and an evidence of the widespread and growing interest of their age group in religious activity which is their own, and which they perceive as meeting their particular needs.

MINISTRY AND MILITARY MOBILITY[22]

A chaplain and a civilian minister were discussing their respective ministries. "I have a parish of transients," the chaplain said. "My people are continually coming and going. They are transferred, on the average, every two years. On any given Sunday I don't recognize half the people in the chapel. This is one of the unique aspects of the military chaplaincy."

"Not any more," the civilian minister replied. "My people are continually coming and going too. I have a church in a metropolitan suburb, with a lot of rising young executives, and they are transferred by their companies just about as often as military men are. Why, I doubt if there are ten families still in my church who were charter members when it was organized eight years ago. You have to remember that the United States has become a nation of transients."

And indeed it has. In modern urbanized America nearly everybody moves frequently. The quiet, rural community where families have lived in the same homestead for five generations and nearly everyone has deep roots, is now the exception rather than the rule.

Yet the chaplain who is sensitive to the implications of his environment is not willing to settle for an easy identification between the problems of military mobility and those of mobile Americans in general. The suburban church and the post chapel do not confront the same kind of mobility. The total institution adds a special dimension to the mobility of military men and their families, and to the ministry of chaplains. No serviceman experiences his relationship to his service simplistically, like that of employee to employer. The total institution of the service is, for him, whether temporarily or permanently, a total way of life.

Military forces are by their nature highly mobile. By definition they must be prepared to move at a moment's notice. No matter how solid and permanent a stateside base may look, it exists only to support the operating forces: the ships, the fighting regiments, the aircraft squadrons, the Fleet Marine Force. Dry as the ground under his barracks may be, the land-based sailor "goes ashore" after work for liberty "on the beach." His base is organized and commanded as if it were a ship. The floor of his office is a deck. The ship is the normative unit for the Navy, as is the fighting division for the Army. So the civilian should not be fooled by the seeming permanence of brick chapels and ivy-covered headquarters buildings. The whole mystique of military service assumes a special kind of operational mobility as a way of life.

There are differences, then, between the mobility of military people and that of Americans in general. These special dimensions added to the military situation can be summarized in terms of: (1) the involuntary nature of personal mobility in the armed forces; (2) the family separation which military mobility requires; and (3) the total mobile environment provided by the armed forces. Let us take a closer look at these three dimensions.

Involuntary Personal Mobility

The rising young executive working for Standard Oil may be transferred by his company from city to city at frequent intervals. But he will always be consulted about those transfers. If he does not like a particular city he will probably have options open to him. If the company is insistent, he always has the option of quitting and going to work for Texaco. Not so with military men. The transfer of the soldier or sailor comes in the form of orders, and he has much less control over his personal mobility than does the civilian.

Further, it is the white collar and executive portions of the civilian population that move most frequently. Blue collar workers, in general, are far less mobile. They may move from rural to industrial areas, or from one industrial area to another, to find work; but such moves are always self-motivated. Laborers, whether skilled or unskilled, are rarely if ever transferred by the employer.

Blue collar equivalents in the armed forces are transferred as routinely as executives. For all military men, "orders are orders." You may state your preferences and submit your requests, but whether or not they are honored will depend on the needs of the service. If you do not like your orders, in the last resort there is no realistic alternative but to grit your teeth and say, "Aye, Aye, sir." The military man has very little control over his personal mobility.

Separation from Family

Another significant dimension of military mobility is family separation. In no other way of life does involuntary separation from family present itself so universally as it does in the armed forces. Quantitatively it varies from service to service. It is probably greatest in the Navy, where long periods at sea are routine. Family separation is common in both the other services, however. Deployed combat units and hardship posts where no dependents are allowed affect a great many soldiers even in the peacetime Army. For many Air Force units, 179-day TDY (temporary duty) assignments—one month at home and 179 days on TDY elsewhere —have been a common pattern since the Vietnamese War. Nearly every serviceman, sooner or later, must undergo some separation from his family.

This aspect of military service leads to a great deal of loneliness. It leads to family tensions and pressures, when mothers must assume the father role as well as their own, and when fathers must be fathers *in absentia.* It leads to special needs when emergencies arise in separated families. Whether he is accompanying the deployed troops or serving in the base chapel at the home port in which families are waiting, this separation is sure to be a major element in the ministry of every military chaplain.

The Total Mobile Environment

A third and perhaps even more distinctive dimension of military mobility is an outgrowth of the characteristics of the total institution, which we examined in an earlier chapter. Military service provides a total mobile environment for its highly transient military personnel. Servicemen routinely conduct their operations in places—at sea, overseas, in combat areas—where a normal community environment is not available. Everything necessary to sustain life and social organization must be taken along. The ship at sea is the extreme example, with its self-contained housing, utilities, food services, shopping facilities, medical, dental, religious, and recreational facilities, and even its own charity drives. Combat units ashore similarly provide a total mobile environment.

Even within the United States, military service takes families as well as service personnel into areas in which they are cut off from the normal facilities of a civilian community. If a new air base is needed, the government does not plunk it down in the middle of Manhattan. It goes to the prairies of Texas or the wheat fields of Kansas where there is plenty of wide open space—but no corner grocery or neighborhood church. The base must be built as a complete community. Where isolation is not a problem, the civilian resources of a small community which would be overtaxed by a large military influx must be supplemented.

In foreign areas, where the standard of living and culture are quite different from those of the United States, a total mobile environment which meets American needs must be provided. American military communities overseas are sometimes ridiculed as "little America" ghettos, complete with Cub Scout packs, backyard barbecues, and an English-speaking Santa Claus in the base exchange at Christmas time. There is justification for the complaint. Many American families in such ghettos pass up priceless opportunities for involvement in another culture and for enriching experiences. But the complainers must remember the involuntary nature of the overseas service of most military families. To live in a charming tatami-matted, paper-walled, non-heated house among neighbors who speak only Japanese can be a delightful experience if you choose it; to have it forced on you is quite another matter. As long as military mobility remains involuntary, American-type communities for those serving overseas will be a necessity in order to maintain an acceptable level of morale.

Even apart from mobile operating units such as ships at sea, in which the total mobile environment has to be taken along to sustain life, the armed forces tend to create for families as well as men a ready-made, self-contained total environment. Military service is a way of life in which people become accustomed to finding such a total mobile environment provided for them wherever they go. The chaplain's place in the military community is itself an outgrowth of this particular kind of mobility. It provides the rationale for such ministry.

Implications for Ministry

There are certain implications for ministry in the involuntary dimension of military mobility. There is a ministry to those seeking to adjust to unwanted assignments, unchosen jobs. There is a ministry to

those trying to make themselves happy in areas they do not like, among
customs and cultures they do not understand. There is a sense of permanence and stability, an at-homeness in even the most unwanted environment, which can be contributed by the presence of the church that is
"built on a Rock."

There are equally straightforward implications growing out of the
family separation which is part of service life. No chaplain who has
watched lonely servicemen aimlessly walking the streets in off-base
towns, who has talked with wives desperate just for the sound of an adult
male voice, can be unaware of the challenge to provide a religious ministry to loneliness. Family tensions, caused or intensified by separations,
increase vastly the need for a counseling ministry. And the crises that
arise in separated families offer the clergyman one of his greatest opportunities.

There are dangers. Some servicemen and their families have a tendency to look upon the services of a chaplain as a "government benefit"
to which they are entitled as part of their compensation. In such a context
there is a downgrading of the elements of personal responsibility and
existential involvement which must be part of a vital religious experience.
But there are redemptive elements, too. The non-church-related young
woman, facing a crisis in the absence of her husband, is not likely to
search out a civilian minister on whom she has no claim. But when the
chaplain is one of the military community "benefits" which her husband
has left her, chances are good she will turn to him. In a highly transient
life, the total mobile environment becomes a substitute for the kind of
stability others may find in the community structures of a civilian neighborhood. It provides a security that would otherwise be lacking. The
presence of a chaplain, as part of the environment, contributes to that
stability and security. The chaplain will minister effectively only when he
understands the unique dimensions of this kind of mobility and responds
to them in a relevant and creative way.

NON-BUILDING-CENTERED MINISTRY

Normative American Christianity is centered in church buildings,
and a church building has a tendency to become the focal point of its own
world. One of the great dangers is that such Christianity may isolate itself
from the real world of real people; that ministers, surrounded by little
groups of like-minded believers, may preach from their pulpits a message
to which no one is listening. The military chaplaincy has helped the
church keep in touch with its times, go where the people are, and say
things relevant to their needs. It constitutes an assertion that the gospel
cannot be kept in a cloister.

The military chaplaincy has never been a building-centered ministry. This is not to say that chapels are not used and appreciated in permanent bases where they are appropriate; no one wishes to do away with buildings and building-centered ministries where they fit the need. But the important thing is that the chaplaincy is not tied to this pattern. Although it must be admitted that at times chaplains do try in an unimaginative way to translate the structures of a building-centered ministry into a society that does not fit them, the chaplaincy has long recognized that what is really needed for corporate worship and Christian community is not a place, but people. Mess compartments, weather decks, tents, and open fields are routinely adapted for worship, and increasingly chaplains are learning to use, rather than trying to change, whatever conditions they find.

A chaplain on a cruiser is not sitting in his church isolated from the world. He has no church building. Even the space in which he preaches on Sunday morning is a mess hall the rest of the week. When his parishioners go to sea, he goes to sea. When they visit Hong Kong, he visits Hong Kong. When they are waked in the middle of the night for a General Quarters drill, he is waked too. When they eat, he eats; when they get seasick, he gets seasick. Despite his non-combatant status he is present with them even in the thick of battle. He learns to know the non-Christians as well as the Christians: what they do, what they think, what they feel.

I served, during the Korean War, as chaplain of a Marine artillery battalion. My parishioners were manning guns, twenty-four hours a day, scattered out all along the sector assigned to them. I would drive my jeep to a battery of 105 mm howitzers and go from bunker to bunker visiting little groups of men in each gun crew. When I had visited all the gun crews and conducted a short service for those men who could come together, I would get back in my jeep and drive on to another battery.

Similar patterns prevailed during the Vietnamese War. Marine chaplains in Vietnam averaged seven church services a week. For the men of Bravo Company, Sunday came on Thursday if that happened to be the day of the chaplain's weekly visit. Nor is this characteristic of combat conditions only. Helicopters (dubbed "holy helos") and bosn's chairs dangling from swaying highlines transfer chaplains from ship to ship at sea. Circuit-riding Air Force chaplains visit airmen at isolated radar sites. The institution of the padre's jeep dates all the way back to World War II. All these are indications of the way chaplains, as the church in the world, are taking word and sacrament to the people, wherever they are.

In many instances the absence of a church building may be an advantage rather than a disadvantage. A chaplain now serving on shipboard, instead of trying to convert the ship's mess compartment into a pseudo-chapel, is taking advantage of its identity as a mess hall to emphasize the significance of communion as a fellowship meal. Another chaplain, a circuit-rider with a group of small ships, has seen small attendance at services as an opportunity for a direct and personal kind of communication; he has added a talk-back session, following the sermon, to his regular liturgy.

Another chaplain, supervising lay leaders aboard each of his destroyers, has prepared an imaginative series of dialogue sermons which he and a lay leader deliver jointly. Even the physical adaptations, though often incongruous, can be a net gain rather than a loss. For the sailor, attending church in well-worn dungarees, who sees the captain's mast stand doubling as a pulpit, or for the soldier or Marine in dust-stained fatigues who sees a pile of ammo boxes used as a communion table, brass shell casings converted into vases or a baptismal font, and parachute nylon for a dossal cloth, the church will never again be quite such an ivory tower proposition, removed from everyday life.

One chaplain, riding the flagship of a fifteen-ship task force, set up an inter-ship radio circuit on Sunday morning. The congregations met simultaneously on each ship, with a lay leader present to lead portions of the service, but with music for congregational singing and the sermon coming by radio from the flagship.

A chaplain aboard a guided missile frigate, given responsibility for closed circuit television programming during a six-month deployment, perceived it initially as a millstone rather than an opportunity for expanded ministry. Nevertheless, he accepted it as a challenge, and in obtaining programming material before departure he included, along with standard TV shows, videotapes and films from church sources, as well as a variety of religious, social, and human relations films from military and secular sources. In addition to such prepared programming, he saw the potential of closed circuit TV as an internal communication system:

> Prior to each port visit, a different department was assigned CCTV programming on that particular port. . . . These presentations differed from the ridiculous to the sublime. Each production was the responsibility of the department assigned with each participant taking full credit for their efforts. . . . We taped and aired on-the-spot interviews from berthing compartments, from the engineering spaces, and from the signal bridge. Helo operations, vertical replenishments, underway replenishments, awards and promotion ceremonies, Career Motivation Council Meetings, and the captain's messages to the crew were all scheduled and aired. What turned

into a highlight was our candid taping of sailors coming through the mess line during mid-rats. The real worth came the following day when, after dubbing in music, we played back the previous evening's taping as part of the day's programming. . . . Everyone on board knew the chaplain was involved and actively engaged with the CCTV. The programming was diverse yet on a high moral plane. My daily television appearances were only two minutes in length. I hope and believe that my messages were timely. I did not come on the air at the same time each day. On Saturdays I always delivered a mini-sermon utilizing the same text I would use next morning. . . . My exposure was magnified greatly by this medium and by the crew's constant knowledge that I was concerned for not only their spiritual well-being but for their welfare and morale.[23]

It would be naive to claim that all chaplains are as creative as they might be in meeting the challenge of a non-building centered ministry. But simply in the nature of things, it is fair to say that the average chaplain conducts more divine services outside of chapels than in them, more services at times other than eleven o'clock Sunday morning than in that hallowed hour, and that he is doing more adapting and experimenting with relevant forms of liturgy and Christian community than is his average civilian counterpart. His situation demands it.

The non-building-centered nature of the chaplain's ministry, together with his place in the military organization, give him an unparalleled opportunity for evangelism. On one occasion a chaplain gave a devotional talk at a breakfast meeting for servicemen in an Armed Forces YMCA. Since the breakfast was free and the place convenient, attendance included some who probably would not otherwise have been listening to devotional talks. The chaplain spoke on the parable of the talents: the man who was given five talents and returned ten, the man with two who returned four, and the one-talent man who buried his. Afterwards the chaplain was cornered by a little group of men who started questioning him and writing notes in a notebook. Shortly one of them asked him, "Chaplain, is it against Navy Regulations to quote the Bible at captain's mast?" The chaplain said he didn't think so, and asked the sailor why he wanted to know.

"I'm going to mast because I got caught running a slush fund," was the reply. "I lend out $5.00 and collect $10.00 back on payday. And since ten for five is exactly what the Bible teaches, I want to quote it to the captain at mast!"

While not necessarily the most fruitful contact that ever took place between a chaplain and an obviously unchurched young man, this encounter is typical of the kind of interchange that goes on continually. The young men and women of the armed forces come from a wide variety of backgrounds, and many of them have had no meaningful contact with organized religion. There is no minister of the church who has a better or more natural opportunity for meaningful encounter with this functionally non-Christian segment of the young adult population than the military chaplain. Chaplains have recognized, earlier in some instances than their civilian counterparts, the significance in ministry of the reconciling witness in secular society. And their place in the military society, their participation in the whole life, not just the Sunday life, of the military community, gives them a ready-made relationship with this secular society.

This is the enormous advantage chaplains have over some other fields of ministry. They do not have to stand outside the lives of these functionally non-Christian young adults, knocking at the door, looking for a way to relate to them, searching for some channel of communication. It is handed to them on a silver platter. On a ship, or in the field, the chaplain shares the life of the men. He knows how good it is to get a shower after a week's manuevers in the field, because he is as grimy and stinking as they are. This is a ministry far removed from church parlors and the niceties of religious symbolism; a ministry in the midst of a kind of life that is thoroughly secular and sensual, often rough and crude, sometimes raw, but life as it is being lived. The chaplain's witness, in this ready-made and intimate contact with a cross-section of America's young adults, to these millions of strong, healthy, bright and skillful, but often spiritually unconcerned and functionally non-Christian young men and women, to the reconciling love of God and its relevance in their lives is a significant contribution to mission in today's church.

ECUMENICAL MINISTRY

A representative of the National Jewish Welfare Board, visiting on one occasion at the Newport Naval Base, was invited while there to attend a meeting of local chaplains. No Jewish chaplain was permanently assigned to the area, where the Navy's Officer Candidate School is located, and local chaplains had been called together to discuss ways of providing religious services for Jewish men and women. As the meeting was drawing to a satisfactory close, the Jewish Welfare Board representative, looking around him, observed, "Only in the military would you find a scene like this—a group of Christian clergymen, Protestant and Roman Catholic, sitting around working out arrangements for Jewish services."

Ecumenism has become a dominant theme in contemporary American religious life. Face with the ecumenical emphasis, older military chaplains have tended to smile smugly and say, "This is nothing new to us; we've had it in the services for years."

In a sense the statement is exaggerated. To say simply that the chaplaincy is an ecumenical ministry might give the impression that denominational differences are ignored and that chaplains are not faithful representatives of the various churches that endorse them. The basic system of the chaplaincy is more accurately labeled cooperative pluralism than ecumenism, and the relationship of the chaplaincy to American religious pluralism will be examined at length in the next chapter.

In a significant sense, however, the ecumenical dimension of the chaplaincy is a unique element in military ministry. Chaplains of all denominations work together in a spirit of cooperation, teamwork, mutual respect, and understanding. They minister to servicemen and servicewomen of many denominations in an atmosphere remarkably free of sectarian tensions. A former chaplain described his experience this way:

> One of my most gratifying memories of my term in the naval chaplaincy is of a truly ecumenical Bible-study group on board a destroyer. Twenty-five men from sixteen denominations crowded every other night into the tiny sick bay to study the Gospel of Mark. They were singularly free from the denominational defensiveness they might have brought to such meetings back home—if you could muster such a group in a parish![20]

The impetus given to the ecumenical movement has been a major contribution of the military chaplaincy to American Christianity. Military chaplains are far removed from the upper reaches of ecumenism, as seen in the interchurch organizations, but they have pioneered in a practical ecumenicity which has helped immeasurably to sell the ecumenical movement at the grassroots level. The effect has been deeply felt both by ministers and by laymen. In the past thirty years a significant percentage of the men and women who make up the membership of the churches have served as laymen or dependents with the armed forces. A significant percentage of America's ministers have served as their chaplains.

The contribution of the chaplaincy has not been one of promoting church union as such. Every minister who enters the military is and remains a clergyman of his own denomination. But he enters a cooperative ministry in which he soon learns that a narrowly partisan denominational viewpoint can do more harm than good. He must work closely with clergymen and with parishioners of many denominations and of other faiths. Some chaplains know little of any church but their own when they enter the military. But they quickly learn that, when it comes to ministering to persons, fine theological and historical distinctions are not nearly so important as they may have seemed back in seminary.

Laymen learn the same lesson. A devout Baptist sailor, serving on a ship whose only chaplain is Methodist, hearing the Word of God truly preached by that Methodist minister and finding his religious needs genuinely met, goes back to civilian life respecting the Methodist church as a true church.

When several chaplains are assigned to the same command, inter-denominational teams are the rule; it would be a misuse of denominational resources to place two chaplains of the same denomination on the same team. A team made up of a Lutheran, a Presbyterian, and a Nazarene, serving a congregation ranging all the way from members of the Church of God to Episcopalians, sharing a building and facilities with congregations of Roman Catholics and Jews, is routine in the military.

Another contribution of the armed forces chaplaincy to the ecumenical development of the American churches should be mentioned. A characteristic of this crisis age of ours has been the presence of American military forces in scores of countries all over the world. Even where there are no permanent installations, American Navy ships, with their chaplains and their Christian congregations, visit ports all over the world. This has brought hundreds of thousands of American churchmen into contact with the worldwide church. On the whole, these American churchmen have responded enthusiastically to contact with fellow Christians of other races, languages, and nations.

I served for a period as senior chaplain of the Chapel of Hope, at the American naval base in Yokosuka, Japan. More than ten Japanese Christian churches in that vicinity have been established, in part, with assistance from the American military congregation, in the years since the end of the Second World War. Numbers of American Christians have worshipped in Japanese churches, visited in Christian Japanese homes, and participated with Japanese Christians in the work of Christ's kingdom. During my tour of duty the congregation of the Chapel of Hope enjoyed a special relationship with a Japanese church in the nearby town of Kurihama, the pastor of which was a retired Japanese Navy captain. Not only did the Americans contribute money to the Japanese church; they worshipped with the Japanese; they assisted the church in sponsoring an English language Bible class at the Japanese Self-Defense Force Academy located in Kurihama; they helped the congregation purchase a building, and men from the Chapel of Hope worked side by side with them over a long period of time, repairing, refinishing, sanding floors, painting, converting the building for congregational use. These and thousands of other laymen and laywomen who have come to know the churches of other nations and people through their military chapel programs have gone back to the United States enriched by the experience. And our churches, too, have been thereby enriched. The military experience has provided by far the greatest grassroots involvement in overseas Christianity in the history of the American churches. The breadth of vision of American Christianity and its attitude toward worldwide Christianity has been greatly affected by the process.

Our starting point at the beginning of this chapter was the recognition that military ministry is not in its essence or its goals different from any other religious ministry. Its outward shape, however—the way in which ministry is done—is a response to the peculiar conditions of military life and the special needs of military people. In this sense, it is a unique ministry.

For more than thirty years now the American churches have committed substantial numbers of their clergymen to this ministry. In that period the number serving at any particular time has seldom fallen below three thousand, and at times it has far exceeded that number. It is strange indeed that a ministry performed by so many clergymen for such an extended period should have received so little scholarly and professional attention.

The churches—and many chaplains—have assumed that military ministry is the same as civilian ministry. This assumption has been attested by the requirement, almost universal among the denominations, that a clergyman seeking a chaplaincy appointment serve for a minimum of two or three years in a civilian parish as a prerequisite to endorsement. A ministerial candidate whose vocational goal is the chaplaincy (and many whose calling to the ministry has come during military service have entered their professional preparation with such a goal), has had no choice but to prepare for parish ministry. Few if any seminaries offer courses in preparation for the chaplaincy, and none offers the chaplaincy as a major field of study. The churches have been content to leave all specialized adaptive training to the chaplains schools, operated by the military services.

It may be high time for a study of the shape of military ministry on the part of the churches and a re-thinking of scholastic and professional preparation for such ministry.

Chapter 5
The Chaplaincy
and Religious Pluralism

The relationship between churches and government inherent in the military chaplaincy may be viewed from two perspectives. Negatively, it may be examined in terms of the question of constitutionality. This has been the perspective of most contemporary opponents of the chaplaincy in its present form. From a more positive perspective, however, the relationship of churches and government present in the chaplaincy may be viewed as a unique form of cooperation, which has been developed in the context of religious pluralism. The American military chaplaincy was the first such chaplaincy in history to take religious pluralism seriously, and to develop structures appropriate to a pluralistic society. In this respect it has become the model for chaplaincies of the armed forces of other religiously pluralistic nations.

THE CONSTITUTIONALITY DEBATE

The constitutionality debate, curiously enough, has originated largely in church circles rather than legal or governmental circles. Initially it was closely associated with the anti-Vietnamese War movement in the churches. We have mentioned earlier the highly critical 1971 book, *Military Chaplains*. This book included a chapter by Randolph L. Jonakait, arguing that the chaplaincy is unconstitutional.[1]

In 1973 the American Civil Liberties Union distributed a study on "Abuses of the Military Chaplaincy" by the same author, and, reversing its long-standing support of the chaplaincy, announced its intention of beginning court tests of constitutionality.[2] This second study by Jonakait, however, had been initiated and jointly sponsored by the Board for Homeland Ministries of the United Church of Christ.

In the same year the report of the Chaplaincy Task Force of the United Church of Christ, the recommendations of which were discussed in Chapter One, included a chapter questioning the constitutionality of the chaplaincy. It looked at both sides of the issue, but marshalled largely negative arguments and strongly implied that a military chaplaincy is unconstitutional. The United Presbyterian Task Force, in the process of studying the chaplaincy in 1973 and 1974, gave considerable attention to the constitutional issue.

The debate on constitutionality has hinged on two clauses of the First Amendment. That amendment begins, "Congress shall make no law respecting an establishment of religion, or prohibiting the free exercise thereof." Opponents label the chaplaincy an establishment of religion, violating the first clause. Defenders have claimed that failure to provide a chaplaincy would deprive those in the armed forces of their right to the free exercise of religion, violating the second. No clear-cut court decision has resolved the tension between the two clauses, but several Supreme Court Justices have given *en passant* opinions in discussing related cases. The clearest such opinion came from Mr. Justice Brennan, concurring in the majority opinion in the case of *Abingdon School District* v. *Schemp*, in 1963:

> There are certain practices, conceivable violative of the Establishment Clause, the striking down of which might seriously interfere with certain religious liberties also protected by the First Amendment. Provisions for churches and chaplains at military establishments for those in the armed services may afford one such example. . . . It is argued that such provisions may be assumed to contravene the Establishment Clause, yet be sustained on constitutional grounds as necessary to secure to the members of the Armed Forces . . . those rights of worship guaranteed under the Free Exercise Clause. Since government has deprived such persons of the opportunity to practice their faith at places of their choice, the argument runs, government may, in order to avoid infringing the free exercise guaranteed, provide substitutes where it requires such persons to be. . . . Hostility, not neutrality would characterize the refusal to provide chaplains and places of worship for . . . soldiers cut off by the State from all civilian opportunities for public communion.[3]

Justice Goldberg, in a separate concurring opinion in the same case, with Justice Harlan joining, agreed that it appears "clear . . . from the opinions in the present and past cases that the court would recognize the propriety of providing military chaplains."[4] Mr. Justice Stewart, in a dissenting opinion in the same case, gave an indication that the chaplaincy is constitutional. The majority in that case made it clear that it thought the chaplaincy might deserve special constitutional treatment. The only Supreme Court justice who has gone on record with an opinion that the chaplaincy violates the constitution is Mr. Justice Douglas, in a concurring opinion in the case of *Engel* v. *Vitale*.[5] One of the most thorough recent studies of the constitutionality issue, citing these and other judicial signals which point toward acceptance of the chaplaincy as constitutional and necessary, is that of Charles L. Greenwood (himself a Navy chaplain and a member of the United Presbyterian Church's task force studying the chaplaincy), published in a 1974 issue of *Church and Society*.[6] Even the United Church of Christ Task Force Report, in its largely negative treatment of the constitutionality issue, conceded that "the prevailing legal opinion, in and out of court, has held that the chaplaincy is indeed constitutional."[7]

No further attention will be given here, then, to the issue of constitutionality. As an institution which predates the constitution, and which has existed in full view of all legal and judicial structures throughout the history of the nation, surely the chaplaincy can lay claim to a presumption of constitutionality until such a time as a court test may indicate otherwise.

The other side of the question, however, deserves attention it has not thus far received. The religiously pluralistic chaplaincy developed by the American armed forces is in some ways a notable achievement. It has set a trail-blazing pattern for a workable tripartite relationship between the persons who make up the armed forces, the churches of a religiously pluralistic society, and a religiously neutral government. The importance of this development is as yet only dimly recognized by the churches.

HISTORICAL DEVELOPMENT OF THE CHAPLAINCY PATTERN

We have noted in Chapter 1 that a meaningful involvement on the part of the churches in matters relating to chaplains did not develop until relatively late in the history of the chaplaincy. For the first hundred years, chaplains answered to the military services alone. The reason for this ecclesiastical vacuum is probably to be found in the basic dilemma faced by the chaplaincy of the new nation: it was an institution based on an established church, in a country without an established church.

The Established Church Background

As we have seen, the desirability of a chaplaincy was not debated during the Revolutionary period, when the armed forces of the new nation were taking form; it was automatically assumed. Chaplaincies had been present in all the fighting forces of western Europe. The basis, however, had always been that of an established church.

It is difficult for Americans today to conceive of the extent to which religious establishment was taken for granted prior to the founding of the United States. Even in the American colonies, an established church had been the normative pattern. Only Rhode Island had a history of non-establishment dating back to the founding of the colony, and the last vestiges of religious establishment were not eliminated in some states until many years after the Revolution. The new nation began without an established religion, not because a majority of its citizens disapproved of establishment, but because different states had *different* established religions.

The First Amendment applied initially only to the federal government. Records of the debate in connection with that amendment make it clear that even Madison, the staunchest adherent of strict separation, had in mind only a national establishment. In fact, that part of the First Amendment dealing with religious liberty did not become applicable to the states until it was applied to them by the Fourteenth Amendment.[8]

The major religions in the forming nation were Congregationalism in New England, Presbyterianism in the middle colonies, and Anglicanism in parts of the South. In addition, there were Baptists, who like the Congregationalists and Presbyterians had their roots in the English Puritan movement. There were smaller groups of Quakers, German Lutherans, and Dutch Reformed in the middle colonies.

The British tradition of the majority of the colonists determined the American military pattern. Armies of the Middle Ages had been raised by feudal lords when occasion demanded, officered by the gentry, and accompanied into battle by the clergy of the region's established church. In England, protected as it was by the English Channel, this medieval military model continued well into the seventeenth century, long after other nations had developed standing armies. The British militia was simply a new form of the medieval levy, commanded by the new equivalent of the old feudal leadership. The Parliamentary Army of the Cromwellian period was the first truly national force in British history.[9]

The colonial militia from which the Continental Army was formed continued the same basic pattern, with elected officers replacing the nobility in providing leadership. Such units, from homogeneous areas, were comprised of persons of the same religion, and the parsons who accompanied them into battle reflected what was essentially an established religion pattern in microcosm.

Even though the Congregationalists and Presbyterians had been dissenters in Great Britain, the chaplaincy tradition with which they were familiar was still that of religious establishment. The Protectorate of Oliver Cromwell had been at least as eager to establish Puritanism as the state religion as had the Royalist forces been to retain the established Church of England. The "New Model Army" of the Puritan Revolution had its establishment of Puritan chaplains, just as the Royalist forces had an Anglican chaplaincy. The Scottish Army of the Solemn League and Covenant had had its Presbyterian chaplaincy representing Scotland's established religion.[10]

Neither the American Anglicans, the Congregationalists, nor the

Presbyterians, then, thought consciously in terms of religious pluralism as the American chaplaincy was established. The local initiative and local choice of chaplains which we have noted earlier as the normative pattern in the Revolutionary period and for a considerable time thereafter merely continued a small-scale version of the established church approach to chaplaincy, with the clergyman representing, in effect, the "established church" of any particular military unit.

Although the Anglicans made up the religious group with the clearest established church background in the Revolutionary period, Tory sentiment was strongest in that communion. There were therefore relatively few Episcopal chaplains. It is impossible to determine how many chaplains actually served with military units during the Revolution, but the best estimate is about one hundred and fifteen. Of these, the largest number were Congregationalists (50) and Presbyterians (21).[11] The principle of choosing chaplains from the denomination to which the majority of the men to be served belonged was nearly universal.

Minority religion chaplains served minority religion units. In the summer of 1776 a German Lutheran, Christian Streit, was appointed chaplain for the German-speaking Eighth Regiment of Virginia.[12] The only Roman Catholic chaplain of the Revolutionary period (and the first to serve with American forces) was Father Louis Lotbiniere, appointed by General Benedict Arnold to serve with a largely French Catholic regiment organized in Quebec.[13] Even as late as 1861, the first Jewish chaplain to serve with American forces was selected by the 65th Regiment of the Fifth Pennsylvania Cavalry, whose commanding officer, as well as many of the officers and men, were Jewish.[14]

The point being made here is that the European (and especially English) background out of which the American military chaplaincy developed was that of chaplains representing a state church and serving a religiously homogeneous military. This pattern was carried over automatically in a localized form into the chaplaincy of the new nation. At this point in American history non-establishment was nothing more than the result of a variety of establishments in the various states, and religious pluralism as it is now understood existed only in a germinal sense.

Recognition of Minority Rights

Very early, however, there was some recognition of minority rights and of a need for some accomodation to the variety of religions existing side by side. As early as the French and Indian War, the Virginia Council, at the request of Colonel George Washington, had appointed a chaplain (undoubtedly Anglican, since that was the established church in Virginia) for his regiment. But at the same time, in 1758, provision had also been made for Dissenting (Baptist) clergymen to serve with the troops when requested.[15]

James Madison is frequently quoted as the strongest advocate among the founding fathers of strict separation of church and state. He opposed a military chaplaincy as an unnecessary politicizing of religion (although he seemed less certain that his reasoning was applicable in "the case of navies with insulated crews"[16]). His reasoning with regard to religious minorities is most clearly expressed in his opposition to a congressional chaplaincy:

> The tenets of the chaplains elected (by the majority) shut the door of worship against the members whose creeds and consciences forbid a participation in that of the majority. To say nothing of other sects this is the case with that of Roman Catholics and Quakers who have always had members in one or both of the Legislative branches. Could a Catholic clergyman ever hope to be appointed a Chaplain? To say that his religious principles are obnoxious or that his sect is small, is to lift the evil at once and exhibit in its naked deformity the doctrine that religious truth is to be tested by numbers, or that the major sects have a right to govern the minor.[17]

The consciousness of religious pluralism, and minority needs and rights, was thus present from the beginning.

Federal Responsibility Supplants Local Option

As long as militia units came from local areas which were relatively homogeneous religiously, little attention had to be given to religious pluralism. And so long as the appointment of chaplains by commanding officers or their selection by the regiment remained the normative pattern, it did not present itself as an issue. It was only as the central government assumed responsibility for the appointment of chaplains (as had been the case with the provision for Dissenters made by the Virginia legislature in 1758) that the necessity for coming to grips with religious pluralism would become inevitable.

Federal involvement in the appointment of chaplains came earlier in the Navy than in the Army. The first ship chaplains had been recruited by commanding officers. As early as 1799, however, Chaplain William Balch was commissioned in the Navy by President John Adams.[18] Thereafter, (although some continued to be appointed by commanding officers or selected by ship's companies, particularly during the War of 1812) the federal government assumed increasing responsibility for the provision of ship chaplains. Of the forty-one known to have served in the

Navy during the second decade of the nineteenth century, eighteen were commissioned by the Navy Department.[19] It must be conceded that many of the Navy Department appointments were political, and that religious pluralism as such received scant attention. Some of the federal appointees were non-ordained; of the eighteen appointed in that decade, only eleven were ordained. One was a Unitarian, one a Presbyterian, and the remaining nine were all Episcopalians.

After the War of 1812, local appointments by commanding officers of Navy ships declined rapidly. In 1823 Secretary of the Navy Samuel Southard issued a directive forbidding appointment to the chaplaincy of anyone who was not an ordained clergyman.[20] Two appointments of chaplains, made by the commanding officers of the *Brandywine* and the *Guerierre* in 1827 and 1828 respectively, were both rescinded by Secretary Southard. The last locally-appointed chaplain appears to have been John F. Girard, who served on the *Potomac* from July, 1840, to September, 1841. Thereafter all Navy chaplains were appointed by the Secretary of the Navy, with increasing attention to their qualifications if not to their denominational distribution.[21]

Local option continued longer in the Army. General Washington had resisted the substitution of brigade for regimental chaplains during the Revolution, since he felt that "the Christian soldier, defending the dearest rights and liberties of his country" should have a chaplain of his own religious persuasion. A brigade was composed of from four to six regiments, and "there might be too many different modes of worship."[22] During the War of 1812, Congress made provision for both brigade chaplains (Act of 29 January 1813) and regimental chaplains (Act of 18 April 1814), but apparently few appointments were made; at the end of the war (1815) there were only four regular Army chaplains, and only one was retained after the war.[23]

In the years following post chaplains were informally and locally procured. The Act of 7 July 1838 officially established the post chaplain system, providing for chaplains (who doubled as schoolmasters) to be employed by local councils of administration. During the Mexican War (in 1847), Congress provided for brigade chaplains to be chosen by all the councils of administration of the regiments making up the brigade. As late as the Civil War, regimental chaplains were still being selected by the regiments, and not until 1861 did ordination become an Army-wide requirement.[24] An 1862 provision for the appointment of chaplains for permanent hospitals, subject to Senate confirmation (Act of 17 July 1862), was the first significant departure from the local option pattern.[25]

As we have seen, federal authorities faced with the necessity for appointing chaplains did not at first give much attention to religious pluralism. The American Navy, beginning with the War of 1812, had modeled itself increasingly after the British Navy, including a preference for the Episcopal church—especially for "officers and gentlemen." We have already noted that of the eleven federally-appointed chaplains during the War of 1812, nine were Episcopalians. By 1840, forty percent of all Navy chaplains were Episcopalians.[26]

When an academy was established at Annapolis in 1840 to train officers of the Navy, Episcopal chaplain George Jones, who had played a significant role in the founding of the school, was the first chaplain—and head of the English Department as well. He became full-time chaplain when the academy was reorganized in 1850, and his successor, Chaplain Theodore B. Bartow, also an Episcopalian, dedicated the first academy chapel in 1854. The service from the Book of Common Prayer became firmly established, and generations of midshipmen became converts to "Naval Academy Episcopalianism." Not until the post-World War II period were modifications made in the Book of Common Prayer chapel service, even when the officiating chaplain was Baptist or Presbyterian.

A similar process shaped the religious preference of the Army's regular officer corps. The Military Academy at West Point had been established in 1802, and the Cadet Chapel was begun there in 1836, with a building erected in 1838. Most chaplains at West Point, until relatively recently, were Episcopalians.

While the nineteenth century brought a *de facto* establishment of Episcopalianism in the officer corps of both services, it also brought increasing public attention to religious pluralism in the services. In the period between the Mexican War and the Civil War, near the middle of the century, there were a number of attacks on governmental chaplaincies and memorials were sent to Congress asking that they be abolished. A series of replies to these memorials, by the Senate and House Judiciary committees, gave evidence of recognition that established church assumptions were no longer relevant, and of increasing attention to questions related to a chaplaincy in a religiously pluralistic society.

Judiciary committees of both houses considered the matter after the Mexican War. The Senate Committee reported that neither the letter nor the spirit of the First Amendment was violated by the military chaplaincy. No privileged or preferred status had been granted to any religious denomination, the committee claimed, nor had penalties been inflicted on any dissenting individual or group. "It is not seen, therefore," the report concluded, "how the institution of chaplains is justly obnoxious to the reproach of invading religious liberty in the widest sense of the term."[27]

The question of preferred status for one religion over others in a pluralistic society appears to have been involved in two other issues relating to the chaplaincy which received considerable attention in the mid-nineteenth century: the question of appropriate dress for chaplains, and the question of the reading of prayers versus free prayer. Both controversies focused more on the Navy chaplaincy than that of the Army, presumably because of the federalized nature of the Navy chaplaincy as compared to the local appointment pattern still normative in the Army.

The debate over the garb of chaplains ranged back and forth between partisans of a plain black suit and those advocating a full officer uniform, between defenders of black buttons and gold buttons. It has sometimes been interpreted by contemporary historians as a reflection of the officer versus clergyman role issue.[28] Undoubtedly this question was involved to some extent. It seems clear, however, that questions regarding different denominational traditions were also, and probably more centrally, involved. An 1844 directive from the Secretary of the Navy requiring that chaplains "while performing religious services on the Sabbath . . . shall wear the Black Silk Gown usually worn by clergymen" (in fact, usually worn only by clergymen of certain denominations), brought far more protest than the requirement in the same order that the ordinary dress of chaplains would be "a Black Coat, with a black velvet collar, and the navy button now in use." A letter written by Chaplain William Colton to the *Independent North American,* in defending the order, recognized that "several religious papers ascribe the introduction of the gown into the Navy as the costume of chaplains to *sectarian* purposes." Himself a Congregationalist, he stoutly denied that "this originated in a spirit of sectarianism, or that there is anything in it which squints at Episcopacy." His defense, however, was itself a recognition that the denominational issue was important in public opinion, and the mandatory black gown for pulpit attire was reversed within a few months, by an order which made the wearing of black gown, plain black coat, or uniform coat optional at divine service.[29]

The other major issue of this period, that of "read prayers," clearly was a denominational question. *Navy Regulations* of 1818 had stated that it was a duty of chaplains "to read prayers at stated periods," and the regulation had remained in effect since that date. The question arose as to whether clergymen of free churches were permitted to offer the extemporaneous prayers customary in their traditions. In January 1859 the

House of Representatives sent a resolution to the Secretary of the Navy, asking, among other things, whether "there is any evidence on file in the department tending to show that non-Episcopal ministers are required by officers of the navy to use the Episcopal liturgy." The Secretary replied that the Department was not aware that the regulation of 1818 had "ever been construed other than to offer prayers at stated periods." To avoid any future misunderstanding, he immediately issued an order (dated 17 January 1859) to the effect that "it is understood that the Navy Commissioners' Regulations of 1818, requiring Chaplains 'to read prayers at stated periods', have heretofore been construed to require them to *offer* prayers, and such will hereafter be the construction."[30]

The increasing concern with religious pluralism is indicated by the request, conveyed in the same congressional resolution of January 1859, for information as to the religious denomination of each person appointed as a chaplain in the Navy since 1813. The fact that the Secretary of the Navy was unable to provide information as to the denomination of thirty-three of the sixty-one chaplains who had been appointed between 1815 and 1856 (the period covered by the report he submitted)—including two then on active duty—is eloquent testimony to the Navy's failure, up until that time, to give much attention to the question of religious pluralism. Later research has shown that of the sixty-one chaplains on the Secretary's list, twenty-four (approximately forty percent) had been Episcopalians, thus confirming the suspicions of the non-Episcopalians who had raised the issue with the Congress.

Development of Genuine Pluralism

The real beginning of a chaplaincy which took seriously the requirements of a religiously pluralistic society can be dated from this debate. It was undoubtedly the source of the naval regulation adopted on 1 June 1860 (and still in effect), that "every chaplain shall be permitted to conduct public worship according to the manner and form of the church of which he may be a member."[31]

The immediate effect did not include a redress of the balance between Episcopal and non-Episcopal chaplains in the Navy. Of the fifty-six Navy chaplains appointed from 1860 through the remainder of the century, the number of Episcopalians continued at approximately forty percent (twenty-three, including two who had joined as clergymen of other denominations, and switched to the Episcopal church while serving). However, the latter part of the century brought into the Navy the first Roman Catholic chaplain (appointed in 1888, and followed by two others in 1892 and 1895) and the first from the Disciples of Christ.

It is not known when the Army and Navy formalized their accommo-
dation to religious pluralism by the establishment of denominational
quotas. It is known, however, that such a system was in effect in the Navy
by 1911. In December of that year, a letter was written by the Secretary
of the Navy to Senator Moses E. Clapp, who had requested the appointment of another Roman Catholic chaplain:

> I find that the next regular vacancy in the corps of chaplains in the
> Navy in the Catholic faith will not occur until 1925. It is possible,
> however, that a vacancy may occur in that faith, either by resigna-
> tion, or otherwise than by retirement, prior to 1925.[32]

PRESENT PATTERN OF COOPERATIVE PLURALISM[33]

The pattern of cooperative pluralism which has evolved out of this
historic development, as we have noted earlier, preserves the interests of
three parties: the government, the individual worshipers who are members of the armed forces, and the churches. The religious neutrality of
the government is derived from the establishment clause of the First
Amendment. The right of the individual American who is a member of
the armed forces to practise the religion of his or her choice is derived
from the free exercise clause of the same amendment. The position of the
first two parties of the tripartite arrangement is thus clearly staked out on
a constitutional basis.

The position of the third party—the churches of America—has been
no less important in the development of the chaplaincy's cooperative
pluralism, but it has been less easily come by. Its basis is the principle,
not precisely defined but generally agreed upon, that the American religious climate is properly one of mutual respect, understanding, and
cooperative co-existence between adherents of different religions. Long
implicit in the constitutional principles and recognized as the ideal, this
principle was slow in reaching full recognition throughout the society. Its
implementation in the chaplaincy has probably made a significant contribution to its belated implementation in the society as a whole.

The chaplaincy pattern of cooperative pluralism, as it now operates,
begins with the appointment of chaplains on the basis of a system of
denominational quotas. The quota system utilizes percentages based on
American church membership as reported annually in the Yearbook of
American Churches, and is designed to reflect faithfully the religious
complexion of the American population at large.

Once appointed, the chaplains who make up the quotas of the
various faiths and denominations are assigned to duty, on ships, military
bases, and with the various air squadrons and combat divisions, on the

basis of continuing attention to the requirements of religious pluralism. A "denominational spread" to meet the needs of as many groups as possible is the goal in assigning chaplains to any given organization or locality.

At the local level the requirements of religious pluralism are met by the assigned chaplains through the operating principle of mutual responsibility. This is a long ingrained tradition in the chaplaincies, accepted by every chaplain as the working basis of his ministry. Each chaplain is obligated not only to serve those of his own faith or denominational group, but also to make provision for those of other faiths and groups. Such provision may be made in several ways. One is the exchange of services among chaplains. This operates in its simplest form when the Roman Catholic chaplain assigned to U.S.S. *Albany* celebrates mass on board U.S.S. *Little Rock,* whose chaplain is Protestant, when the two ships are in proximity, and vice versa. In the Navy there are standard procedures for coordinating the exchange of denominational coverage in Navy ports and in operating units at sea, with the staff chaplain of the senior commander having responsibility for coordination, and with all other chaplains having the responsibility of informing him of needs for denominational services and their own availability.

When chaplain exchanges will not suffice, the services of civilian clergymen, where available, are used. Lists of English-speaking clergymen of various religions in frequently-visited ports are a standard resource for shipboard chaplains deploying to the Mediterranean, the Far East, or other operating areas. At permanent bases, all three services utilize civilian auxiliary chaplains to provide denominational services.

In the absence of either chaplain or civilian clergyman, provision for those of other faiths is made by lay leaders, appointed by commanding officers and trained by chaplains to conduct religious worship for their own group. The Roman Catholic church designates authorized military lay leaders as "eucharistic lay ministers," who can distribute the sacrament in the absence of a priest. Lay leaders are provided not only for Protestant, Roman Catholic, or Jewish congregations, but also for Latter-Day Saints, Christian Scientists, Eastern Orthodox, and others as needed —in short, for any religious group present in sufficiently large numbers to form a regular worshipping congregation.

The individual chaplain's part in this religiously pluralistic ministry may be summed up in terms of the following responsibilities:

1. The chaplain is generally responsible for meeting the religious needs of all personnel of the command he serves by scheduling divine

services in the command or offering access to services elsewhere, for all groups, insofar as it is possible.

2. He personally provides the liturgical, sacramental, and pastoral ministries for those in the command who are of his own faith or denominational group, on as inclusive a basis as his own church and the churches of those being served will permit.

3. He arranges for the services of other chaplains, auxiliary chaplains, civilian clergymen, or lay leaders in the command, or sends "church parties" (groups of worshippers) elsewhere, to meet the needs of those he cannot serve personally.

4. He holds himself in readiness to assist other commands which may need his services to provide for personnel of his faith or denominational group.

Distinction between Administrative and Religious Responsibilities

A major reason for the effectiveness of the religiously pluralistic ministry in the armed services is to be found in the chaplaincy's clearcut distinction between the administrative area, in which the chaplain functions without regard to his denominational affiliation, and the religious area, in which he functions entirely as a representative of his own church.

Organizationally, the American military chaplaincies are fully integrated. In contrast to the chaplaincies of certain other nations, where there are parallel Protestant and Roman Catholic chaplaincies, each with its own Chief of Chaplains and organizational structure, our chaplaincies are administratively unified. A Roman Catholic senior chaplain may and frequently does supervise the work of a group of chaplains made up not only of other Roman Catholics but also Protestants of a variety of denominations, and perhaps Jewish, Latter-Day Saints, and Orthodox chaplains as well. The same title, "chaplain," is used to address priests, rabbis, and ministers alike. The Chief of Chaplains may be of any religion. Administratively there is no distinction.

Religiously, however, each chaplain's ministry is determined by his own church. The right of the chaplain to conduct public worship—and by implication his entire ministry—in accordance with the rites, rules and practices of his own church is carefully detailed in the official regulations of all the services. This clear distinction between the administrative area, which is completely integrated, and the religious area, which is completely uncoerced, is the working basis of the chaplain's ministry to a pluralistic society. The principle is summarized in the phrase that has become the motto of the Navy Chaplain Corps, "Cooperation without Compromise."

The "Protestant Program"

It is not with regard to "cooperation without compromise" between Protestants, Roman Catholics, Jews, and those of other religions, but with regard to the so-called "Protestant program" in the services that misunderstandings most often arise. Certain fallacious statements are sometimes heard:

"Chaplains are forced to give up their denominational identity and are known only as 'Protestants'."

"Every serviceman who is not Roman Catholic or Jewish is considered a Protestant and must take part in the Protestant program."

"The armed forces have developed a 'Military Protestant Church' which competes with the various Protestant denominations in communities where bases are located."

None of these statements is true. A source of much of the confusion is the widespread use of the term, "General Protestant Service." Technically speaking, there is no such thing. A service is conducted by a chaplain who, though he may represent any one of a number of denominations, considers himself a Protestant. It is open to all worshipers who, whatever their denominations, consider themselves Protestant. Such a service may legitimately be called a Protestant service. Certainly this is a more convenient term for use in the plan of the day or on the bulletin board than "Service Conducted by a Methodist Chaplain Open to Protestants of all Denominations." But the term "Protestant Service" carries with it no implication of enforced conformity.

There is no established liturgy for such a service, nor even a normative pattern. Every chaplain is entirely free to follow the liturgy and forms of his own denomination, with such adjustments as his denomination may permit, and he may care to make, to the fact that the worshipers come from many denominations. The fact that most chaplains of Protestant denominations do make such adjustments is not an indictment, but an indication of their desire to be relevant. Such adjustments are by no means mandatory. Military worshipers are accustomed to a variety of liturgical forms—and to frequent changes in liturgical forms as chaplain follows chaplain—and they take it in their stride.

It is by no means required, or even expected, that all Protestant laymen will attend the services conducted by any particular chaplain, or that all those who do attend will find their needs fully satisfied. Every effort is made to supplement the available "Protestant services" with various denominational communion services and sacramental ministries where needed and to encourage contact between laymen and their own denominations.

Protestants, however, are accustomed to cooperating, worshipping together, and crossing denominational lines. The various denominations endorse chaplains, expecting them to cooperate in such a fashion. Workable patterns have been developed through long years of experience. For these reasons, the cooperative Protestant program in the military provides a viable system that meets the needs of most Protestants most of the time.

The key to such a program is voluntarism on both sides, clerical and lay. Without any coercion on the part of the military, chaplains generally find that they can serve Protestants from a broad denominational spectrum; and far from finding themselves compromised by so doing, they find it an exciting and challenging ministry. Laymen, for their part, find equally without coercion that they can be served by chaplains from a variety of denominations; and far from being compromised, they find it a richly varied and rewarding form of church life. The significant thing is not only that it works, but that it works well. As we noted in the last chapter, it is properly labeled religious pluralism rather than ecumenism. But nevertheless, it has set a pattern for *practical* ecumenism which, as successive generations of young Americans have passed through the armed forces in the years since the Second World War, has contributed immeasurably to the growth of the ecumenical movement.

The workable pattern of cooperative ministry established by the chaplaincies within the armed forces still falls considerably short of solving all the problems of government-sponsored religion in a pluralistic society.

Chaplains themselves have achieved an admirable level of cooperation. The reasons are not hard to find. In the first place, the military pressures in an authority-based system are such that chaplains must find ways to work together if they are to work at all. Military commanders, with little knowledge of or taste for the fine points of sectarian hair-splitting, are notably impatient with religious warfare. Second, group pressure is a factor. Studies of social groups have established clearly the tendency of members of such groups to resolve their differences in mutually acceptable ways. Chaplains working in a religiously pluralistic environment, with clergymen of all religions, tend to be influenced by each other in the direction of cooperation and accomodation. Third, there is undoubtedly an element of internal pressure. By a self-selection process, those clergymen who enter the ecumenical ministry of the armed forces are likely to be those naturally inclined to cooperative attitudes and ecumenical accomodation. Finally, the trust level among chaplains, built up in a system that has worked well and fairly over a long period of time, provides an element of reassurance.

CHURCH STRUCTURES FOR COOPERATIVE PLURALISM

The churches which sponsor chaplains and back their cooperative ministries have, however, made far less progress in the direction of cooperative activity than the chaplains themselves. In tracing the history of chaplaincy development in the pluralistic context, we noted that much of the initiative came from the government rather than the churches.

Today there exists a group of civilian clergymen, usually called "endorsing agents," who meet periodically in connection with chaplaincy affairs. They cover what is probably a wider denominational range than any other religious group in history. Meetings include not only Roman Catholic, Orthodox, Mormon, and Jewish representatives, but Protestants ranging all the way from such non-affiliating groups as the Associated Gospel Churches and the Independent Fundamental Churches of America to the liberal denominations of mainline Protestantism. The representatives work together with an easy informality, on a first name basis. They are not, however, an organization, and they would stringently resist being so regarded. Some would find it impossible, on principle, to belong to the same organization as others. They come together only at the invitation of the chaplaincies. Meetings were formerly sponsored separately by the Chiefs of Chaplains of the various services, but in recent years the three chiefs have generally acted jointly, through the Armed Forces Chaplains Board, in calling such meetings.

Tentative movement in the direction of some autonomy for this group has begun. In 1974 an informal *ad hoc* committee of Washington-based endorsing agents by common consent extended an invitation to the three Chiefs of Chaplains to attend a meeting hosted by the group. There have been no steps toward formal organization or fixed membership, however, and it does not appear likely that such steps will be taken.

The General Commission on Chaplains

The closest thing to a church-sponsored cooperative organization for dealing with the chaplaincies is the General Commission on Chaplains and Armed Forces Personnel, which has been mentioned several times previously. The present membership of this organization consists of thirty-three Protestant denominations, ranging from such theologically conservative groups as the Church of the Nazarene and the Christian Reformed Church to such liberal groups as the United Church of Christ. Most of the major (in size) Protestant denominations are represented with the exception of the Southern Baptist Convention and the Lutheran bodies. These however, send observer/consultants to meetings of the

General Commission, and on some occasions observers from the Roman Catholic Military Ordinariate and the Jewish Welfare Board attend as well.

While the General Commission represents the most successful attempt on the part of the churches to join forces in supporting a cooperative chaplaincy, even this organization has depended heavily on government initiative to bring the constituent churches together. As we have noted before, its antecedent was the Washington Committee on Army and Navy Chaplains, established in 1914 by the Federal Council of Churches.

The impetus behind the formation of this committee came not from the churches but from a Navy chaplain, George Livingston Bayard, who in 1913 appeared before a meeting of the Federal Council of Churches in Baltimore to urge its establishment. Such a committee was authorized, and the Washington Committee was formed the following year. Chaplain Bayard spearheaded the committee in its formative stages, and he formulated the bill which was passed by Congress in 1914, providing a chaplain for each 1,250 military personnel.[34]

Other major steps in the development of the General Commission came also at government initiative. As the United States entered the First World War, the Secretary of War, Newton D. Baker, requested a central accrediting agency to endorse the chaplains being recruited for wartime expansion. It was in response to this request that the Federal Council's Washington Committee was transformed into the General Committee on Army and Navy Chaplains, representing the thirty-two constituent bodies of the Federal Council. The chairman of the reorganized committee negotiated an understanding with both the Secretary of the Navy and the Secretary of War "by which it was agreed that the Federal Council should have authority to investigate and nominate all Protestant candidates for the chaplaincy and that applications already on file in the departments should be sent over to the Washington office of the Federal Council."[35]

The World War I period represented the high water mark of Protestant cooperation in dealing with the chaplaincy. During that period the General Committee took an active role in establishing quotas for various denominations on a percentage basis. By attention to ministerial qualifications and by insisting on evaluation by denominational officials rather than letters from fellow-ministers, it hastened the demise of appointments based on patronage or political considerations. It ended the long-time dominance of Episcopal chaplains in the Navy; of the 162 Navy chaplains appointed during the First World War, fewer than ten percent were Episcopalian, as compared with forty percent throughout the eighteenth century. It raised education standards, insisting on a college degree and giving preference to those with seminary training.[36]

At the beginning of World War II, the government once again requested the convenience of a single endorsing agency for Protestant chaplains. This time, however, a number of denominations preferred to make their endorsements directly to the military services. In the post-World War II period, even more denominations established their own endorsing procedures. Some continued to channel their endorsements through the General Commission, but its activity as an endorsing agency, except for a few small denominations, became largely a formality. The agency has continued to serve as a forum for discussion of matters of common interest by a large number of denominations, including those with a consultant relationship as well as member denominations. But its credibility as an agency authorized to represent all Protestantism did not last beyond the brief period of the First World War, and has been increasingly eroded in the post-World War II period.

Denominational Agencies

In the period immediately after the Second World War attention was on demobilization. The Korean War at the beginning of the fifties, however, brought another military build-up, and the twenty-year Cold War period from then until the Vietnamese War was marked by large standing armed forces. During this period all the major denominations built up their own bureaucracies for dealing with the armed forces. The vested interests of denominational officials operating from their own denominational contexts brought a further erosion of cooperative structures.

The issues raised during the Vietnamese War brought increasing interest in church circles in the establishment of church control over the chaplaincies. The religious pluralism of American society requires, however, that the churches work together to establish such control. No structure for such cooperation is presently in existence. In 1972 an American Baptist Navy chaplain was tried by General Court Martial on a charge of adultery. Chaplaincy officials of his church took the position that such a charge was within the province of church oversight rather than military law, and disputed the right of the Navy to try him.[37] Following his acquital, these American Baptist officials sought to enlist the support of the other churches in asserting this principle of denominational control. There was much discussion in the General Commission, but no structure existed for broader-based initiatives, and nothing happened.

Within the military, among chaplains themselves, however, cooperative pluralism is a working reality. If denominations have not been able thus far, on their own initiative, to join forces sufficiently to assume full control of the ministries of chaplains, it is certainly true that they have backed their chaplains in the cooperative patterns worked out within the services. It is the creative partnership of churches, armed forces, and military churchmen, rather than the churches alone, which has blazed new trails in cooperative religious pluralism.

Problem Areas

There are, of course, problems. One has to do with the place of evangelism in such an environment. For many religious traditions, the making of converts is a central thrust; a religious environment which did not permit the sharing of the Good News and the bringing of others into the household of faith would not be regarded as fully meeting the spiritual needs of believers. Well over ninety percent of Americans, however, consider themselves to be adherents of or believers in some religious group, and in such a society the evangelism of one group is usually at the expense of some other group.

In civilian society, where all religious groups operate autonomously, the right to evangelize is not questioned. Within the cooperative pluralism of the armed forces, with all denominational activities carried on as part of a single coordinated "religious program" under command sponsorship, it can conceivably be an issue. It is less likely to be a problem in practise, however, than in theory. Large numbers of young adults of all religious traditions are for all practical purposes religiously uncommitted, and it is from the ranks of the uncommitted that most converts are made. A "no proselytizing" ground rule is generally recognized by chaplains, in the sense that positive efforts on the part of a chaplain to persuade a person to leave a religion to which he is actively committed are unacceptable. However, conversions from one major faith to another at the initiative of the person concerned are quite common. For a chaplain to give religious instruction and provide assistance in such an instance is routine. Practically all chaplains rejoice when a religiously uncommitted serviceman, regardless of his formal religious background, becomes an active, committed member of some fellowship of faith.

It is not correct, therefore, to regard the chaplaincy as a ministry of "maintenance" alone, in which the evangelical thrust central to many religious groups must be played down. On the contrary, the annual statistics revealing the number of young adults who find an active religious commitment while in the armed services are impressive indeed.

In 1973 a Jewish group took public issue with the Chief of Navy

Chaplains on a question having to do with "Key 73," a nationwide Christian evangelistic emphasis with which a substantial number of Protestant and Roman Catholic religious groups cooperated. Information and materials relating to Key 73 had been distributed to chaplains, and its executive director had been invited to speak to a conference convened by the Chief of Chaplains. The Jewish group, identifying Key 73 with Christian evangelistic approaches to Jews which were believed to have been made in some cities, objected. The reply of the Chief of Chaplains was fully in keeping with the cooperative religious pluralism pattern. He indicated that he had been assisting a substantial group of Christian chaplains in carrying out an emphasis of *their own churches,* and that he would at any time give the same kind of assistance to Jewish chaplains.

A pluralism-related problem, more troublesome than evangelism for some, is one experienced by chaplains as they seek to clarify their own identity and mission within the military. As we have noted before, the goals of religious ministry are established by the churches rather than by the military, and in a pluralistic society the churches have a wide range of goals. The military approach to doing things is characterized by great precision as to the nature of the mission, the tasks, and the functions to be performed by any unit or group. In this context, chaplains have grappled long—and unsuccessfully—with the problem of stating their own mission with military precision. Such generalizations as the Army chaplaincy's traditional motto, "Bringing men to God and God to men," have been easily come by. But specificity as to what this means—the military always moves on to break down mission into specific tasks and functions—has been illusive.

The Navy Chaplain Corps in 1969 brought together approximately seventy-five senior chaplains for a five-day conference, the major task of which was to be the formulation of mission, task, and function statements for the corps. The job proved so formidable that the conference never got beyond the first stage. Its product was a one-paragraph mission statement:

> The mission of the Chaplain Corps, comprised of representatives of the religious bodies of the United States, is to provide professional direction to the Naval establishment in religious matters and to promote the spiritual, religious, moral, personal and corporate wellbeing of members of that establishment, their dependents, and other authorized persons by providing ministries appropriate to their rights and needs.

Sufficiently general to be acceptable to all, the statement provided no more real specificity than "men to God and God to men." Its less-than-earthshaking significance is attested by the fact that following the conference it languished for four years before it was dug out, and, with minor modifications, made "official" by the signatures of the Chief of Chaplains and the Chief of Naval Personnel.

Meanwhile, chaplains continued their search for a common definition of their ministry. In 1973, when the twenty-five regional Pacemaker workshops of Navy chaplains sought to identify the major concerns and professional needs, it appeared that the desire for a definition of ministry was still occupying a high place—second on their list of priorities. What it means for chaplains serving military people to "provide ministries appropriate to their rights and needs" is still a question on which there is little agreement—but a great deal of searching.

In addition to widely differing definitions of religious ministry in different religious denominations and traditions, the diversity of contemporary ministries provided under the sponsorship of the "servant church" for secular society must be taken into account. The involvement of chaplains in "people-serving" ministries not directly related to chapel-centered or liturgically oriented religious programs, which will be examined in some detail in Chapters seven and eight, parallels a similar movement in many civilian churches. There is no single definition of the ministry of clergymen in a religiously pluralistic society. Living with pluralistic definitions of their mission is not easy, particularly in a military environment where precision of definition is more comfortable. Chaplains, however, have no choice but to accept it.

A related problem in a religiously pluralistic ministry is one felt with special strength by younger chaplains and those with strong social concern. Such chaplains would like for conferences of chaplains, or the Chief of Chaplains in their behalf, to take positions or make pronouncements on controversial social, moral, and ethical issues of the day, as their denominational church groups do.

Chiefs of Chaplains have generally taken the position that an official pronouncement from the chaplaincy of a military service would come from an arm of the government, and could not be made from the same stance as could a similar statement from an independent denomination. They have advised chaplains to participate in their own denominational structures for such pronouncements. However, even in the context of intra-corps discussion, chaplains represent such a wide range of backgrounds and orientations that they are seldom able to agree on controversial issues. The inability of a group as pluralistic as the Chaplain Corps to reach a consensus on these issues, regarding which clergymen often have strong feelings, is frustrating.

A final problem related to religious pluralism has to do with the homogenizing effect of cooperative ministry, particularly as it affects Protestant Christianity. The effect of cooperative pluralism on religious faith itself is probably both good and bad. On the positive side, it brings about a decrease in petty sectarianism and contributes to the ecumenical movement. But on the negative side, it may lead to a weakening of those aspects of Christian witness which might be controversial (but may nevertheless be regarded by some as central) and a blurring of focus.

We have noted earlier that Protestant chaplains and laymen of most denominations generally work together in a single "Protestant program" in a military command. Does this result in a watered-down, least-common-denominator religion, as some critics have charged? Does something of this same homogenization affect Catholic, Orthodox, and Jewish ministries in the ecumenical environment of the armed forces? And even more basically, does the military environment of pluralistic ministry distort such a least-common-denominator religion with nationalistic, patriotic, or militaristic influences? These questions will be addressed in the following chapter on questions related to civil religion.

Chapter 6
The Chaplaincy
and Civil Religion

George H. Williams, in his essay on the history of the military chaplaincy, advanced the theory that the Army and Navy have tended to become "denominations" for the chaplains of the respective services. In part he was speaking in terms of polity, suggesting that relationships and institutional controls within the military chaplaincy have replaced the comparable relationships and institutional controls provided by the various denominations for their clergy.[1] But in addition, he suggested at one point that the Army and Navy "denominations" of the chaplains have supplanted civilian ecclesiastical bodies in more substantive ways, both with respect to the replacement of "competitive denominational differences" with a common denominator religion, and the tendency to "descry in Protestant or Christian America with a 'manifest (continental) destiny' the larger church in which they, with their fellow officers and men, constituted the militia of Christ."[2] This, in effect, is a charge that chaplains have substituted a civil religion for church-oriented religion.

Such charges have been leveled repeatedly, and not entirely without grounds. Denominational officials, particularly those representing churches with a strong sense of the distinctiveness of their own traditions, have repeatedly warned chaplains against participation in a "military religion." Every chaplain has met career military families whose members are faithful church-goers, but who have no denominational affiliation, identifying only with military chapels. Observers have noted that there is often a liturgical similarity in various Protestant military chapel services, regardless of the denomination of the officiating clergyman (and that clergymen from free churches often become high churchmen in the military).

Other charges have to do with the using of religion for national, patriotic, or military purposes. Complaints have been raised about such activities as an invocation given by an Air Force chaplain in Oklahoma at the ceremonial welcoming of a new cargo aircraft to the inventory of the United States Air Force.[3] Every critic of the chaplaincy has his horror story, like that of the American Civil Liberties Union study describing a chaplain who "replaced the Gloria Patre (sic) with 'My Country 'Tis of Thee' . . . and with great gnashing of teeth . . . loudly exclaimed, 'It is the chaplain's job to do everything he can to help his commanding officer whip the troops into a fighting frenzy.' "[4]

Military Chaplains, the polemical book published in 1971 by Clergy and Laymen Concerned about Vietnam, included a chapter purporting to demonstrate that chaplains are communicating a "military religion."[5] Written by Daniel Pinard with sociologist Peter Berger, the article was based on a claim to have analyzed "educational materials disseminated by chaplains." In content, this military religion was accused of linking God and country. Although the authors stated that "we were impressed by the fact that our materials contain relatively few statements that openly identify America and its political institutions with the will of God," they found circuitous linkage in such things as the title of a book of prayers, *Strength for Service to God and Country,* the front cover of which is "emblazoned with an American eagle in full martial splendor."[6] Military religion, according to their analysis, also legitimates military authority, justifies participation in war, and seeks to further the concept of the "wholesome soldier."[7]

If one leaves aside the undemonstrated implication that such teachings are all or even central in what chaplains teach, a legitimate point can be made. A great many chaplains would, without a moment's hesitation, readily agree that they try to provide "strength for service to God and country," that they see a relationship between God and country, that they consider military authority legitimate, that they find participation in war justified under some circumstances, and that they prefer "wholesome soldiers" to unwholesome ones. Most chaplains would deny vehemently that such teachings are central in their gospel. But many would admit that they are sensitive to the charges and not completely comfortable with the situation.

Such charges, and the practices underlying them, are a problem both for thoughtful chaplains and for the churches viewing the work of chaplains. Any substantive effect of the military situation on the content and practice of religion is probably a result of at least two factors. One in religious pluralism, which we looked at in the last chapter, and the possible tendency in cooperative ministry toward homogenization and common denominator religion. Another is patriotism, along with the close identification between the military way of life and national purposes. Both of these factors are aspects of what is commonly known now as civil religion. The relationship between the chaplaincy and civil religion is an important issue in any comprehensive examination of the military chaplaincy.

CIVIL RELIGION AND ITS VARIOUS MANIFESTATIONS

Only recently has civil religion been clearly identified and discussed as a religious dynamic in the United States. The contemporary popularity of the term and the concept are traceable in large measure to an essay by sociologist Robert N. Bellah on "Civil Religion in America," first printed in *Daedalus* in 1967 and since widely quoted and reprinted.[8]

The phenomenon is, of course, much older, and it has been dealt with in a variety of ways by earlier commentators. Rousseau first coined the phrase in *The Social Contract* and prescribed the content of a simple civil religion, acceptable to all, which he considered appropriate for state sponsorship. While the founding fathers did not use the term, and may or may not have been influenced by Rousseau, similar ideas on the part of Enlightenment thinkers had wide currency in the Revolutionary period, and the idea, if not the term, is reflected in their writings.

Prominent among more recent American proponents of civil religion was John Dewey, who in the 1930's propounded a "common faith," drawn from those common elements of religious experience shared by all Americans, with the non-essential elements in traditional religions (in Dewey's thought, generally the supernatural elements) eliminated, and commended as a basis for national life and morality.[9]

In the 1950's, the Jewish philosopher Will Herberg, in the book *Protestant—Catholic—Jew*, which first appeared in 1955, described what he called the "civic religion of the American Way of Life." The American Way of Life, he said, is the common faith which provides an "overarching sense of unity" to American society. It synthesizes all that Americans, on the existential level at which life is lived rather than the conceptual level of traditional belief systems, consider to be good, right, and true. "It embraces such seemingly incongruous elements as sanitary plumbing and freedom of opportunity, Coca-Cola and an intense faith in education —all felt as moral questions relating to the proper way of life. The very expression 'way of life' points to its religious essence, for one's ultimate, over-all way of life is one's religion."[10]

Herberg's American Way of Life embraces belief in God and tolerance in religious matters. He makes it clear, however, that although it is the "common religion" of American society, it is not the so-called "common denominator" religion, composed of beliefs to be found in all religious groups. It influences and is influenced by what Herberg calls the "official religions" of America—Protestantism, Roman Catholicism, and Judaism—but is distinct from them. It is repudiated as religion by some groups—certain churches of immigrant-ethnic background, certain Lutheran and Reformed churches, sections of the Catholic Church and those with an "explicit and conscious theological concern" (in fact, Herberg appears to include in this category all those who take their own religions seriously as operative in life)—but for the remainder, Herberg considers it to be the operative national religion. Its influence, he says, has secularized and devitalized the historic Jewish and Christian faiths, and on the whole he tends to view it quite negatively.

The civil religion identified by Robert Bellah is neither Dewey's common denominator religion nor Herberg's Coca-Cola and education religion, though it is related to both. He sees it as an authentic religious dimension of national life. Its central symbol is God, belief in whom played a significant part in the founding of the country and its constitutive documents. Its essence is a national recognition of God's sovereignty, which has safeguarded the nation from absolutism. Although the operative source of political authority is the will of the people, the will of the people lacks ultimate significance because the nation stands under higher judgment. The American tradition has recognized a deep obligation, both collective and individual, to carry out God's will on earth. The seeking of God's approbation and subjection to God's judgment are recurring themes. The theme of sacrifice for the nation (seen, in a sense, as sacrifice for God) is a prominent one. God is associated with law and order, with right and justice.

Unlike Rousseau and Dewey, Bellah did not devise such a civil religion and recommend it to the body politic. Rather he described the civil religion he observed as operative in American history. His body of religious symbol and belief, imbedded in the founding documents of the nation, enunciated by the founding fathers, has been central in American life, he says. Its themes have been prominent in nearly every presidential inaugural address. Its rituals are embedded in patriotic ceremonies, Memorial Days, Thanksgiving Days, inaugurals and state funerals. It has had deep meaning in times of national crisis.

The civil religion of Americans, says Bellah, is clearly distinguished from, but by no means antithetical to, the personal and denominational religions of American life. It is selectively derived from Christianity but clearly not the same thing as Christianity. The average American has seen no conflict between the two.

Bellah's evaluation of American civil religion is strongly affirmative: "I would argue that the civil religion at its best is a genuine apprehension of universal and transcendent religious reality as seen in or, one could almost say, as revealed through the experience of the American people."[11] Like all religions, it has at times been distorted and deformed. The "religion in general," the "religion of the American Way of Life," and the "American Shinto" derided by critics are aspects of civil religion, Bellah believes, but at its worst rather than its best. He feels that civil religion at its best has made a significant contribution to the American tradition —notably in guarding against absolutism by positing a higher standard above the will of the people—and should be regarded as a valid religious manifestation.

If Dewey, Herberg, and Bellah may be regarded as representative of three historical perceptions of civil religion, it might be noted that the perceptions differ significantly with regard to the relationship between civil religion and the personal or denominational religions to which Americans give their spiritual allegiance. Dewey regarded the "common faith" of Americans as superior to denominational religion and favored substitution of the former for the latter. He felt that all uncommon and exclusive elements in denomoninational religion should be eliminated. Indeed, he considered the very notion of a particular religion to be anti-religious.[12] Herberg sees the substitution of the religion of the American Way of Life for the historic faiths as a dangerous trend. His perspective would regard this kind of civil religion as a threat to personal and denominational religion. Bellah would see civil religion as occupying a different sphere from the personal and denominational religions of Americans, with neither threatening the other and with both recognized as valid and authentic religious dimensions of life.

CHAPLAIN INVOLVEMENT IN CIVIL RELIGION

No clergyman comes into closer contact with civil religion—in all its versions—than the military chaplain. As a clergyman serving persons of many different denominations, he is frequently in contact with "common denominator" religion: working together with laymen of various religions, in ecumenical services, conducting or participating in worship for persons of other religions. The temptation is always before him to modify his own gospel in this direction.

As a member of an institution which exists to serve a national purpose and which is a major focal point for much of the nation's patriotic sentiment, he is no stranger to veneration of the American way of life, particularly in its patriotic manifestations. As a clergyman member of the military institution, his very presence is seen as a symbol of the national relationship to God. He is almost always expected to be a participant—usually with an invocation and perhaps a benediction as well—on ceremonial occasions. He offers prayers at Change of Command ceremonies, ship commissionings, unit anniversaries, and training course graduations. Chaplains have even been called on to pray at cocktail parties commemorating such events as the Marine Corps Birthday, or at judo tournaments sponsored for dependent children. Memorial services, all too frequent during times of combat, may be formal command-sponsored events at which the entire unit is paraded. Military funerals are also occasions which combine military ceremony and religious rites.

Until 1972 numerous chaplains officiated at divine services where attendance was compulsory, such as recruit training centers and the service academies. In 1971 chaplains had the curious experience of hearing senior Naval authorities claim in a court of law that the divine services conducted at the Naval Academy chapel were "entirely secular in purpose," provided solely as an element in the training of young midshipmen to become officers and gentlemen. Such an interpretation (had it been accepted by the chaplains themselves) would have placed the entire liturgical ministry of the chaplains involved in the category of civil religion. The problem was solved, however, by the elimination of compulsory church attendance throughout the military services, following a Circuit Court decision in 1972 that it was unconstitutional.

The relationship of weddings to civil religion as opposed to denominational religion is one which should be explored by the entire ministerial profession. The number of church, chapel, or clergy-performed weddings which are genuinely acts of and within the Christian community, as was originally envisioned for the rite or sacrament, may be quite small. Many such ceremonies for straightforward young adults today are re-written to omit explicit references to the Christian community, or to replace St. John with Kahlil Gibran. The problem of requests to perform religious marriage ceremonies for persons whose relationship to church or synagogue is tenuous at best is particularly acute for chaplains. They are ministering to a population made up largely of young adults, at the marrying age. Relationships with their parishioners are often highly transient and temporary. The environment of the total institution encourages these military young adults to feel entitled to the use of a chapel and the services of a chaplain, and it encourages chaplains to feel obligated to provide such services.

Yet while weddings which are genuinely acts of the Christian community in the fullest sense of the word may be rare, the desire for a church or chapel ceremony and for a religious blessing of the union are in most instances genuine, even if poorly rationalized and articulated. It may be that the ministerial profession needs to develop a separate rationale for weddings performed by clergymen in the tradition and in line with the values (real, if limited) of civil religion at its best, quite distinct from that of denominational weddings. In such an event the clergyman could stop agonizing over his inability to impart true religious depth to the weddings of semi-agnostic young adults, or the alternative heartlessness of turning down a request from a couple whose desire for the blessing of God is genuine, if vague and formal.

A final category of chaplain activites which may be related to civil religion is participation in such endeavors as the character guidance, moral leadership, and human goals programs with which they have been prominently associated. Such programs are never regarded by military command as part of the explicitly "religious" program in which the chaplain represents his church. The goals may be the teaching of ethical conduct, the facilitation of personal growth, training in human relations, assistance with human problems, or the elimination of injustice and discrimination—all of which may also be goals of the servant church. They are "official" programs in which participation is usually mandatory; yet an element of common denominator religion has almost always been present in them. The chaplain generally regards his own participation as part of his explicitly religious ministry. This major element in the civil religion dimension of military ministry and the problems associated with it will be dealt with separately in the next two chapters. For the present we will examine the general concept of civil religion and the chaplain's relationship to it.

Many chaplains are highly ambivalent in their attitudes toward the kinds of activities listed above. They tend to view the nation, those values associated with its history and traditions, and the military services as valid and necessary instruments of national policy and defense. Were this not the case, it may safely be assumed that in most cases they would not have volunteered for service in the military. All chaplains are, and historically always have been, volunteers. There is an element of self-selection in volunteering for ministry in the nation's military forces which would automatically eliminate most of those clergymen who have a negative view of the nation and its military forces.

It follows that most would tend to affirm those symbols and beliefs which Bellah describes as central to civil religion at its best. The sovereignty of God over the nation; the national obligation to follow God's will; the judgment of God over the nation's conduct; the religious dimension of national crises and sacrifices—all these could be expected to strike a responsive chord with persons who have made vocational choices both for the church and for the military. It may be assumed that chaplains are naturally disposed to participate enthusiastically in acts and ceremonies which affirm these values.

Yet there are a number of factors which might lead the chaplain to view civil religion negatively. As a church professional, whose relationship to his own church comes first, both temporally and vocationally, that chaplain regards his role as a clergyman of church-oriented religion as his primary responsibility, far more important in the overall scheme of things than the civil religion ceremonies.[14] The sheer number of civil ceremonial requirements may begin to impinge on his primary responsibility: the eighth request for an invocation at the base Little League play-offs, the Army Wives' Club bazaar, or the meeting of the Navy Relief Society Advisory Board, may be onerous. Further, it quickly becomes apparent that many of those military leaders who feel most strongly about the requirement for prayer at the Change of Command ceremony or about compulsory church attendance for cadets at the Air Force Academy, are not personally involved in the religious community of the chapel or denominational church.

The Herberg view that the religion of the American way of life is a threat to church-oriented religion is widely shared by those who take church-oriented religion seriously, and the chaplain sees many illustrations of military people for whom the military-patriotic version of the American way of life does appear to be the operative religion. He even observes chaplains who seem to fit the category—young flag-wavers who take pride in wearing a forbidden pistol into combat, or older burnt-out cases with regimental patches sewed to their stoles, who appear to have nothing left but God-and-country ceremonials.

Denominational officials are likely to be suspicious on this score. The "Praise the Lord and Pass the Ammunition" syndrome, popular during the Second World War, has long since become unfashionable in church circles. Finally, the attacks on the chaplaincy, particularly with regard to subservience to military commanders and military values, which grew out of the Vietnamese War, have made chaplains themselves sensitive and defensive. As a result, chaplains are highly ambivalent with regard to civil religion.

Research on Chaplains and Civil Religion

In 1971 Leonard L. Ahrnsbrak, himself a Navy chaplain, conducted research in connection with graduate study at Princeton Theological Seminary on "Role Conflicts Among Navy Chaplains in Light of American Civil Religion." He posited a religio-cultural matrix for the chaplain's ministry in which both civil religion and church-oriented religion (Ahrnsbrak used the term "Judeo-Christian tradition" to describe America's denominational religions) are present. His hypothesis was that the presence of these two religious dimensions is a significant factor in causing role conflicts among Navy chaplains. The research instrument was a questionnaire, sent to 150 active duty Navy chaplains (a 15% random sampling), 51 retired chaplains (10% random sampling) and 42 inactive duty reserve chaplains (5% random sampling). His overall return rate was sixty percent.

The research findings were not always precisely measurable. Particularly difficult to evaluate was the section dealing specifically with civil religion, since it is not at all sure that the respondents understood the context (it would have been necessary to have read Herberg and Bellah) or the thrust of the questions. It was not clearly demonstrated that there is a relationship between the role conflict which he found (as have many other studies) and the responses regarding activities he identified with civil religion. In general, however, he concluded that the research supported his hypothesis. The data suggested that the religio-cultural matrix in which the chaplain's ministry is performed does contribute to role conflict.[15]

Particularly telling were the answers to questions regarding activities associated with civil religion. A great deal of ambivalence marked responses to the question, "What reason do you give for a chaplain participating in change of command ceremonies? Dedication of non-sacred buildings? Funerals for non-religious deceased persons?" Many answers from active duty chaplains justified participation and were interpreted by Ahrnsbrak as positive answers, but they were often defensive in tone:

> . . . all changes of command need the blessing of God and his guidance. Although the officer taking command may have no relationship with the established church or have morals that are high I feel that we are ministering to the entire crew.
>
> . . . the chaplain is to show a sacred dimension to all of life and death. He can do this effectively if he wants to—attitude is a big factor.
>
> . . . There is a psychological need to "do something." I am glad to help make the "something" Christian.
>
> . . . change of command and funerals . . . are for the most part, a ministry to the gathered congregation, valid.
>
> . . . by his very presence he is a sign, a symbol of a set of values different, perhaps, from others. He certainly has as much right to be there as anyone else.

Other answers were interpreted by Ahrnsbrak as neutral, although mixed might have been a more accurate description of some of them:

> . . . the import of such participation can be slight, unknown, even impossible to distinguish, but there can be an impact.
>
> . . . Why not? What is a sacred building? What is a non-religious person? Who in hell can judge that? a "pious" chaplain?
>
> . . . religious window dressing—tradition—"God is on our side."

Other answers were negative:

> I have grown to have a great aversion for this type of ceremony, change of command, graduations, dedications, etc. If ordered to go,

I go, and make an effort to offer a prayer that is meaningful to *and of* the persons present there. I think that very often the presence of the Chaplain is symbolic and mechanical (or, as a friend said, he indicates when the thing begins, and when it is over), with the symbolism being pretty token toward God. I do feel, though, for the people present, and perhaps it is often an opportunity to say something to them, or rather *with* them, to God. I see no point whatsoever in a Chaplain appearing at the burial of a person who had no contact with religion in his life, unless it would be clear that he might be able to offer his help to the family. I do truly deplore formalistic ceremony which has no solid basis behind it.

. . . the most tension filled area of my ministry involves the very functions mentioned in this question. At times I have felt that a proper response of a Christian Chaplain would be to cease from or refuse to participate in the "witch doctor roll" of change of command ceremonies, dedication of ships, etc.[16]

There was considerably less ambiguity in responses to a group of three questions having to do with required chapel attendance. Ninety-two percent of the active duty responses indicated that the chaplain should have a voice in deciding whether chapel attendance should be required. Seventy-five percent said midshipmen should not be required to attend chapel, and in a parallel question, seventy-six percent gave negative responses to the statement: "It is in the national interest to require future officers to attend chapel services." (This was at a time when the matter was before the courts, and the Navy's defense of required attendance was along the lines suggested by this statement.) Seventy-six percent said recruits should not be required to attend chapel.

It is interesting to note that retired chaplains and inactive duty chaplains (who are civilian clergymen) split much more evenly on required church attendance than did the active duty chaplains. The retired group split 52% to 48% in favor of required attendance for midshipmen, and 67% to 33% in favor of required attendance for recruits. This presumably reflects the feelings of an earlier era when compulsory church attendance was widely accepted. However, even more interesting is the sentiment of the civilian clergymen (inactive duty chaplains), who split 50%–50% on required attendance for midshipmen, and 41% to 59% against required attendance for recruits. Active duty chaplains have no monopoly on ambivalence about civil religion.

The stronger negative response from active duty chaplains may well reflect the discomfort of more direct involvement. The fact that such chapel attendance was still compulsory at a time when so large a percentage of active duty chaplains opposed it was interpred by Ahrnsbrak as a factor in role conflict.[17]

At the very least, the Ahrnsbrak study gave persuasive evidence that their involvement in civil religion presents some problems to chaplains. In December, 1973, a cassette tape on civil religion and chaplains was distributed by the Chief of Navy Chaplains as part of a continuing series of specially prepared taped resources, thus recognizing the need of chaplains for some assistance in sorting out the issues.[18]

TYPES OF CIVIL RELIGION

There is no question that both civil religion and church-oriented religion are present in the chaplain's ministerial environment. Indeed, both are present in the environment of every American clergyman, although civil religion is undoubtedly more prominently present for the chaplain than for others. The question is whether both are *legitimately* present—whether civil religion is, as Bellah claims, an authentic religious dynamic in which the chaplain may participate with integrity and without betraying his church vocation.

Ahrnsbrak, in a segment of the tape mentioned above, suggests that it is important for the chaplain to differentiate his civil religion from his own particular brand of Christianity or Judaism in the practise of his vocation. It would probably also be helpful for chaplains to differentiate between various types or manifestations of civil religion, and Ahrnsbrak's analysis suffers from his failure to do so. Differing attitudes toward different types may be appropriate. To lump together Herberg's Coca-Cola-and-faith-in-education American Way of Life and Bellah's national submission to God as a higher judge leads to confusion, not clarification. From the perspective of church-oriented religion, Herberg rightly deplores the tendency to substitute the American Way of Life, even with its emphasis on religious tolerance and generalized "faith in faith," for dynamic participation in a denominational community of faith. The so-called "American Shinto" which chaplains from time to time encounter, if its effect is to substitute country for God, the flag for the cross, and good citizenship (or wholesome soldiership) for Christian commitment, is probably another version of the same thing, and equally illegitimate.

Bellah, however, is talking about something quite different, and he has considerable justification for regarding the God-centered themes and symbols of America's civil religion (every theme and symbol he identifies with American civil religion *is* God-centered) as a valid and genuine apprehension of transcendent religious truth. Bellah is helpful, in this regard, in pointing out the worst aspects of civil religion ("religion in general," "American Shinto," and "religion of the 'American Way of Life' ") in contrast to its best aspects. Here (as in church-oriented religion also) we are justified in affirming the best while guarding against the worst. It may be helpful, at the risk of over-simplification, to distinguish between the three kinds of civil religion, using the descriptions of Dewey, Herberg, and Bellah to differentiate them.

1. Common denominator religion

Common denominator religion consists of those beliefs and symbols which are held in common by most people. Although the "common faith" recommended by Dewey in the 1930's was a desupernaturalized version derived from religious experience, most contemporary common denominator approaches seek to combine rather than discard particularized religions, focusing on those elements common to the great majority of the denominational religions in the Judeo-Christian family. Some Americans (atheists and adherents of Eastern or non-Judeo-Christian religions) would not accept them, but since practically all American religions belong to the Judeo-Christian family, the vast majority would.

Common denominator religion is an element in all forms of civil religion, including that described by Herberg and that described by Bellah. The official theism of the United States, incorporated in such national statements as the motto, "In God We trust," the Declaration of Independence assertion that we are endowed by our Creator with certain unalienable rights, and the added phrase in the Pledge of Allegiance, "one Nation under God," reflects a common core of beliefs present in all American religions. The particular themes which make up the *content* of common denominator religion are seldom challenged, since by definition common denominator religion consists of beliefs held by all. All clergymen and churchmen who participate in ecumenical services of any kind, who work together in common endeavors, or who participate in joint ministries, do so on the basis of those elements of their respective religions which they hold in common. The fact that others hold the same beliefs makes them no less vital as part of the belief systems of denominational communities of faith.

Common denominator religion becomes objectionable to adherents of church-oriented religion when it seeks to stand on its own, or becomes a substitute. This is the negative connotation usually attached to the phrase. If Dewey's "common faith" is the prototype, his reception was frosty because he suggested that this common faith could become a religion in its own right, replacing the denominational religions. A member of a church-oriented community of faith need have no inherent objection to affirmation of those elements of his faith, simply because they are shared by others.

2. "American Way of Life" religion

Herberg's observations provide the prototype here. He labeled those things to which Americans are obviously devoted, as evidenced by their operative choices, as their religion. Certainly the American Way of Life he described is a core of common values and a unifying force among Americans. Whether operative choices are necessarily the ultimate values may be debatable. It may be that the definition of what constitutes a religion is the issue here.

The patriotic dimension of the American Way of Life is the aspect of this form of civil religion which chaplains encounter in a special way. The real danger for them is the parochial use of religion for nationalistic purposes, the identification of God's will with the national will, when God becomes a means rather than an end. The most serious problem in the realm of civil religion is not with the American way of life itself, but with its elevation to the status of a religion, its substitution for more authentic forms of religion. If it replaces denominational communities of faith, or if it devitalizes them as Herberg claims it does, it is highly questionable. Either in the materialistic form which Herberg decried or the patriotic form with which chaplains are most familiar, it is probably, as Bellah suggested, civil religion at is worst rather than its best.

3. The God-centered dimension of national life

Civil religion, as Bellah described it, is the God-centered dimension of national life, an expression of religious faith interpreted in the light of American historical experience. It does not replace or oppose denominational religions; it coexists with them as an added dimension, an additional aspect of valid religious experience. This is the definition of civil religion which, following Bellah's exposition, has gained general acceptance.[19]

We are therefore justified in adopting this as the understanding of civil religion with which we are dealing when we conclude that it is an authentic religious expression in which chaplains may legitimately participate. The Dewey and Herberg versions may be recognized as aspects of civil religion, but they are distortions, unacceptable manifestations to be guarded against as one affirms the validity of civil religion at its best.

CLARIFYING THE RELATIONSHIP OF CHAPLAINS TO CIVIL RELIGION

With this as the operative definition of civil religion, we are in a position to make some observations which may assist in clarifying the relationship between the chaplaincy and civil religion. First, it might be noted that few churches and few clergymen would deny that civil religion (so understood) has some authenticity and validity. Few civilian clergymen or churchmen would refuse on all occasions, as a matter of principle, to offer prayer at public ceremonies or to affirm the sovereignty of God over national life and the nation's obligation to seek to follow his will. For chaplains, the problem of their relationship to civil religion differs only in degree from that of other clergymen and churchmen. As members of an institution which in itself embodies patriotic symbolism and national purposes, they naturally encounter it to a greater degree in their own professional life. As members of both the church and the military, and therefore living symbols of the relationship between God and country, they are likely to be invited to take part in civilian church activities on civil religion occasions, such as Independence Sunday or Memorial Day. But aside from the degree of involvement, there is no essential difference between chaplains and civilian churchmen at this point. If participation in civil religion is legitimate for the church at all, it is legitimate for chaplains.

Second, it might be noted that civil religion can never be completely separated from church-oriented religion. Ahrnsbrak describes the relationship of civil religion to denominational religion as a symbiotic one—civil religion draws its life from the Judeo-Christian tradition and a threat to one is a threat to both. Whether in its worst form or its best, civil religion draws from and reflects elements of denominational religion. Furthermore, when a clergyman participates in ceremonies or exercises of civil religion, there will always be elements of his denominational religion present with him: exposure, witnessing, a theology of presence, even a form of pre-evangelism. At the same time, however, it might be noted that a denominational religious leader participating in civil religion is justified in regarding the two as separate kinds of activities, each with its own context and justification. There is no inherent conflict between the two.

Since civil religion responsibilities are more prominent in the ministry of chaplains than in other ministries of the church, the chaplain has some special obligations:

1. A chaplain must have a thorough understanding of what civil religion is, its uses and its misuses. He should be familiar with its various manifestations, and he should be quite clear as to the limits of *legitimate* civil religion.

2. A chaplain may, as Ahrnsbrak suggests, sort out his attitudes toward his civil religious involvements by regarding it as a separate re-

sponsibility from his basic responsibility of leadership in denominational religion. He can legitimately function in both areas, and, indeed, in his particular profession, he must.

3. He must continually guard against distortions of civil religion and the dangers of allowing it to get out of proportion. An ecumenical ministry in a religiously pluralistic environment makes common denominator religion always a temptation. In the military environment, the danger of allowing religion to become a means to an end, a tool of national purposes, is particularly grave. "American Shinto" is to be avoided at all costs. The chaplain must guard against the substitution of civil religion in any form—even at its best—for the community of faith he represents.

The relationship of the chaplain to civil religion is likely to remain one of tension, but it need not be destructive tension. Rightly understood and carefully safeguarded, civil religion can have a legitimate place in his ministry. To this end, chaplains are in need of guidance and assistance from their churches. The appropriate relationships must be determined, in the last analysis, by the churches themselves. As clergymen in direct and continuing contact with civil religion, chaplains can assist in this task —but only as representatives of their churches working within the church context.

Their involvement in civil religion is such that their objectivity may sometimes be open to question. The churches can assist them in this and other such areas by arranging seminars and conferences, and offering study opportunities in which they meet with civilian teachers and leaders to work on the issue. For the churches to allow the chaplains to work out their own independent accomodation with civil religion would be a serious error. But for the churches to deal with civil religion without taking advantage of the insights, the first-hand experience, and the deep involvement of their chaplains in the issue would be an equally serious error.

Chapter 7

Character Education

One of the major manifestations of civil religion in the armed forces, and one of the most controversial of the activities of chaplains, is character education. We noted in Chapter 3 that the goals of religious ministry are determined by the churches rather than the military services. They are therefore likely to be peripheral to the operationally-oriented goals of the military. The organizational precariousness of the chaplain's position under these circumstances leads to a good bit of discomfort. A psychic need to be needed, a desire to find a more central role in the organization, and a search for firmer levels of funding and support are all natural in this situation.

More positively, chaplains have an obligation to serve the entire institution. This is clearly an expectation of the churches and one of the church-derived goals of their ministry. As a result of these two factors, the chaplaincies in the post-World War II years have devised a series of programs, variously known as character guidance, character education, moral leadership, the Protection of Moral Standards Program, and the Human Self-Development Program. Related efforts have been known by a variety of other names. In this discussion the term "character education" will be used to cover the entire field, except when another title is used in a particular historical context.

In general, the term refers to a series of chaplain-centered programs, which have received considerable emphasis in all three services throughout the post-World War II period. These various programs have all shared the following characteristics:

1. They have been designed and promoted by chaplains, but adopted as "command" programs under line sponsorship, the participation of chaplains as instructors or discussion leaders being viewed as a military staff function rather than an ecclesiastical function.

2. They have been viewed as separate and distinct from the "religious" programs in which chaplains function as clergymen leading church-oriented religious activities.

3. Religion (generally a form of civil religion) has, nevertheless, been an element in the content and orientation of all such programs.

4. The basic aims of the programs have been the teaching of morality, the fostering of human growth and self-realization, and the enhancement of interpersonal relations.

5. The programs have been aimed at *all* military personnel, regardless of religious or non-religious preferences, and attendance at classes and discussion sessions has generally been compulsory. They have frequently been incorporated into command training schedules for all hands, along with training in rifle marksmanship, fire fighting, first aid, and personal hygiene.

In most instances specific programs described in this chapter are those of the Navy. Comparable programs have been and still are present in all three services, and the issues they raise are equally applicable to all services.

EARLY ANTECEDENTS OF CHARACTER EDUCATION

Concern by chaplains about the morals of the troops and the moral conditions of their environment is as old as the chaplaincy itself. So is the conviction of commanders that one of the functions of chaplains is the protection of moral standards for the entire command. George Washington's first expressed interest in the chaplaincy, during the French and Indian War, was to find a "gentleman of sober, serious and religious deportment, who would improve morale and discourage gambling, swearing, and drunkenness."[1]

Efforts to promote moral character have been made by military commanders throughout American military history, if not always for the sake of morality as an end in itself, then on the basis of the purely utilitarian consideration that certain moral virtues make for a more efficient and effective military organization. Early efforts of chaplains to promote general morality were unorganized and dependent on individual initiative, but were a continuing emphasis. Drury's history of the Navy chaplaincy contains sections, in each historical period, dealing with the morality of the sailors of the day and the efforts of chaplains to improve it. The legitimacy of this area of concern for chaplains is taken for granted.

The earliest *Chaplains Manual,* issued in 1918 by Chaplain John B. Frazier, the first Navy Chief of Chaplains, described an early "moral lecture" program:

> There is one phase of a very difficult but very important subject that can and should be presented by the Chaplain in a series of lectures, delivered once a month. The reference is to social hygiene. . . . While the Surgeon is the logical person to speak on this theme from a medical standpoint, the Chaplain will find that a wise presentation of its moral, social, and professional aspects will carry just as much weight as does the fear of physical contamination.[2]

As early as 1921 Navy chaplains in recruit training stations were working on a formal program of lectures, presented on company time to recruits. Such a program was in operation in most of the recruit centers by 1923, and from then on "moral lectures" by chaplains were a regular part of recruit training.

The Character Education Movement of the Fifties

In the period immediately after the Second World War, there began what was probably the most massive, intensive, and carefully organized attempt at character building through education ever attempted under secular sponsorship. The heyday of the character education movement in the armed forces extended through the decade of the fifties, coinciding with the height of the Cold War period, in which large standing armed forces, with a draft that required a period of military service from nearly every able-bodied young male American, was a major fact of American life. Since the character education program was designed and operated for the military services by their chaplaincies, it represented the most massive experiment ever conducted by a group of clergymen in extending their influence beyond the context of religious faith. Its aims were high—"to build a strong moral, ethical, and spiritual foundation in the Navy" was the stated purpose as described in the Navy's long-standing directive on the subject.[3]

The fifties were, of course, the high point of the so-called "revival of religion" in the postwar period. Church membership was at an all-time high, as was formal adherence to religious values. The influence of chaplains within the military establishment also reached a high water mark. The climate was never more favorable for a massive experiment in the clergy-dominated teaching to a general adult population of moral values derived from religious systems. It is probably accurate to say that character education was the dominant institutional interest of the chaplaincies during the period. Large budgets were made available, and substantial investments of manpower and effort were poured into the endeavor.

Although the program suffered a marked decline after the fifties, it still exists, in one form or another, in all the services. In its original form it was continued longest in the Army. Until 1972 monthly standardized lectures, prepared by the Army Chaplains' Board, were sent to all chaplains for use in a program of instruction which theoretically reached all troops. Character Guidance continued until that time to be listed in the Army's regulatory manuals as a major responsibility of all chaplains.

In 1972 the Army's Character Guidance Program was replaced by a Human Self-Development Program. Implementation is optional with individual commanders, and attendance is voluntary. Materials prepared by the Chaplains' Board are designed for a discussion format with groups of twenty or less. Such materials are distributed quarterly.

In the Air Force, character education is now limited to the Air Training Command for airmen and officers in first term student status. The thrust has moved from moral instruction to clarification of values. Each chaplain team at a given institution works within broad guidelines to assist the airmen in identity formation and values clarification.

Except in recruit centers, the Navy's servicewide character education program has been, for all practical purposes, dead since the middle sixties. Its basic directives, however, have never been cancelled. They remain, ignored, on the books. The publications developed in the fifties still remain in the publications system, and periodic attempts have been made to revive it, including several current efforts. Its basic goals, furthermore, have been incorporated into several other programs which have come and gone with varying degrees of success—the Personal Enrichment Program for young adults in the Submarine Force, at which we have already taken a look, and a Personal Response Program during the Vietnamese War. Character education remains, then, a live issue which must be examined in detail in any analysis of the contemporary military chaplaincy.

Post-World War II Beginnings

The post-World War II character education movement began with a reexamination of the long-established practice of having chaplains give moral lectures to recruits. The Army's Universal Military Training Experimental Unit at Fort Knox, Kentucky, in 1946–47, provided for moral instruction by chaplains. It was regarded as highly successful. On the basis of this experience, a letter, signed by the Secretary of War in January, 1947, initiated such a program throughout the Army. A circular, published in August, 1948, directed the establishment of Character Guidance Councils from the Department of the Army down to the batallion level. When the U. S. Air Force became a separate service, it carried over the Army character guidance program, which was established by Air Force directives in November, 1948.[4]

In 1946 the Navy reexamined the moral instruction included in Recruit Training, and devised a new series of ten "lectures on moral and ethical subjects" which were included in 1947 in the Curriculum for Recruit Training. Titles of the ten lectures were: (1) The Navy Way; (2) A Man's Obligation to His Folks; (3) The Navy Man and his Religion; (4) Looking Ahead; (5) The Case for Continence; (6) Taking a Chance; (7)

The Finishers; (8) Self-Command; (9) The Navy Man and Marriage; and (10) You're on Your Own.[5]

In 1950, representatives of the three Chiefs of Chaplains met to review what was by then known as character guidance instruction given to recruits. Over an eight-month period they developed and tested a series of six "Armed Forces Chaplains' Visual Presentations," consisting of lecture outlines with visual aids in the form of a black flannelgraph board on which lecture symbols were placed. These were adopted by all three services.

The period of massive emphasis on character education was initiated with a letter, dated 26 May 1951, signed by Secretary of Defense George C. Marshall and addressed to the secretaries of the three services. It said, in part:

> It is in the national interest that personnel serving in the Armed Forces be protected in the realization and development of moral, spiritual, and religious values consistent with the religious beliefs of the individuals concerned. To this end, it is the duty of commanding officers in every echelon to develop to the highest possible degree the conditions and influences calculated to promote the health, morals, and spiritual values of the personnel under their command.

In the Navy and Marine Corps this directive was implemented by the Chief of Naval Personnel and the Commandant of the Marine Corps in a joint letter, issued on August 23, 1951. It stated that the protection and development of moral standards is a responsibility of leadership which must be shared by all non-commissioned and petty officers as well as the general and flag officers, the commanding officers, and the subordinate officers who bear the direct responsibility. It directed commanding officers to "insure that all personnel are reached by group instruction and by personal interviews on all matters that promote the realization and development of moral, spiritual, and religious values, consistent with the religious beliefs of the individual concerned."

The "Cradle-to-Grave" Program: Recruit Training

With character education thus given official sanction throughout the Navy and Marine Corps, the Navy chaplaincy moved ahead full steam to develop a program which would be "a continuous process for all personnel in whatever area of service they may happen to be, whether in Recruit Training, Service School, Officer Candidate School, service with the Fleet, or on duty on Foreign Station."[6]

For implementation of the program, these various areas of service were broadly classified into three levels or phases, the first dealing with the newly enlisted recruit, the second with enlisted and officer schools in which advanced training is given to potential leaders, and the third with general duty in the fleet, at Naval stations, and overseas.

The "Chaplains' Visual Presentations," already in use for recruit training in all three services, became the first level of the Navy's total character education program. Subjects covered in this series included: (1) Religion in the Navy; (2) The Case for Continence; (3) Marriage and Family Life; (4) Responsibilities (to God, to others, and to the self); (5) Moral Principles; and (6) Citizenship. The series was essentially a straightforward content-centered combination of civil religion and common denominator moral principles.

The Chaplains Division of the Bureau of Naval Personnel prepared a series of eight films, primarily for use with this series. As time went on it was put into more general use with character education throughout the Navy. Titles were: (1) The Golden Moment (introduction to character education); (2) Men of the World (servicemen's public relations); (3) Let's Get it Straight (alcohol education); (4) To be Held in Honor (sex and marriage); (5) Pulling Your Weight (responsibilities); (6) Religion in the Navy; (7) You Think it's Luck (gambling); and (8) The Chaplain Comes Aboard.

Second Level: Schools for Future Leaders

In the four-year period from 1952 to 1956, teams of chaplains were assigned to commands of various types to develop character education curricula for the other two levels of instruction. The second level was that of leadership training. A character education curriculum was planned for service schools, at which petty officers and future petty officers are prepared for enlisted leadership. A team of six chaplains was sent to the Naval Training Center at Bainbridge, Maryland, in June, 1952. In the curriculum they produced the emphasis was shifted from moral principles and their application in life to personal values and growth. Utilizing the findings of the behavioral sciences, they devised "guided discussions," involving class participation, but following a controlled and predictable pattern. Accompanying visual symbols for use on the black flannelboard were produced to reinforce the highly standardized "discussions."

The series, which was entitled "Our Moral and Spiritual Growth Here and Now," began with a slide lecture called "Your Navy Chaplain and You." This was followed by discussion outlines covering six major areas, with four supplemental discussions for use in those service schools having courses of longer duration. The areas covered, with the titles of the guided discussions provided for each area, were: (1) Need and Urgency (orientation to the environment of the immediate present); Discussion: "Let's Look Around." (2) Self-Understanding and Personal Worth; Discussion: "Let's Look at Me." (3) Discrimination and Choice of Values ("the individual as he examines his values of the present moment and the choices necessary to transform them into a positive system of values related to the Eternal"); Discussions: "Let's Weigh My Values: How Important is What I Want?" and "Let's Examine my Choices: Which Way am I Going?" (4) Constructively Resolving Tension; Discussion: "Can I Learn to Take It?" (5) Responsible Freedom and Natural Rights; Discussion: "Let's Look at my Freedom." (6) The Power of a Controlling Purpose; Discussion: "What Keeps Me Going?"

Supplemental discussions were provided for longer schools: (1) What's Happening to Me?" (Personal concern and the importance of developing high moral standards. Charts rather than flannelboard symbols were used with this presentation). (2) "Here I Am" (The importance of selecting a positive course for growth and development). (3) "How Important is What I Want?" (Examination of personal values and the relating of values to behavior, life's goals, and the welfare of others. A chalk and blackboard presentation, this was provided as an alternative to the two discussions on value and choices in area 3). (4) "Let's Look at Me —A Leader: Here I Am Out Front" (How to develop the characteristics of forceful leadership).[7]

This series, which depended heavily on the behavioral sciences, was probably the best of the curricula developed during the fifties. It utilized a "guided discussion" technique, but allowed for a considerable measure of flexibility. It emphasized the *process* of growth and decision-making rather than content, and it marked a definite break with the "moral lecture" concept of series one. Common denominator civil religion, a prominent element in the first series, was present less directly as an undergirding for the general orientation, but not so extensively as explicit subject matter in this series.

The Chief of Naval Personnel and the Chief of Naval Air Training published instructions in 1953 and 1954 incorporating character education periods in the curricula of Class "A" (first level) service schools. In these schools the materials from the "Moral and Spiritual Growth Here and Now" series were widely and successfully used for many years.

Third Level Curricula: General Service

In September 1953, steps were taken to prepare curricular materials for use by chaplains at the third level of the "cradle-to-grave" program

—general duty afloat, ashore, and overseas. Three teams of chaplains were established. One, assigned to the Atlantic Fleet Destroyer Force, headquartered at Newport, Rhode Island, developed a series for shipboard use. Published in 1955 as Series 3, under the title, "Because of You," it provided discussions "for use over a four year period at the rate of five discussions per year for all personnel afloat." The subject matter was essentially duplicated every other year, though with a difference of approach. Titles (with explanatory phrases as given in the curriculum's table of contents) were as follows:

Year One: (1) "What Good are You?" (The intrinsic worth of the human person); (2) "The You in the USA" (Why we are here: personal responsibility to country); (3) "She Loves Me, She Loves Me Not" (Responsibility in sex and marriage); (4) "Drinks and Drunks" (Responsibility and the use of alcohol); and (5) "People are Not Fireproof" (Penalties of avoiding responsibility).

Year Two: (1) "A Square Deal" (Meanings and applications of justice); (2) "Show Me the Way to Go Home" (Meaning and importance of home); (3) "With Malice Toward Some" (Existence and impact of prejudice); (4) "Free for Nothing" (Principles and practices of honesty); and (5) "Who's Who" (Importance and evaluation of recognition and acceptance).

Year Three: (1) "What Makes a Man a Man" (Responsibility and character); (2) "What's Right with America" (Evaluation of country in the light of personal responsibility); (3) "What is This Thing Called Love" (Truth and error about love and sex); (4) "You Said a Mouthful" (Responsibility in the use of speech); and (5) "Front and Center" (Attempts to avoid responsibility and the consequences thereof).

Year Four: (1) "Made in America" (Principles and ideal of justice and democracy); (2) "Happy Days Are Here Again" (Meaning and importance of desire for happiness); (3) "Heart Failure" (Importance of charity in human relations); (4) "The Sweat Treatment" (Meaning and dignity of work); and (5) "Wish You Were Here" (Responsibilities on "liberty" or shore leave).

As may readily be seen from the topics and explanatory phrases, this was a content-centered rather than a process-centered series. Series 2 had departed almost entirely from the teaching of moral principles, and had espoused instead the facilitation of personal development. Its emphasis had been on the process of growth. Series 3, emphasizing content, returned to a heavy dose of moral principles. There was some emphasis on human personhood, particularly with regard to personal responsibility, but with a conceptual approach. The repeated use in the explanatory

phrases of "meaning of . . . ," "principles of . . . ," "importance of
. . . ," and "penalties of . . ." provides a clue to the didactic nature of
the series.

The materials continued the "guided discussion" methodology developed for Series 2, but applied it in a somewhat rigid and mechanical
way. Where Series 2 had used the guided discussion to lead a group
through a process of self-examination and examination of choices, designed to encourage growth, Series 3 used questions to elicit predictable
responses for the purpose of building a rational "case" for a particular
viewpoint. There was little leeway for variation by either chaplain or class.
The effect was that of a participatory lecture or sermon, in which the
group was used to make certain points. The introductory materials described the method:

> The guided discussions in this manual are actual representations of
> experiments conducted with varied groups of naval personnel. The
> chaplain who studies these materials carefully before attempting to
> use them should experience little difficulty in grasping the objec-
> tives, thought content, and particularly the "direction" deliberately
> evoked in each discussion. The chaplain can feel secure in knowing
> that the answers given to discussion questions are actual and typical
> answers given by men themselves; he can safely anticipate answers
> of a similar nature in many instances. However, since every group
> differs, the chaplain may not receive "typical" answers, so that it is
> gravely important that he himself know the direction in which he
> wants the group thought to move, the objectives he wants achieved.
> His sincerity alone is not adequate. Incalculable harm can be done
> in a poorly guided discussion. Not only can it quickly degenerate
> into a "free-for-all," or a "gripe" session, but the entire group can
> be seriously misled by one member of the group whom the chap-
> lain's lack of preparation and knowledge of his subject have left him
> unable to control and "use" for the good of the group.[8]

An illustration of the use of the guided discussion in this series is
found in the introductory portion of the second in the series, "The You
in the USA":

> Intro: (Chaplain begins immediately with question directed at vari-
> ous individuals selected at random in various sections of group.)
>
> What are you doing here? Why are *you* here?
>
> (Slight initial confusion may be met by question. Men may ask what
> chaplain means. Insist that confusion be resolved by group itself.)
>
> (Go on with further questions as noted.)
>
> How many of you are in the Navy because you personally want to
> be? Let's have a show of hands.

(It is to be expected that a few may raise hands. Write *Want* on board, and tally figure beneath it.)

Now then, if so few are here because they personally want to be, whether it is for schooling, travel, pay or what have you, then why are the others here? Let us have some further answers.

(Several answers will be given such as: Get it over with; Navy sold me a bill of goods, etc.)

Apparently a sizeable number do not really want to be in the Navy, would definitely prefer being elsewhere, or in some other job. This would mean that a large number are here in the Navy because we must be; in a sense we cannot help it.
Let us analyze this. Why is it so? . . . What answers can we give to the question: Why must we be here?

(Answers point up conditions of world at large, ordinarily centering upon communism.)

Most of these answers come out to pretty much the same thing, do they not—the condition of the world at large? . . .[9]

The title of the discussion from which this excerpt is taken, "The You in the USA," points up another characteristic of the "Because of You" series. Patriotism became an explicit subject to be taught in character education classes. It was the only subject included in all four years. In addition, references to the founding fathers, anecdotes from American history, American "principles," the pledge of allegiance, and historic documents (most of them direct reflections of civil religion) are heavily larded throughout the discussions of the series. An appendix provided a large number of illustrative anecdotes for optional use. The largest number were listed under "Patriotism," but many in all categories were stories from American history. In effect, the appendix is a short reader in civil religion.

Religion itself, which had been the subject of one lecture and a prominent element in most others in the first series (recruit training), but which had been present less directly in the second, was once again explicit in the subject matter of the third series. Common denominator religious concepts—God, the created order, natural law, God's moral law, the Ten Commandments, divine reward and punishment, faith, the Bible—were frequently used, often (in sermonic fashion) in the concluding portions of a discussion. In a very real sense the "guided discussions" of Series 3 could be labeled sermons of a civil religion.

When used as directed, the "Because of You" series was quite effective. In the context of the anti-God communism and pro-God Americanism which was characteristic of the fifties, it was undoubtedly reasonably acceptable. Many chaplains, however, objected to the parroting of their prepared lines in a staged dialogue, and some considered the procedure to be downright manipulative. Further, operational commitments and shipboard pressures made the covering of "five discussions a year for all personnel afloat" (even where chaplains were present on shipboard) much more difficult than in recruit training and schools, where teaching was the primary mission. Widespread indifference on the part of line commanders meant that in most cases the attempt was made only if a chaplain pushed it. In addition, although the curriculum was published at what was probably the high-water mark of the character education movement, the decline set in rapidly. As a result, even on those ships where it was attempted, the effort had largely expired long before year four of the first four-year cycle was reached.

In September 1953, teams had also been ordered to the Naval Training Center at San Diego, California, to prepare materials for use in continental U. S. shore stations, and to Sasebo, Japan, to devise a series for use in the Far East. The latter series, although labeled Series 5, was completed first and was published in 1955 under the title, *My Life in the Far East.* The subjects covered (with explanatory phrases as given in the table of contents) were: (1) Do I Ring True? (personal integrity); (2) How Shall I Live? (right and wrong choices in conduct); (3) What Do I Want? —Americanism or Communism; (4) What Do I Show to Others?—Ambassadors of the United States; (5) What About Women? (6) What About Liquor? (7) What About Narcotics? (8) What About the Black Market? (9) Moral Standards Beyond the Dateline; (10) My Home of the Future (the effect of conduct in the Far East on future marriage); (11) The Best Years of a Man's Life (constructive use of freedom in the Far East); and (12) Marriage—Where and to Whom? (marriage to nationals of Far Eastern countries).

Prepared in straightforward outline and essay format, the series employed no gimmicks. The preface gave few instructions: "It is assumed that this material will be used by the instructor as a guide, but that each instructor will formulate his own discussion plan and questions."[10] Common denominator religion was taken for granted, and brought in explicitly on occasion, though not so frequently as in Series 3. There was one session on Americanism and some American heritage material. The civil religion element was clearly present. For the most part, however, the series concentrated in a down-to-earth way on those moral problems encountered most frequently in the Far East. Acceptance among chaplains was fairly general. Since commanding officers of ships and stations in the Far East were (and are) faced with far higher rates of venereal disease, drunkenness, narcotics usage, and (in those days) black marketing than in the United States, and since relationships with foreign nationals of the host countries were a continuing problem area, the direct relationship to operational readiness was almost universally perceived. Character education sessions of this kind were therefore much in demand, and the series was widely used for a long period.

Series 4, the last of the major published curricula, entitled *This is My Life*, was published in 1956 and intended for use at shore activities. Departing from a treatment of moral conduct as such, it sought to teach a personal religious, philosophical, and behavioral orientation out of which moral choices could be made. Fine in theory (particularly from the perspective of clergymen), the result was something less than satisfactory in practice. The team responsible for development of the series produced five presentations, the major part of the three-year preparation period being devoted to an elaborate series of test runs at seven Navy and Marine Corps commands in the San Diego area.

The themes were: (1) My Equipment (Human nature); (2) My Value (Personal worth); (3) My Rules (Natural Moral Law); (4) My Relationships (Group living); and (5) My Development (Character). The format was called a "directed discussion," with preliminary guidelines to the instructor indicating that "questions, short responses, and repetitions indicate the interplay between the leader and the group." In effect, however, the written presentations were in outline and essay form.

The content was a startling (and ill-fitting) combination of straight Roman Catholic Thomistic theology in presentations one (human nature) and three (natural moral law) and behavioral science in presentations four (relationships) and five (growth and development). Presentation two (human value), less easily labeled, might be called a combination of behavioral science and common denominator religion.

The heavily theological content made presentations one and three the most explicitly religious of all character education materials developed during the period. It was not, however, civil religion. Presentation one, in addition to a discussion of the "order of natures" (material, vegetive, animal, human, angelic, and divine), and a discussion of human nature (physical and spiritual, with the powers of the soul: intellect, free will, and immortality), provided appendices giving "proofs for the existence of God" and "proof for existence of spiritual soul."[11] Presentation three covered the laws of man's nature (material, vegetive, animal); the Eternal Law in the Mind of God; the Natural Law of reason (and its relationship to Divine Law); Natural Law as universal and immutable; and the results of disobedience to Natural Law. It provided an appendix on "other kinds of laws which flow from the Eternal Law in the Mind of God," human positive law and divine positive law.[12]

Despite the inclusion in the book of elaborate statistical evidence from pilot runs to show that the material was understandable and effective, it had little appeal to bluejackets. The Thomism was rejected almost unanimously by Protestant chaplains. In addition, by the time it was published the character education movement was well past its crest. As a result, it was rarely used.

Final Efforts

Two final chaplain teams were assigned in the summer of 1955: one to the Officer Candidate School in Newport, Rhode Island, to complete level two by developing materials for officer training, and a second to the U.S. Naval Retraining Command in Portsmouth, New Hampshire, to develop a special series for personnel in confinement. The first was completed as a conventional character education curriculum, and some use was made of the materials in the limited officer training situations for which it was designed.

The Retraining Command team went beyond its original mandate and ultimately developed a "Handbook for the Guidance of Chaplains in Institutions of Confinement." Entitled *The Man Within*, this handbook was issued for limited circulation by the Chaplains Division of the Bureau of Naval Personnel in 1956. It provided a thoughtful examination of the context of ministry with confinees: the offender, the offense, and the nature of confinement. As part of an analysis of the chaplain's attitudes and ministries, it included a discussion of character education lectures and their utilization. No specific suggestions were made as to content; attention was given rather to the necessity of making such lectures appropriate and useful.

The largest section of the handbook was devoted to "group work," to be used by the chaplain as an extension of personal counseling. In addition to a discussion of the possibilities and advantages of such group counseling and the chaplain's role as enabler, it gave reasonably detailed procedures for setting up such a program, the dynamics of the group, various techniques to be used by the enabler, and abbreviated verbatims of three sessions of a sample group. Soundly incorporating the insights of the then-youthful field of group dynamics, the handbook would still be useful as an introduction to group counseling today. In shifting the emphasis from the lecture and the pseudo-participation of the guided discussion to genuine group participation, the Retraining Command team was probably the most forward-looking of the Navy's character education teams of the fifties.

The concept of character education underwent a gradual evolution as the movement ran its course during the fifties. Beginning as "character guidance" on the basis of simple moral instruction, it gradually became "character education," a more ambitious attempt to mold character. What was meant by "character" was never precisely defined, but, increasingly, simple ethical teaching was replaced by a broader emphasis on growth and development of the whole person. Lectures gave way to group discussion. An attempt to teach moral principles was replaced by an attempt to encourage the development of personal value systems.

As this emphasis developed, increasing use was made of the insights of behavioral sciences. Particularly useful was the growing knowledge of group dynamics from the disciplines of sociology and social psychology, following the pioneering work of Kurt Lewin. Useful also was the new school of humanistic psychology just coming into prominence in that period under the leadership of Abraham Maslow, Carl Rogers, and others. The self-realization values of humanistic psychology became increasingly the values of a character education focused on personal growth.

RELATIONSHIPS TO LINE COMMANDERS

A recurring issue throughout this period was the relationship of chaplains to line officers, in the development and sponsorship of the program. In conception, philosophy, and design, character education was a chaplains' program. Chaplains had originated the idea, promoted its adoption, written the curricula, taught the classes, and served as the staff administrators at every level. As a "chaplains' program," however, it was associated by line officers with the voluntarism which characterizes religious observances. It was regarded as suspect by hard-headed pragmatists to whom "character" meant an old sea-dog.

To achieve its goals, however, the program had to be carried out under line auspices, with the "clout" of military command behind it. From the beginning, therefore, an attempt was made to sell it as a command program. Starting with Secretary Marshall's memorandum of 26 May 1951, long known as the "charter of character education" (the original draft of which had, of course, been written by a chaplain), command responsibility had been emphasized. "It is the duty of commanding officers at every echelon . . . ," that memorandum had said. The various directives, circulars, and orders which put the program into effect were invariably signed by line commanders and went out through command channels for command implementation. But no one was fooled about the realities. There were a number of line officers and enlisted leaders at every level who, like General Marshall himself, were thoroughly sold on and became personally involved in this approach to leadership. In general, though, line officers were ambivalent, continuing to regard it as a "chaplains' program."

There was much ambivalence in the chaplaincies, also. A religious dimension had to be maintained in the program (and, indeed, was in every curriculum developed) in order to retain chaplain interest and commitment. But it had to be common denominator religion. Civil religion generally, as Herberg noted, tends to be regarded as a threat by those most strongly committed to denominational religion. The common denominator religion of character education was so regarded by many chaplains. Other chaplains, particularly in recruit centers and service school where teaching such classes was the major activity for some, felt that it tended to get out of proportion, consuming time clergymen should be devoting to church-oriented religious leadership.

The religious issue was further complicated by the fact that the program was sold to its consumers as "non-religious":

> In his specific religious ministry the chaplain may find ample means of ministering directly to personnel of his own religious persuasion. . . . But in his key position as advisor to the command in moral matters the chaplain can aid *all* personnel directly. . . . He can help create the environment conducive to the moral and spiritual welfare of all hands. . . . However, the Character Education program is *not* a religious program. Confusion on this issue is both dangerous and unnecessary. It is true that the Character Education program attempts to promote the realization of moral, spiritual, and religious values. This no more makes it a religious program than the food a man eats makes a man. . . . At no time is any chaplain charged with carrying out a religious ministry contrary to his own creed, or the spirit and tenets of his own church. He may not be so charged. Participation in the Character Education program must not violate this maxim in any respect. If such violation is to be avoided, three facts must remain clear. (1) The Character Education program is not a religious program. (2) The chaplain must never be charged with expressing religious doctrines contrary to his own creed. (3) The participation of chaplains in the program must not lend it a religious "tone."[13]

Such obscure distinctions satisfied neither chaplains nor line officers. The program was thus involved in serious contradictions on this score. Neither side found character education's non-religious religion entirely acceptable.

With line leadership divided and the chaplaincy also divided, then, commitment to the experiment was somewhat less than total at every level. In an attempt to deal with these factors, the long-range strategy of the chaplaincy was to enlarge the scope of the program to include elements other than the character education classes taught by chaplains. Character education became part of a larger "Moral Leadership Program." This, in turn, was incorporated into an even more general "Leadership Program." In the late fifties, staff responsibility for development and administration of the effort was shifted from the Chaplains Division of the Bureau of Naval Personnel to a specially created Leadership Office in that Bureau. A line captain was placed in charge of the office, although his key staff assistants continued to be chaplains. Leadership teams, with both line and chaplain members, were set up at various fleet centers, to oversee and assist with implementation of the program in ships and stations.

Early on, there had been attempts at the local level to involve persons other than chaplains—both officers and petty officers—as instructors in character education classes. Here again, the basic contradiction led to mixed results. The curricular materials prepared by and for clergymen were regarded as impossible by gunnery officers and bosn's mates. But when these line leaders discarded the prepared materials and launched out in their own several directions, the results were unpredictable—at best something other than the kind of character education originally envisioned. By the early sixties, when the Leadership Office in the Bureau of Naval Personnel ceased to be chaplain-dominated and began to turn out leadership materials by and for non-chaplains, the movement was already moribund.

For all practical purposes, the movement had died before stage three materials—those for general duty on ships and shore stations—were put into wide-spread use. The *My Life in the Far East* curriculum, which as we have noted offered a practical, down-to-earth approach to problems encountered by commands in the Far East, continued to be used on local initiative by chaplains on duty in that area for many years. None of the other curricula reached a significant level of utilization, however. *Because of You* required a mechanical parroting of canned materials which few chaplains were willing to give. *This is Your Life* departed from the civil religion basis of the rest of the program and launched out into a traditionalist Roman Catholic natural theology which was widely rejected. Both languished on storeroom shelves.

By the beginning of the sixties the original character education movement had run its course. The special Leadership Office in the

Bureau of Naval Personnel continued in existence for some years, but the chaplaincy was less and less involved. No one officially killed the program. A directive requiring character education sessions in recruit training and certain schools and stating that such sessions "should be included in the command program of naval leadership" afloat and ashore was reissued in 1962. It then remained uncancelled on the books for more than ten years. All the curricula remained nominally current in the publication system, available on order. They were, however, largely ignored. In recruit training and schools where such classes continued to be required, chaplains gradually discarded outmoded materials and used whatever they saw fit. All too often they fell into the habit of giving *pro forma* lectures on any subject they considered appropriate.

In the end the character education experiment of the fifties probably foundered because of the basic ambiguity of its nature. Sold as a command program, it never genuinely enjoyed command support and sanction, except from that minority of line officers with a deep concern for morality and human growth as ends in their own right. Numerous attempts were made to demonstrate its validity as an essential contribution to the military mission, but without success. Those commanders who saw the necessity of building "a strong moral, ethical and spiritual foundation in the Navy" as a military requirement were the already-convinced, and they remained a minority. For the majority it was always a "chaplains' program," associated with religion, and regarded as a militarily non-essential extra.

As a chaplains' program, however, it never enjoyed the full support of chaplains either. Many of those who saw their ministry primarily in church-oriented terms perceived it as a religiously non-essential extra— at worst a threat to religion, at best a consumer of time better devoted elsewhere. Its slow demise in the sixties was mourned by few in either the line or the Chaplain Corps.

Chapter 8

Personal Growth and Human Relations Programs

The decline of the character education movement of the fifties did not end the dynamic it had expressed. It has been followed by other chaplain-designed programs with the same general characteristics: programs intended for the entire institution rather than religious congregations only. None has received the massive attention and support, or assumed the messianic proportions, of the great experiment of the fifties, but all have met the same general institutional and personal needs.

The major focus of these programs in the sixties shifted definitively from a simplistic teaching of morality to a far more complex approach to the promotion of personal growth, the development of values, the formation of identity, and the enhancement of human relations. In the process, behavioral science became an increasingly important resource and standard. These developments continued trends which, as we have noted, began during the character education movement of the fifties. Despite the evolution, however, the new programs have represented a continuation of the same dynamic.

PROGRAMS OF THE SIXTIES:

The LEAD Program

We examined in an earlier chapter the efforts of chaplains to adapt their ministries to the young adult age group which makes up most of the military population. In that context we looked at the LEAD (Lay Enrichment And Development) program, devised in the mid-sixties for the young sailors who man the Polaris submarines and who have no chaplains with them while on patrol.[1] The GRADE (Group Religious And Devotional Expression) phase of the LEAD program was specifically religious in focus—although the ecumenical context of lay leader training, along with the careful limitation to non-sacramental functions and non-controversial content, led to a predominance of common denominator religion.

The other half of the program, however, PEP (Personal Enrichment Phase) carried on the personal growth and development emphasis of the earlier character education movement. The young adult "issue areas" on which it focused—the young adult as a social being, the young adult and sexuality, the young adult and his search for life meaning and value, and the young adult and vocation and leisure—were of general rather than specifically religious application. It was intended for the whole crew rather than sectarian groups. With its elaborate audio-visual reference system, it offered in effect a "mechanical character education program." A further parallel was the evolution of the program: from chaplain origins to implementation under line sponsorship, gradual transfer to line leadership, and slow decline. By 1972 PEP—the Personal *Enrichment* Phase of LEAD—had been turned into PIP—Personal *Information* Program—under line officer leadership, and the LEAD program had gone the way of most character education and personal growth programs.

The Personal Response Program of the Vietnamese War

Another program which went through the same basic evolution—design by chaplains for the entire institution, selling as a "command" program, turning over to line leadership, and gradual death—was the Personal Response Program developed during the Vietnamese War. Originally devised by chaplains serving with the Marine Corps, its focal point was cross-cultural understanding between American Marines (later sailors as well, when substantial numbers were brought to Vietnam in connection with the "Riverine" forces) and the Southeast Asian nationals with whom, in the unique milieu of the Vietnamese War, they were thrown into intimate contact. Elaborate curricular materials were developed to enable chaplains to teach servicemen the customs, values, and behavior patterns of the Vietnamese, Montagnards, and later, Thais. At the height of the movement, such instruction was theoretically being given to every American Marine or sailor deployed to the area. Line officers and NCO's, led and trained by chaplains, were used as instructors along with the chaplains themselves. Since the subject matter was limited to a relatively narrow range of conduct—cross-cultural understanding and behavior—the explicit religious content which had been present in earlier programs was missing. However, the heavy emphasis on Southeast Asian religions in the content of the curriculum gave the classes a "comparative religion" dimension. Beyond this, an elaborate attempt was made to provide a religious rationale for chaplain involvement, on the basis of a theology of reconciliation.

The issue of the chaplains' rationale in developing the program, over against the rationale of line commanders in funding and sponsoring it, became far more complex in connection with personal response than it had been in connection with earlier forms of character education. "Winning the hearts and minds of the Vietnamese people" became a major military objective. Chaplain instruction to American troops aimed at cross-cultural understanding had, therefore, clearly recognizable military values.

Furthermore, the American-Vietnamese interaction thus encouraged became an important source of military intelligence. In the Army, whose chaplains developed a program quite similar to that initially devised by Marine chaplains, Personal Response was identified openly with "psychological warfare." In the Marine Corps, the program was placed under the G-3 (Operations) staff section. It was regarded by military leadership as having direct and immediate military payoff, and sometimes "sold" by chaplains to line commanders on this basis. As a result, the discomfort of other chaplains at having their ministries "used" for military purposes became extreme. Personal Response became the most controversial and probably least accepted of all the character education efforts attempted by the Chaplain Corps.

The purely human dimensions of the program, however, were recognized and applauded by at least part of the line leadership. As an inter-cultural relations program, applicable all over the world where American sailors and Marines are in contact with foreign nationals, it became one of the foundations of the Navy's Human Goals program. It is not accidental that this human goals emphasis came to the forefront during the period in which Admiral Elmo Zumwalt, who had been a strong supporter of Personal Response during his tour of duty as Commander of Naval Forces in Vietnam, was Chief of Naval Operations.

The "Behavioral Science Versus Religion" Issue

The perceived issue of behavioral science versus religion became increasingly important within the chaplaincy in connection with the Personal Response and LEAD programs. Personal growth and interpersonal relationships had replaced moral principles as the focal point, and a non-religiously-oriented approach to the development of personal value systems had replaced the religiously based morality which had enjoyed consensual support in the fifties. The behavioral sciences provided the methodology—the group process—and, to a considerable extent, the values as value-oriented humanistic psychology and sociology became popular.[2] The explicitly religious content of the earlier character education efforts was separated (in GRADE) from the Personal Enrichment Phase (PEP) of LEAD, and was omitted entirely in the Personal Response Program, which dealt only with cross-cultural understanding.

A considerable number of chaplains selected for postgraduate education under Navy sponsorship chose fields of study in the behavioral sciences. In many instances they were then given specialized assignments in the LEAD or Personal Response programs, where they came to be regarded, and to regard themselves in some instances, as specialists. Some came to consider themselves primarily behavioral scientists rather than clergymen. For the most part, however, they regarded their work as religious ministry. Some tension developed between this group of chaplains and those with more traditional concepts of ministry. Many of the more traditional chaplains had little enthusiasm for the new programs or for participation in them.

ATTEMPTS TO REVIVE CHARACTER EDUCATION

Efforts to revitalize character education itself began in all three services at the end of the sixties. A significant increase in racial unrest and a proliferation of problems related to drug use occupied attention at the highest military levels. All three chaplaincies, seeking to contribute toward solutions to these serious problems, began to reexamine their generally moribund programs of character education.

The Air Force Chief of Chaplains, acting under this impetus, called together a conference of chaplains, representing all grades, to study the issue and make recommendations. The result, known as the "Bridge Report," recommended that the Air Force not go back to the old pattern of chaplain-run mandatory character education instruction. It recommended, rather, that chaplains work with other staff persons concerned with values and behavior as a resource for command programs. At the headquarters level, chaplains worked with agencies such as the Information Office, which prepares monthly "Air Force Now" films which are seen by all airmen.

Character education has been retained as a formal program in the Air Training Command, both in basic and second level training. Airman recruits spend a half day with chaplains in the first week of their training. Presentations, however, are not standardized. Individual chaplains prepare their own, with the focus on identity and values.

The Navy's first major effort to revive character education was in recruit training commands. A special project was established in the Chaplains' Department at the Recruit Training Center in Orlando, Florida. An initial pilot project, conducted by one chaplain who had just completed special postgraduate education, experimented with small group interaction following a human relations training model. Such an approach proved impractical because of the large number of chaplains required as group leaders. This pilot project, however, had included a careful study of the psychological and social needs of recruits at various stages of their training. The final model focused on these needs, using larger groups of recruits in a classroom setting, but retaining as much open discussion and group interaction as possible.

An evaluation conference was convened by the Navy's Chief of Chaplains in 1971 to determine whether the Orlando model of character education should be introduced in other recruit training centers. There was a wide divergence of opinion among chaplains as to whether the process model of meeting social and psychological needs of recruits, with no explicitly religious content, was appropriate for chaplain-led character education. Some felt, with considerable support from line commanders, that the classroom experiences were valuable to the recruits, but that chaplain instructors were not required. They felt that non-clergyman behavioral scientists, or even specially-trained petty officers, should be utilized as instructors.

Their view prevailed. The chaplains who had developed the program were assigned the task of training petty officers to conduct the classes—an experiment which was later regarded as successful. Another group of chaplains in another recruit center was assigned the task of developing new materials, focusing on values, for chaplain use in recruit character education. Their product, known as the VDM (pronounced "vidim" and standing for Values and Decision Making) program, is now in use at the San Diego Recruit Training Center.

In 1970 a "Human Factors Training Program" for midshipmen was initiated at the U. S. Naval Academy at Annapolis. The program was developed by a chaplain with specialized education in behavioral science (psychology) and considerable experience in group process. He trained the regular brigade chaplains to function as group facilitators. The approach was basically that of human relations training, following a T-group or sensitivity training model. Its major goals were in the areas of personal adjustment, self-understanding, and interpersonal relationships. Beginning with the plebe class (entering midshipmen) and focusing initially on their adjustment to the new environment, the program was later expanded to include other midshipmen, squad leaders, and even faculty members.[3]

A third major effort within the Navy's Chaplain Corps to revive character education began in the Second Marine Division at Camp Lejeune, North Carolina, in 1972. Utilizing chaplain leaders in small group discussions (eight to eighteen Marines), it has been labeled the "Human Meaning Program." A brief description comes from the division order officially introducing the program:

The need to focus on moral problems and values is urgent in view of the social problems confronting our division personnel. To meet this need, the Human Meaning program is designed as a means of motivating the individual Marine to maintain high standards of personal conduct and assist him in finding meaning in life . . . The Human Meaning Program is *not* a new program, but a contemporary approach to Character Education. The content of Human Meaning sessions will deal primarily with human values in the context of concrete life situations. The methodology will be "discovery learning" (in-depth group discussion) in which each participant through the sharing of ideas and experiences may discover for himself what is important for the improvement of his personal life and his relationships with others.[4]

After seven months in operation, both the chaplains and the line commanders in the Second Marine Division considered the program successful and planned to expand it.

Although some discussion of moral standards was retained in the Human Meaning Program, the major emphasis in most newer versions of character education has been shifted from moral instruction to personal growth and human relationships.

One exception to this general trend is a new chaplain-initiated course on morality, which became part of the curriculum of the U. S. Naval Academy in the 1974–75 academic year. Utilizing a text written by a chaplain, the required (but non-credit) course is entitled "The Professional Officer and the Human Person." It deals with such issues as the morality of warfare, the demands of honor, and moral arguments over the dropping of the atomic bomb on Hiroshima, as well as contemporary problems such as drinking, drug addiction, and racism.[5]

The Human Self-Development Program

By far the most ambitious of the current attempts of the military chaplaincies to revive character education is the Army's Human Self-Development Program. As we have noted before, the original Character Guidance Program persisted far longer in the Army than in the other two services. It remained in effect, relatively unchanged, from its inception in the late forties until 1971. Its theme—"Duty-Honor-Country"—reflected a continued emphasis on patriotism and moral principles. It remained basically a chaplains' program (though under command sponsorship, of course), with standardized assigned topics each month for chaplain-led classes, utilizing materials provided by the Chaplains' Board.

Late in 1971, Army Regulation 600–30 of 19 October 1971, entitled "Human Self-Development Program," replaced Army Regulation

600–30 of 1 July 1970 entitled "Character Guidance Program." Continuity with the older program was maintained, with emphasis on moral leadership, the "basic truths, principles, and attitudes that undergird our nation's heritage," and the "moral foundations of dedicated citizenship."[6] The chaplain continues to be the instructor in most instances. The regulation specifies that the instruction and program "will remain nontheological and nonsectarian. These sessions are separate and distinct from the voluntary religious program of the command which is the proper sphere of voluntary denominational religious activity."[7] Instruction remains obligatory during basic training (four hours) and advanced individual training (two hours).

Despite these evidences of continuity with character guidance, however, the Human Self-Development Program is significantly different in approach. Most importantly, it is (beyond the basic and advanced individual training level) a voluntary program. The company commander can use it or not, as he sees fit. In some units where it is used, attendance is voluntary. Because it is voluntary, it has been generally deemphasized, and many chaplains are not involved. The instructional method is group discussion rather than lecture. The chaplain-enabler seeks to involve the troops, and there is considerable emphasis on process, rather than content alone. Ideally, groups are no larger than twenty, although larger groups are sometimes accepted. The program is offered as "a vehicle whereby the commander can address today's challenging problems of racial tensions, drug abuse, poverty, dissent and moral behavior."[8] The Human Self-Development Program is far more flexible than was character guidance, with voluntary and adaptive use of training texts and instructional packets. It seeks to be broad in scope, with classroom sessions regarded as only one aspect of the program. The establishment of Human Self-Development Planning Units, with membership including the medical officer, inspector general, information officer, and unit sergeant-major among others, is required in all commands, down to the battalion and company levels when feasible. As was the case in earlier character education programs, however, classroom sessions receive the greatest emphasis and carry the main burden.

Instructional materials, prepared by the Chaplains' Board, are issued quarterly. A typical pamphlet, published in February 1973, was entitled "Manhood." It contained materials for four sessions: (1) Manhood: Putting it Together; (2) Manhood: Hacking It; (3) Manhood: Opting to Live; and (4) Manhood: Living with your Limits. Along with conceptual material for possible presentation by the instructor, resources included a wide range of questions for discussion; gaming (the widely-used "NASA Exercise," designed to demonstrate the superiority of group decision-making to that of individuals, is included); suggested films; numerous poetic and literary illustrative references; and a bibliography.[9]

Despite its fresh approach and its flexibility, the Human Self-Development Program is in some ways strongly reminiscent of the Navy's character education programs of the fifties, particularly the "Moral and Spiritual Growth Here and Now" curriculum which sought to move from lecture to discussion, from content orientation to process orientation, and from moral principles to personal growth. The assignment of Army chaplains to the leadership departments of nearly all service schools, which began in 1972, is also reminiscent of the use of chaplains in the Navy's Leadership Program of the late fifties and early sixties.

It is quite clear that the overall dynamic of all the recent attempts to revive character education is essentially the same as that of the character education movement of the fifties. The general characteristics of all these programs have been quite similar to those of the original model: (1) each was originated within the chaplaincy, but implemented as a "command" program under line sponsorship; (2) each has been viewed as separate from the explicitly "religious" program led by chaplains; but (3) religion (generally common denominator civil religion) has nevertheless been an element in either the content or the orientation of all such programs, and chaplains in specialized assignments related to them have regarded their work as religious ministry; (4) the basic aim in each case has been the fostering of morality, values, personal growth, or interpersonal relations; and (5) each has been aimed at all personnel in the units concerned, without regard to religious or non-religious preference.

It is also worth noting that most of these programs (except those current revivals of character education which are still in formative stages) have followed the same general life cycle as character education: (1) birth within the Chaplain Corps; (2) implementation under the sponsorship of line commanders; (3) evolution into a line-led program; and (4) slow death, or transformation into something other than the original intent of the Chaplain Corps. We are therefore justified in examining the entire character education movement, both the earlier version and the present versions, together with the related human growth and relationship programs, as a single aspect of the work of chaplains in the armed forces.

VALUES OF THE PROGRAMS

It is important to observe that while each of these programs has been controversial and most (except the new ones in an early stage of the cycle) have "failed" in the sense of being discarded or radically modified, some things have been accomplished. Certain needs have been met, some of them organizational and some personal.

1. Effect on the Institution

The effect of character education and related movements on the military institutions in terms of moral standards taught or maintained, personal growth achieved, and human relations improved, is, of course, impossible to estimate. The original character education program set out to "build a strong moral, ethical and spiritual foundation" in the military. The achievement was obviously somewhat less sweeping. Such statistical studies as were made during the heyday of character education in the fifties, purporting to measure the level of morality "before" and "after" character education (usually in terms of reduced VD rates, disciplinary cases, etc.) were virtually meaningless. None demonstrated causality, or measured the effect of any other factors which may have been at work. None demonstrated any sustained change over a period of time. The same has been generally true of all such programs.

Every chaplain who participated conscientiously, however, has had knowledge of individual persons who were affected positively, either through the program itself or through relationships established in the context of the program. Any quantity of personal change may be presumed to effect some measure of institutional change. Secondary institutional effects, resulting from organized and continuing attention to moral, personal growth, and human relations issues, and from the thought and discussion generated within the institution, have also been factors clearly present. It is certainly reasonable to conclude, therefore, although measurable changes cannot be demonstrated "scientifically," that there has been an effect on the institution. Entirely apart from pros and cons regarding the contribution of such a process to the military mission, in purely human terms this effect on the institution may be regarded as positive and worthwhile.

2. Organizational Needs Met for the Chaplain Corps

We have noted in Chapter 3 that the ministry of religion is always viewed as peripheral to the operationally-oriented goals of a military organization. As a result, chaplains always occupy a precarious place in the organization, dependent on temporary coalitions with interested authority figures, with a low priority for money and support and high vulnerability when cuts are made.

A service-wide program affecting everyone, with compulsory par-

ticipation under command auspices replacing the voluntarism characteristic of religious participation, and with a rationale that ties it to the
overall military goals, changes this. Money becomes available. During the
character education period in the fifties, far more funding went into the
development of curricula, making of films, and support of additional
billets, than is ordinarily obtainable for support of religious ministry. The
same was true of the LEAD and Personal Response programs in the
sixties.

Every such venture into a general non-religious program, justified
in terms of military rather than church-oriented goals, sets in motion
counter forces from the churches and from the clergy role within chaplains themselves. Thus each, in a sense, carries the seeds of its own death.
There is a genuine organizational need, however, to be needed, to be
more central and less peripheral, to seek more funding and support, to
acquire greater power. Such a program, while raising other problems,
does, nevertheless, at least temporarily meet that organizational need.

3. Personal Needs of Chaplains Met

A regularly structured place in the operational schedule (classes in
the training program) pulls a chaplain out of his religious limbo into the
mainstream. It gives him a clearly describable responsibility in a highly
structured organization. He no longer feels compelled to explain himself
to people who keep asking, with a chuckle, "What does a chaplain do the
other six days of the week?"

A character education or human growth program may also meet
personal needs of clergymen increasingly disenchanted with the institutional church and worship-oriented ministry and frustrated by the small
numbers involved in chapel-centered programs. Such clergymen may feel
that human self-realization is a more relevant religious expression than
ancient creeds, and may be looking for a non-church-related serving
ministry to the whole society, although they may be unwilling to forsake
their professional identity as clergymen.

Charges have been made that chaplains are clergymen who failed
in the civilian church. If the implication is that chaplains are incompetent
cast-offs from the church, the charge is probably refuted by the high level
of selectivity, the fact that far more apply than can be accepted, and the
careful screening done by denominational endorsing officials. However,
it is probably true that many chaplaincy applicants are clergymen who
have experienced some discomfort in church-oriented ministry and are
looking for a ministry of a different kind. Some chaplains who have
become deeply involved in character education and related programs,

and for whom such activity has become central in ministry, may find here the answer for personal needs of this kind.

4. Benefits to Religious Ministry

Each of the programs we have examined has been, at least in part, a valid expression of civil religion. As we have seen in Chapter 6, civil religion rightly understood does have legitimacy and can appropriately claim part of a chaplain's time. Further, it is generally conceded that chaplains have a religious obligation to provide a serving ministry for the entire institution. As ethical instruction, facilitation of personal growth or enhancement of interpersonal relationships, these programs provide a service related to the chaplain's field of competence. They have given opportunities for constructive contact with the entire military institution, which chaplains have found to be door-openers for more specifically religious ministrations. The counseling ministry offered by chaplains to the whole institution has been enhanced; many initial contacts in class or small groups have later led to more personal relationships in counseling. The programs have provided a way of demonstrating the relevance of religious faith to all of life.

The various character education, personal growth, and human relations programs, then, have brought a number of positive accomplishments. Perhaps even more important, they have met institutional and personal needs. Psychological and organizational forces have tended to thrust the chaplaincy repeatedly into such activities, and will probably continue to do so.

The appropriate place of such activities in the ministry of chaplains is still, however, an open and hotly debated question. The main issue for chaplains has never been whether or not these programs are good and worthwhile, but rather whether or not they are the business of chaplains. The protection of moral standards and the building of character, the promotion of personal growth, the enrichment of personal lives, the fostering of cross-cultural and interpersonal understanding, the development of human values and meaning—all these are life-enhancing endeavors which chaplains, probably without exception, support and applaud. But should they be the responsibilty of chaplains? And if so, how do they fit into the religious ministry for which chaplains have been ordained and endorsed by their churches? Is it appropriate for some chaplains to be involved full-time in such programs, and for many to be heavily involved part-time? Is this the kind of activity for which the churches provide military chaplains?

HUMAN GOALS IN TODAY'S MILITARY

The question will continue to arise, not only as old character education programs are continued and new ones devised, but in connection with a number of other emphases currently receiving much attention in the armed forces. At the end of the sixties the enormous increase in drug use among military personnel led to the crash development of programs aimed at drug education, counseling, and treatment of drug users. In the early seventies specialized programs for alcoholics were added. During the same period interracial tensions—reflecting developments in civilian society—reached a critical stage in the military. Crash programs were initiated to promote racial understanding and equal opportunity for minorities.

The chaplaincies were already at work in all these areas when the Secretary of Defense enunciated human goals for the armed forces, and line commanders began to be seriously concerned. Chaplains of all three services had been sent to postgraduate school for specialized counseling training in connection with both drug and alcohol abuse. The chaplain effort had been a rehabilitative one long before the military shifted from punitive to rehabilitative approaches. Chaplains had long been involved in race relations programs, through counseling and the traditional ombudsman function, as well as through religious leadership and teaching. They had pioneered in the use of black-white encounter groups, and in black studies programs at the unit level. Chaplains involved in some of the character education and personal response programs had acquired considerable expertise in the small group process and in human relations training. Many were skilled in group counseling. Therapeutic groups in disciplinary commands and brigs and growth groups of various kinds under chaplain leadership were common.

The Navy Chaplain Corps had pioneered in contemporary methods of adult education, and its advanced course at the Navy Chaplains School, established there in 1968, was the only significant Navy-run course with a human relations orientation. As a result of all these factors, the Chaplain Corps contained the only substantial pool of professionals trained in the behavioral sciences and human relations skills when the drug and race crises burst on the Navy at the end of the sixties. A number of chaplains were therefore brought into the Washington staff of the official (known initially as the Assistant Chief of Naval Personnel for Human Resources Management) responsible for designing programs in these fields. Others were used in positions of field leadership. The Navy's first course for line officer and enlisted human relations specialists was designed and conducted by the Chaplains School staff.

When the Air Force, during the same period, developed its crash program to deal with race relations, there was an urgent need for film resources. The Air Force Chaplain Film Inventory was found to be a readily available source of films on race and human relations.

Unlike the character education movement of the fifties and the LEAD and Personal Response programs of the sixties, all of which had originated and and been designed by chaplains, the Human Relations programs of the early seventies (all of which were, in 1973, combined into an overall Human Goals program) were from the beginning command programs, under line officer direction. The chaplains involved in them have, therefore, been isolated from Chaplain Corps structures and from church-oriented religious ministry. This fact, together with the increasing numbers of chaplains with behavioral science training and identification, has brought something of an identity crisis to the chaplaincy.

THE ROLE DEFINITION ISSUE

Questions about the chaplains' role in connection with human relations activities have reached to the highest levels of military leadership. In April 1972, the Chief of Naval Operations directed that a study be made

> to appraise the current and future role of the Chaplain Corps in meeting the spiritual and temporal needs of Navy personnel. Such a study should address the . . . availability of post-graduate education (particularly in the social sciences) for Chaplain Corps officers and subsequent utilization of this education; and envisioned additional roles of the Chaplain Corps in fulfilling not only their historic chaplain roles but in meeting the new problems we face today and in the future.[10]

The issue was most critical, however, among chaplains themselves. Those chaplains who came to be regarded as behavioral science specialists and who became heavily involved in "people-oriented" programs under line sponsorship were viewed with suspicion by traditionalists, with the implication that they had in some fashion left the ministry. One chaplain, in 1971, applied for and was granted a transfer from the Chaplain Corps to the line, where as a line officer he continued to work as a human relations specialist. At least two other chaplains requested, but were denied, transfers to line officer status.

These were exceptions. Most of the chaplains employed full or part time in human relations projects regarded their activities as forms of religious ministry. The need for clarification was reflected in recurring attempts within the chaplaincy to "define ministry." As late as October, 1973, the series of Pacemaker Conferences sponsored by the Chief of

Navy Chaplains identified "definition of ministry and communicating the role of the chaplain to command" as the second most important item in a prioritized list of issues before the Corps. Other concerns in addition to that of human relations versus traditional ministries were involved, but the question of the place of the programs we have been discussing in ministry was certainly high among the concerns reflected.

To the extent that the chaplaincy has worked out its own answers to questions regarding definition of ministry and role, such answers have of necessity been pluralistic. The basic professional identity of chaplains, as the Chaplain Corps suggested in its response to the CNO request mentioned above, is determined not by the Navy but by the churches.

The military's responsibility in role definition has to do with establishing the *conditions* of religious ministry and defining the human needs to which its chaplains, as religious professionals, are expected to respond. It is neither the responsibility nor the right of the military to define the basic role and mission of clergymen as anything other than the religious ministry for which their churches ordained them.

Religious leadership, as defined by church-oriented religion, is seen by chaplains as central in their own role. A 1971 study by Aronis of chaplain role and identity listed six functional roles and their ranking by chaplains in order of importance. The three roles which are explicitly religious in the church-oriented sense—pastor/counselor, liturgist-preacher-priest, and religious educator—were ranked first, second, and third. Another part of the same study asked chaplains to rank in the order of importance thirty specific activities. The top priorities of the resulting list were weighted heavily in the direction of activities related to church-oriented religion, with divine services first in importance. The people-oriented functions associated with Human Goals emphases, and traditionally regarded as derivative expressions of religious faith, were clustered lower in the list.[11]

In the light of institutional duality and the church-derived identity of chaplains, these findings are not surprising. Their role in the military must be seen as basically the ministry of religion in the church-oriented context. However, a role definition for chaplains in terms of church-oriented ministry does not exclude people-oriented activities outside the church context.

There is no single definition of ministry in a religiously pluralistic society. All definitions identify ministry as "religious," and all would regard it as "people-oriented." However, the meaning of the term "religious," the relationship between "religious" and "people-oriented" activities, and the extent to which secular people-oriented activities would

be regarded as inherently religious would all be subject to varying interpretations. There is a respectable body of opinion in the contemporary
religious world which considers secular human relations activity, in set-
tings unrelated to institutional churches or formal worship, to be fully as
authentic a religious ministry as is traditional chapel-oriented ministry.

From this perspective, a chaplain working full time in a drug program or a race relations program, reporting to the Human Resources
Project Manager and having no regular divine service responsibilities,
would be regarded as engaged in a specialized ministry, but a fully religious ministry. Such a definition may be a minority opinion within the
contemporary religious world; the majority in the religious community
would probably adhere to a more explicitly church-related definition of
"religious" activity. It is, however, a valid contemporary definition, and
one which the chaplaincy, in a context of religious pluralism, recognizes
and makes provision for. The military cannot define religion for itself; it
must follow the lead of the American people and accept a variety of
definitions.

The ministry of religion takes different functional forms in response
to different human needs. Thus the ministry of religion under institutional church sponsorship varies widely in rural parishes, inner-city
parishes, hospital chaplaincies, or foreign missions. It is a normal expectation that the functional form taken by the ministry of religion in the
Navy would be determined by the specialized environment and the needs
of the people served.

A professional role definition for chaplains in terms of ministry of
church-oriented religion, therefore, does not mean that the mission of
chaplains is limited to church-oriented functions such as ministration of
sacraments and religious ordinances, preaching, and religious education.
The ministry of religion in all American religious traditions has historically embraced a wide range of humanitarian concerns. Chaplains in
pastoral assignments in ships and stations, long before the development
of character education or special human relations programs, have been
involved, as part of their religious ministry, in a wide range of people-
oriented activities. These have included the traditional chaplain ombudsman activities; educational and counseling activities in the fields of race
relations and drug abuse; welfare activities; many family-oriented activities including marital and pre-marital counseling, weddings, and family
newsletters or videotape "familygrams"; counseling and assistance to
persons in disciplinary trouble, and a wide range of other kinds of personal counseling; and a number of expressions of personal concern such
as visits to men on watch, to the sick, to homes, to men in confinement,

etc. All these activities are part of the ministries of chaplains to the entire units they serve; it is impossible to draw a line between their "religious" and "secular" dimensions. They are all strongly supportive of current people-oriented Human Goals emphases of line commanders.

Navy chaplains who were surveyed recently regarding their activities during one seven-day period reported that they spent an average of 48.4 hours that week in such people-oriented activities as those listed above. Chaplains in afloat commands averaged 52.3 hours of the week in such activities. Afloat chaplains reported that an average of 79% of their total working time is spent in these people-oriented activities. The remainder of their time, spent in liturgical, sacramental, and specifically church-related activities is, of course, also people-oriented. The statistics are drawn out only to point up the fact that the distinction drawn by some superficial observers between chaplains' religious ministry and military "people-oriented" programs is not supported by factual data.

The Navy Chaplain Corps study of its contemporary role and mission, made in response to the CNO directive referred to above, concluded that:

> The current understanding of the role and mission of the Chaplain Corps reflects not a static adherence to a "traditional role," but a dynamic exploration of the appropriate contemporary role. It emphasizes: (a) religious ministry as central in the chaplains' role and mission; (b) a pluralistic understanding of the nature of religious ministry, in accordance with the religious pluralism of American society; (c) chaplains as religious leadership professionals, representing their own churches and religious groups; and (d) the "people-oriented" nature of religious ministry.[12]

In 1973 this general understanding of the relationship between the ministry of chaplains and the Human Goals initiatives of the Navy was incorporated into an instruction issued to all commands in the U. S. Atlantic Fleet:

> Chaplains are clergymen trained and ordained by their respective denominations for religious ministry. Their basic purpose in the Navy is to provide such religious ministry. While different denominations in our religiously pluralistic society have differing approaches to religious ministry, all are concerned with the whole person. Thus, the Navy's people-oriented initiatives related to human goals and resources are not in conflict with, but are related to and supported by, the religious orientation of chaplains. Contemporary training for the ministry of religion includes a substantial emphasis on the behavioral sciences. As a group, chaplains have a high level of education in the behavioral sciences. They provide a

significant resource for Navy programs related to human goals as long as they are utilized in ways which do not interfere with the ministry of religion for which their churches ordained them and made them available.[13]

Need for Church Guidance

The issue of the involvement of chaplains in character education and in more general programs related to human goals is one in which the churches should have a key role. At its heart it is a question of the definition of religious ministry, and only the churches are in a position to answer it. The answer will, of necessity, be a pluralistic one, in view of the American religious situation. The chaplaincies, in allowing and defending the involvement of chaplains in a wide variety of serving ministries to the entire institution as well as in the traditional provision of religious services and activities, are reflecting what they perceive to be the attitude of the churches. Indeed, the chaplains *are* the churches in their own segment of society, and their participating influence helps to shape the position of the churches at large.

There is no issue, however, on which there is a greater need for guidance from the whole church. While there is good evidence, as we have seen, that the chaplaincies have tried to be faithful interpreters of church attitudes and practises, a more active role on the part of the churches in articulating their own attitudes is called for. Cooperative structures—those in existence and new ones that may be devised—should debate, along with the chaplaincies, the propriety of what the chaplains are doing. Denominational officials responsible for chaplain supervision should explore with their own chaplains their involvement in these fields.

Do the churches approve a full-scale attempt on the part of the chaplaincy to revive the character education movement of the fifties? How do such activities fit into the chaplain's mission as an ordained religious leader? What proportion of the time of chaplains should be given to them? Where explicitly religious elements are present in such programs, is it a civil religion which is fully compatible with denominational religion? Do chaplains appropriately assume some responsibility for the moral conditions in a military environment? What about the compulsory element in character education and human relations programs designed for all hands? Is even civil religion appropriately made obligatory? At what point, if any, does humanity-affirming, person-serving, growth-producing activity which is entirely separate from a church or chapel context cease being religious ministry and become the province of non-church-related behavioral science? When clergymen become convinced that their vocational future lies entirely in these activities and are unwilling to return to chapel-oriented ministries, what should be their status? Should they seek to become line officers or do the churches wish to continue to sponsor their ministries? When activities (such as Personal Response), which are viewed by chaplains as ministry of reconciliation between persons, are apparently viewed by military commanders as psychological warfare and a source of intelligence, are the churches willing for chaplains to continue their involvement? These and other questions remain far from fully resolved. It is a major responsibility of the churches that sponsor the military chaplains to help those chaplains resolve them.

Chapter 9

Directions for the Future

We have been examining in some detail the ministry of military chaplains, particularly those aspects of military ministry which are distinctively different from civilian parish ministry. We began with the recognition that a military chaplain receives his basic professional identity from his church, and that he shares with all other ministers the basic mission and goals of religious ministry. The external form of his ministry, however, is determined by the other institution to which he belongs, the military service. We examined the nature of the military institution, and we looked at the place of chaplains and chaplaincy within the military organization. We looked at the unique shape of military ministry, within the institutional and organizational setting. We looked at the relationship of the chaplaincy to two American religious phenomena which have helped to shape it: the religious pluralism of American society and the civil religion which is an element in the faith of Americans. We then examined in some detail certain controversial aspects of chaplain activity which are manifestations of civil religion—character education and human relations programs. We have repeatedly found a need for guidance, direction, and greater involvement from the churches.

In this concluding chapter we will attempt to pull together some of the implications of various aspects of the chaplaincy we have been examining, particularly as they impinge on the future of the military chaplaincy.

Since the American withdrawal from the Vietnamese War, the military forces of the United States have been reduced in size from a little over three million to a present total of about two million. In the climate of détente with China and the Soviet Union, there is hope for further reductions in the future. There is every indication, however, that the United States intends to maintain her status as a world power for the foreseeable future, and that she will therefore retain sizeable armed forces.

Discussions of the armed forces chaplaincy in church circles tend, at times, to become confused with the pacifist/non-pacifist debate over whether or not there should *be* armed forces. That is, of course, a legitimate debate, in which churchmen have engaged for twenty centuries and will undoubtedly continue to engage. From our immediate perspective, however, it is not the point. Realistically, we recognize that the United

States does have large armed forces and is likely to continue to have them. Realistically, we also recognize that the churches will continue to provide ministries to military men and women. Starting with these assumptions, the question of whether the present form of military chaplaincy provides the best available ministry to the military is very much to the point.

The anti-chaplaincy movement which began during the Vietnamese War has cooled considerably. There are still some, however, who propose the substitution of a civilian chaplaincy to the armed forces or a radical "de-militarization" of the chaplaincy. It is necessary, therefore, to examine this question in some detail.

SHOULD THE CHAPLAINCY BE CIVILIANIZED?[1]

We looked in Chapter 2 at Erving Goffman's concept of the total institution, and at the characteristics of the military service as a total institution. We also examined in Chapter 4 the "total mobile environment" which the institution provides for its members, wherever they go. This background, and particularly the strong sense of the difference between insiders, who share the life of the total institution, and outsiders, who belong to another world, casts some light on the question. Military chaplains are insiders; this is the whole point of their institutional duality. Civilian chaplains to the armed forces would be outsiders.

Should clergymen serving a total institution be insiders or outsiders? Most of the issues currently being debated—the wearing of the uniform, the holding of rank, the authority of commanding officers over chaplains, their accountability to military law—may be regarded as aspects of this insider-outsider question. As we noted earlier, the proposal of the United Church of Christ task force for a "demilitarized chaplaincy,"[2] together with the assumption that such a chaplaincy could remain part of the military from which it had been demilitarized—insiders with respect to advantages, but outsiders with respect to constraints imposed by a total institution—is somewhat naive. The realities of total institutions generally, and the armed forces in particular, are such that a demilitarized chaplaincy of this kind could only be a civilian chaplaincy. Ministers serving the armed forces will either be insiders, full members of the armed forces subject to military command, or outsiders, ministering to, but not part of the armed forces. It is not likely that the churches can have it both ways at once.

Freedoms and Constraints

Each form of ministry would bring some freedoms and some constraints. A ministry by civilian outsiders would be free to pass judgments on the military command structure and its mission, unaffected by personal involvement. It would be free to urge disobedience of orders, which the organization Clergy and Laity Concerned about Vietnam apparently wanted Air Force chaplains to do during the Vietnamese War. It would be free not just to counsel, but to make common cause with dissidents. But it would be limited in its access to people. It would be limited in its ability to accompany military people wherever they go—particularly in the most stressful situations, such as combat, operations in which national security is a significant factor, and extreme isolation. It would be limited in its access to the power structure for affecting change. And, of course, the more it exercised its freedoms to take an adversary stance over against the military authority structure—total institutions being what they are—the more limited would be its access to people and structures. Outsiders are more free to be prophets than pastors.

A ministry by military insiders, on the other hand, is completely free in its access to people and structures. It is free to share the lives— including the moral ambiguities—of military people. It is free to take its ministry into the whole of the military society, under all conditions. Because of the long historical development which has led to well-recognized relationships with the churches and a clear understanding that chaplains are clergymen first and members of the military second, it is free to proclaim an authentic religious message within the institution. It is free to engage with the power structure to affect the quality of life within. But it is limited by the necessity of conforming to military law and regulations. It is limited by the reality of military authority. It is limited by the self-interest of ministers who identify with the institution of which they are a part. Insiders are more free to be pastors than prophets.

The categories are not, of course, so sharply differentiated as to be mutually exclusive. No one in any total institution is completely an insider. Every military man or woman maintains a private preserve untouched by military control. Chaplains, in particular, are prevented by their institutional duality from full military identification. As clergymen whose first loyalty is to their churches they are, in a real sense, "outsiders on the inside."

Nor does the dichotomy between pastoral and prophetic functions represent a simple "either-or." Within the limits established by acceptance of military legitimacy and authority, chaplains clearly have prophetic responsibilities. Internal diversity, judgment, and criticism are not only proper at the appropriate time and place, but necessary to institutional health. Acceptance of military command does not require the wearing of a muzzle. As we will see in the next section on the sociological function of a military chaplaincy, ministry to the institution itself (as distinguished from the pastoral ministry to the persons who make up the institution) is inherently a prophetic function. Some of the proudest moments in the history of the chaplaincy have been those moments when military clergymen stood up and were counted on issues of consience or conviction. A chaplaincy entirely devoid of prophetic dimensions would be a poor instrument of the Lord's work.

Conversely, a ministry by civilian chaplains who were outsiders in the sense that they were not members of the military, obviously could provide a large measure of pastoral care. Clergymen serving churches near military bases have done so for years. The distinction between insiders and outsiders is by no means an absolute one.

But the distinction is none the less real. It is one of the characteristics of a total institution—particularly the military—that there is a clearly-perceived line between those who are members and those who are not, and a deeply-felt sense of common identity within the institution. The distinctions being drawn here are, broadly speaking, valid ones. And the military chaplaincy is clearly, in this sense, an insider ministry.

Much of the current debate within the churches has thus far focused on the problems and ambiguities of the insider ministry as provided by the present chaplaincy system. The United Church of Christ task force report mentioned earlier gave little attention to alternatives, and the American Civil Liberties Union report, also mentioned earlier in this book, gave none.[3] Concerned churchmen, before they can have a basis for serious decision-making, must take a careful look at two additional areas. First, they must examine the positive aspects of the insider ministry and the extent to which problems and dangers are outweighed by advantages and creative opportunities. Second, they must examine carefully the alternative outsider ministry.

Positive Aspects of the Present System

The insider ministry of military chaplains clearly has many positive aspects, as we have been noting. One of the few contemporary critics to give any attention at all to the positive side was Robert McAfee Brown in the concluding essay of the Cox book. He noted, on theological grounds, the obligation of the servant church to reach out to all, to take its ministry into the world, even the sinful parts of the world, with a theology of presence—as, he conceded, chaplains are doing.[4] The positive aspects must be weighed against the negative ones. (In fairness to Brown, it should be noted that he found the balance to be on the negative side, largely because he considers modern warfare so evil that it cannot be legitimated by a theology of presence.)

While chaplains would agree that they face problems and temptations as insiders in the armed forces, they would point out that other
clergymen also do in their ministries. Concern about advancement and
status and pressures from whatever establishment wields power and pays
salaries are not military monopolies. Chaplains would claim that most of
them have maintained their integrity as witnesses to the faith they were
ordained to proclaim, just as most civilian clergymen have. Despite their
military allegiance, they believe their first loyalty is to God. They believe
they are providing authentic ministries and that they have a record of
positive accomplishment. It is probable that the rank and file in the
churches would agree with them, despite the parade of hostile witnesses
cited by Clergy and Laity Concerned, the American Civil Liberties Union,
the United Church of Christ task force, and others. And in the view of
the millions of Americans who have passed through the armed forces in
the post-World War II years, the rank and file probably have a sound
basis for judgment.

But we do not have to depend on reading the rank and file opinion.
The churches have readily available a method of testing the claims of
chaplains. Every denomination has officials charged with responsibility
for overseeing its military chaplains: the members of its chaplaincy committees or boards and staff executives. It is strange indeed that no systematic attempt has been made to obtain a full evaluation from these churchmen, the only ones who regularly visit and observe chaplains in their
work, receive their reports, and deal with their problems. While some are
former chaplains and bias is undoubtedly present in the group, they are
nevertheless those chosen by the churches to represent their interests in
dealing with the military. A study of the collective opinion of these civilians, as to the freedom, the effectiveness, and the authenticity of the
ministries of chaplains, would be a valuable contribution to the debate.

Examining the Alternative

Second, the proposed alternative of ministries to the armed forces
by civilian outsiders needs a much more careful examination than it has
thus far been given. The United Church of Christ task force report gave
an exhaustive critique of the problems of the present system, but only the
scantiest attention to the untried alternative it proposed. Its demilitarized
chaplaincy was only sketchily outlined. The one analogy cited—that of
lawyers in courts martial who report to the Judge Advocate General
rather than the local commander—is not especially relevant. The sole
function of such trial lawyers not only permits, but requires, their total
non-involvement in the everyday life of the people with whom they deal.

But it is hard to envision religious ministry totally non-involved with the life of the military community.

Even less attention was given by the United Church of Christ task force to its proposed civilian ministries. The American Civil Liberties Union study gave none at all. In 1972 the General Commission on Chaplains published a lengthy feasibility study of civilian chaplaincy for the armed forces,[5] but neither of these studies referred to it. At a minimum, those churches interested in substituting civilian ministries to the armed forces should institute and fund a variety of pilot projects to provide an empirical data base for evaluation. Undoubtedly the armed forces would cooperate, since the objective would be the provision of the best possible ministry.

Beyond this, a thorough study should be made of the wealth of data already existing on various outsider ministries to the armed forces. The Military Academy at West Point has a civilian chaplaincy. What are its characteristics? For many years a civilian church existed on government property in the middle of the Naval Training Center at Great Lakes, Illinois. Similar churches have functioned for periods on other military installations. Why were they discontinued? What has been the experience of the thousands of denominational churches located in the vicinity of military bases (including some small bases with no chaplains assigned, for which they have provided the only available ministries)? In particular, how well have they succeeded in forming ecumenical coalitions to offer non-competitive ministries to military communities? What kind of impact have they had on command structures? What has been learned through the Servicemen's Centers in certain overseas areas for many years sponsored by the National Council of Churches? The data available on outsider ministries should be given the same searching study as the insider ministry of chaplains.

Following the 1973 publication in the *Christian Century* of an article by the author in which these questions were raised, syndicated columnist Lester Kinsolving investigated the civilian chaplaincy at the U. S. Military Academy. He reported in his column:

> The Rev. James Ford, chaplain of the United States Military Academy, told this column, "I'm not really a civilian chaplain, because I'm paid and housed by the military." No such pay or allowances accrue, however, to West Point's Catholic chaplain. Father Robert McCormick is pastor . . . by appointment of the Archbishop of New York. . . . Despite his civilian status, Father McCormick did not take to his pulpit to denounce the widely publicized (and severely deplored) "silencing" of a Catholic cadet named James

Pelosi. . . . "When you're part of an organization you can be more effective by working within the organization," Father McCormick told this column.[6]

If civilian chaplains identify with the institution, would any of the weaknesses of the chaplaincy in this area be corrected? If they do not identify with the institution, how effective would their pastoral ministries be?

Careful study should also be given to existing models of secular civilian agencies serving the armed forces. There is no doubt that a considerable measure of accomodation between a civilian chaplaincy and the military services could be achieved. A number of civilians serve the armed forces under cooperative arrangements. Civilians work on every base, and technical representatives of civilian firms even go to sea on Navy ships under certain conditions.

The closest analogy would probably be the American Red Cross, which has a corps of career field directors serving the armed forces. Such field directors work under an elaborate legal agreement which spells out relationships. They wear their own uniforms. They are extended many courtesies by the military: office space on bases, access to non-classified military areas, use of government communication facilities, even simulated rank for certain purposes. But there should be no illusion as to where they stand. They are outsiders, performing clearly defined functions in a limited area, and are so regarded by servicemen and women. Are these the conditions under which the church wants to express its pastoral concern for young adults in the military?

Theology of Involvement

It would be a mistake, however, for the churches to make wholly pragmatic decisions based on study of the effectiveness of alternative models of ministry available. For at its heart, the issue of insider versus outsider ministries is theological. The question of the churches' involvement or non-involvement in the military, centering on whether or not clergymen should be full-fledged members of the armed forces, depends in the last analysis not only on one's pacifist or non-pacifist stance but also on one's concept of mission. Is there a theology of involvement in the world? Is there a place in the church's mission for Christian professionals within the secular structures, sharing the lives of those served, participating in the ambiguities and contradictions of their existence, seeking to minister to and even sometimes modify the structures of which they they are a part? Or does the mission of the church require its professionals to sit above the social and institutional structures of the world as "come-outers," unsullied by participation, free to urge disobedience, passing judgment as outsiders?

A dialectical kind of theologizing might conclude that both are needed. The military needs prophets, pronouncing judgment from the outside, but it also needs pastors who share the life within a total institution. Insiders must belong to the total institution in order to serve it, and this inevitably means subjection to military command and conformity to military law and regulations. Most chaplains regard the full sharing of life within the armed forces—wearing the same uniform, obeying the same regulations, enduring the same stresses and ambiguities as their parishioners—as their most priceless asset in mission. They see such involvement as a theological imperative.

THE SOCIOLOGICAL FUNCTION OF A MILITARY CHAPLAINCY

The primary concern of church and military alike, when the future of the chaplaincy is considered, is the effectiveness of chaplains and their ability to be authentic ministers of Christ in a military organization. We have seen that the chaplaincy is generally an effective ministry, meeting the special needs of military people. There is, however, another contribution made by the presence of representatives of the churches as insiders in the total institution, a contribution which is relatively independent of the effectiveness or ineffectiveness of individual chaplains. It is useful for a moment to look at the chaplaincy from a sociological perspective—in terms of the dynamics of social groups rather than individual persons—and at the function thus served by having chaplains in the military.

Historically, the presence within the military of a group representing religious values and humanitarian concerns has been socially significant. Beginning with George Washington's call for gentlemen "of sober, serious and religious deportment, who would improve morale and discourage gambling, swearing, and drunkenness," the presence of chaplains has brought a much-needed religious and moral dimension into a kind of environment in which these dimensions are easily forgotten.[7] We have seen in historical sketches in previous chapters the contributions of early chaplains in advancing education, eliminating inhumane punishments such as flogging, and improving the quality of life for the individual soldier or sailor. In March, 1859, the Judiciary Committee of the House of Representatives described the sociological contribution:

> The spirit of Christianity has ever had a tendency to mitigate the rigors of war, if as yet it has not been entirely able to prevent it; to

lend to acts of charity and kindness; and to humanize the heart. It was true philanthropy, therefore, to introduce this mitigating influence where, of all other places, its fruits were to be more beneficially realized, namely into the Army and Navy, and to abolish it, in this Christian age of the world, would seem like retrograding rather than advancing civilization.[8]

In the last two chapters we examined a parade of programs aimed at the promotion of morality and human growth: Character Education, Moral Leadership, Personal Response, Human Meaning. Many of these programs came to grief. Some that survived evolved, once they were removed from chaplain control, into something other than their chaplain progenitors had intended. As "programs," none may in the long run survive. From the religious perspective, there may be some question as to whether or not they should. But they are important as attempts to wrestle with religious and human values in a non-religious and sometimes inhumane institution. The significant contribution is the continual input of these values and the continuing interaction thus initiated.

In 1970 and 1971, when the My Lai atrocities in Vietnam were much in the public attention, I was often asked, "Where were the chaplains at My Lai? How could such things have happened if chaplains in Vietnam had been doing their job?" The implication was clear, especially to those —numerous in that period—with strong anti-military feelings. There were charges that such atrocities were commonplace in Vietnam, that chaplains must have been aware of them, that they had failed to take a moral stand against them, and by their silence condoned them.

I had no personal knowledge of the Vietnamese War, not having served there. I was, however, deeply ashamed that a My Lai could have happened in the armed forces of which I was a member. And I was sufficiently concerned about the charges regarding chaplains to inquire among the numerous chaplains I knew who had served there. I found not a single one who had knowledge of an atrocity such as My Lai and had remained silent. (It was later revealed in testimony at the Calley trial that a chaplain, who had heard indirectly of the incident, had been instrumental in bringing it to command attention at one echelon.) Many, however, told me of other incidents in which a potential My Lai did not happen, or was ameliorated, or a brutality was punished.

War is always brutal, and it brutalizes those who engage in it. No war has been without its atrocities. But they have been the exception rather than the rule in the American armed forces, and when discovered they have almost always been severely punished by military authorities themselves. I am convinced from my own experience with men in combat in another war, and from my talks with chaplains who served in the Vietnamese War, that My Lai was not normative, that chaplains generally did not condone such conduct, and that because of their presence there were far fewer such incidents than might otherwise have been the case.

It is also evident that vast numbers of soldiers and Marines in Vietnam, under the leadership and influence of their chaplains, devoted millions of dollars and countless hours of work to building and repairing hospitals and orphanages, feeding the hungry, caring for the sick and dispossessed, and otherwise showing human concern for the people of that tragically war-torn land.

We have discussed earlier the "Personal Response" program of chaplains in Vietnam. Whatever may have been its military use or misuse, this project in cross-cultural understanding taught hundreds of thousands of American troopers to see the Vietnamese as persons rather than "gooks." There is substantial evidence that during the Vietnamese War, as throughout American military history, the sociological effect of the presence of representatives of the American churches and their religious values has been of great significance.

We looked in some detail in Chapter 2 at the characteristics of total institutions. As total institutions, the military services are in many respects closed societies, with their own customs, conventions, and standards. The stereotype of the dangerous "military mind," often depicted in cartoons, articles, and books, is greatly overdrawn; military minds reflect nearly as much variety as civilian minds. But the danger of such a malign influence developing within the military institution would be far greater were not the Christian and the Jewish minds present, in dialogue with the military mind.

Even if it were possible, from the standpoint of individual persons "performing ministry," to substitute civilian clergymen for the military chaplaincy, there is grave question as to its sociological wisdom. Leaving aside all questions of relative effectiveness, cost, the impracticality of a civilian chaplaincy in shipboard and combat situations, and the problems of denominational coordination, it is probable that the most serious loss from civilianization would be this loss of the influence of an insider chaplaincy on the institution itself. A chaplaincy might well be justified on these grounds alone, as a contribution of the churches to American society.

It is hoped that this study's analysis of the military chaplaincy, as an insider ministry by persons who are not only full members of the clergy of their churches but also full members of the military institutions they serve, has established the viability and validity of this ministry. The questions raised by advocates of a civilian ministry to the armed forces, however, need not receive an either/or answer. Though a continuation of the chaplaincy in essentially its present form is fully justified and desirable, modifications of present patterns are obviously possible and undoubtedly desirable in some areas. A more accountable chaplaincy, closely watched, continually encouraged, fully backed, and genuinely shaped by the churches would be helpful to churches and armed forces alike. Far too many chaplains feel isolated and ignored by their churches, and far too many churches give military ministry a low priority. Real help from the churches in correcting the abuses, dealing with the problems, and living with the ambiguities of military service is long overdue.

The answer may lie in pluralism, as the United Presbyterian task force suggested. Continued insider ministries by uniformed chaplains within the armed forces are needed. Increased efforts on the part of the churches to provide complimentary civilian ministries are also needed. We will look later in this chapter at some steps the churches can take to supplement as well as to help shape the chaplaincy of the future.

QUESTIONS REGARDING UNIFORMS AND RANK

Part of the general questioning of the chaplaincy which began during the Vietnamese War and has continued to a lesser extent in the postwar period had to do with the propriety of chaplains wearing uniforms and holding rank.

The uniform issue is simply another way of raising the question as to whether chaplains should be full-fledged members of the armed forces. The question has been addressed in considerable detail already. If the need for "insider" ministries by persons who are fully part of the military organization is accepted, the uniform must be accepted also. Most chaplains, as we have noted, find the wearing of the uniform to be a bond between them and other insiders in the total institution. Those who object to a chaplaincy in principle, on grounds that the churches should not be involved in the military, will continue to object to uniforms; but for those who accept an "insider" chaplaincy, it is a non-issue. As such it will not be further addressed here.

The question of rank for chaplains, however, merits further attention. It would be possible for chaplains to be part of the military service in which they minister without holding rank. British Navy chaplains wear uniforms, and they hold the equivalent of rank (fully recognized among themselves) for administrative purposes. But they do not wear rank insignia on the uniform, and in theory the chaplain is presumed to take on

companies integration into the organization. The danger of a kind of subserviency that negatively affects ministry, resulting not only from the fact that commanders in many instances prepare the fitness reports on which promotions are based but from the whole structure of military authority, cannot be overlooked. But neither should it be overemphasized. Undue concern about the issue reflects a misunderstanding of the nature of military command and military relationships. Chaplains are not nearly so much at the mercy of commanding officers as outsiders think. Commanders are sometimes envisioned as absolute autocrats who can do anything they wish. Actually, they are hemmed in by numerous regulations and restrictions, particularly in the field of personnel administration. A military service, as we have noted earlier, is a bureaucracy, and one of the characteristics of bureaucracy is the building in of safeguards for the protection of bureaucrats. In order to give a low mark or make a negative comment on a fitness report, a Navy commanding officer must first show the chaplain what he is saying, giving him a chance to prepare a written rebuttal. While this is not always the case in the Army and Air Force, both services have appeal provisions which are open to a chaplain. For a commanding officer to institute disciplinary action of any kind against a chaplain, there must be a violation of a regulation which can be formally proved.

Commanding officers are themselves survivors of a selection system which places a high premium on good judgment and sound administration. Most of them are persons of religious faith, with a high regard for religious values and a sincere interest in the chaplain's ministry. Even if they are not themselves religious persons, they know that it is in their own best interest as commanders to have as effective a religious program as possible. Because they are accustomed to a staff system in which they depend on technical "experts" as their advisors in specialized fields, and because they do not consider themselves to be experts in the field of religion, they tend to keep hands off. They are often reluctant to interfere in the performance of ministry, even when interference is needed. For these reasons, the power of the fitness report, as it is related to rank and advancement, is not likely to be as big an element in the distortion of ministry as outside observers sometimes suspect.

Entirely apart from formal rank titles, some system for the evaluation of professional performance is necessary, as is some system for the recognition of age, experience, leadership ability, and determination of pay grades. It may be argued that an informal, haphazard, "free enterprise" system (the systems in many civilian denominations might be so characterized) would be better than a planned and formalized system. In a military organization, however, a formalized system is likely to be more acceptable.

It is undoubtedly true that temptations of rank and status sometimes motivate chaplains, just as high-steeple churches and larger salaries sometimes motivate civilian ministers. It is a debatable question, however, whether the institutionalization of rank in the military service makes it more of a problem than the subtle forms of rank and status in other areas of ministry. It is certainly a more open concern in the military. The chaplain wears his rank on his sleeve or collar, and everyone knows what it is. When he is passed over for promotion, everyone knows that, too, and it is much harder to live with than the failure to get a call to First Church, known only to the minister's wife and the pulpit committee. But the problems in this area may be balanced by the fact that the whole process is open and aboveboard. Many chaplains are more aware of the danger of rank and status than are their civilian colleagues whose rank and status are less public, and they may in some cases try harder to overcome it.

The question of whether the rank of the chaplain is a barrier in his work with enlisted persons is also one to which no definitive answer can be given. Sometimes, clearly, it is a barrier—particularly if the chaplain concerned is one of the minority overly conscious of rank. Chaplains generally have been of the opinion that the potential barrier can be readily overcome by the chaplain's own manner and attitude. The 1965 United Presbyterian Position Paper on the chaplaincy said that

> surveys of those of our church who have served as chaplains show that a strong majority of them believe rank to be necessary for the chaplain to operate effectively in behalf of the men, and, on the other hand, that it is not a real barrier between the chaplain and the enlisted men unless that chaplain makes it so.[11]

In 1968 the Chaplains Advisory Council of the Presbyterian Church, U. S., canvassed the active duty chaplains of that denomination (fifty-four respondents) on their attitudes toward a number of issues. The report of the study stated:

> Chaplains . . . reveal considerable sensitivity to the ambiguities of officer status and military rank for chaplains. Only three saw no effect on ministry. The largest number (36) saw rank and officer status as having an effect on ministry, sometimes as a handicap, sometimes as an advantage. Twenty-six felt that the effective chaplain can readily overcome the handicap, and the same number (26) indicated that the handicap is outweighed by the advantage of being fully a part of the society in which the chaplain ministers. Only one

saw officer status and rank as such a handicap that the church should develop an alternative form of military ministry.[12]

In some instances, as this report indicated, rank is seen as a definite advantage. The U. S. Navy Chaplains School has used as a training device for chaplains a series of taped conversations of groups of enlisted men. One such tape included a discussion by a group of five men on the rank of chaplains. One sailor recalled a chaplain who "wanted everybody to call him captain," much to the disgust of all, but the general consensus was that in most cases a chaplain is a chaplain, and the rank didn't matter much. One member of the group, however, said that when he had a problem and needed the help of a chaplain, he wanted the highest ranking chaplain he could find, because "he can get things done."

My own experience has been that whatever initial barrier exists can easily and quickly be overcome. At the time of my promotion to the grade of Rear Admiral, I wondered if this would continue to be the case, since flag rank is relatively rare and most enlisted men do not often deal with admirals. I have found that I have to work far harder to overcome this element in my relations with other chaplains (for whom flag rank in the Chaplain Corps has special meaning) and in official relations with officers than in counseling relationships with enlisted persons, whose mind-set is on "chaplain" when they seek counsel, and who frequently pay no attention at all to the rank.

One evening as I was standing the watch as duty chaplain for the Norfolk Naval Base, I received a telephone call at the duty chaplain's office from the officer of the deck of a destroyer, asking me to come to the ship to talk to an enlisted man with a serious problem. When I got out of my car on the pier, the quarterdeck of every ship in the area was thrown into a panic by the unexpected arrival of a flag officer, and I was surrounded by a chorus of bos'n pipes and announcements of "Attention to port!" or "Attention to starboard!" The officer of the deck of the ship I boarded nearly swallowed his moustache when he discovered that the duty chaplain he had summoned was an admiral. The one person who was completely unperturbed was the seaman who had asked to talk to a chaplain. We talked for nearly an hour, in a perfectly normal and reasonably productive counseling session. His only recognition of rank came as I was leaving, when he looked at me curiously and said, "You an admiral? I never talked to an admiral before."

Few chaplains would deny that there are dangers and problems connected with rank and officer status. Probably the greatest danger is the spiritual danger to the chaplain himself, who may be led to forget on occasion that his sole purpose in the military is to be a minister of the gospel. But it is by no means clear that the dangers are any greater than the comparable dangers to any clergyman. Who can say that the temptation to work for advancement to the grade of colonel is any greater than the temptation to work for a call to First Church? Or that subservience to the military power structure is any greater than subservience to the financial power structure which raises the budget of First Church? Or the ecclesiastical power structure? Who can say that the barrier of officer rank insignia is any greater than the barrier of the coat and tie signifying upper middle class status, or the clerical collar? It is quite possible that the barriers are less rather than greater, since formalized rank is such an ubiquitous part of the military way of life that it is taken for granted.

Because chaplains are themselves always interested parties, and because their judgment may be clouded by self-interest, it would be a mistake for the churches to rely on their opinions alone. This, like all other aspects of the chaplaincy, should be kept under continual supervision and review by the churches. Here again, the civilian churchmen charged by the denominations with responsibility for supervising chaplain ministries would be a good source of substantiating data.

The basic issue, however, is whether the dangers and problems associated with military rank and status outweigh the advantages. The advantages, of course, have to do with being fully a part of the military institution to which they are ministering, being fully a participant in the lives and problems of the people who make up the institution, sharing with them all the normal conditions of life—of which rank is certainly one. The advantage of this insider status has been discussed at great length in this book, and will not be repeated here. Most chaplains clearly feel that their position as full members of the military community is an enormous advantage over the sort of ministerial segregation they have experienced in the civilian parish. It gives them tremendous opportunities for real relationship and real service that they would not otherwise have.

THE CHURCHES AND THE CHAPLAINCY

In looking at the question of the civilianization of the chaplaincy, we noted that in addition to the insider ministries provided by chaplains, there is also a need for outsider civilian ministries to the armed forces. A pluralistic approach, as suggested by the United Presbyterian task force, would provide both. We also noted that there is a need for the denominations to provide closer supervision, stronger support, and greater interest in the ministries of their chaplains. In this section we will look at some of the ways the churches can participate more actively in their ministry to the armed forces in the future, and some of the ways in which the churches themselves will benefit from greater interaction with their chaplaincies.

Civilian Ministries to the Military

While civilian ministries, as we have seen, could not replace the military chaplaincy without serious loss of effectiveness, there is unlimited opportunity for civilian ministries to supplement and cooperate with the ministries of chaplains. This is particularly true in the continental United States where numbers of civilian churches are located in the vicinity of military bases. These churches are already serving large numbers of military personnel and families, and in "service towns" such as Norfolk, Virginia, or San Antonio, Texas, churches in which more than half the membership is military-related are not uncommon.

The suggestion is sometimes made that in areas where civilian churches are available, no military chaplains should be provided. In late 1973, the House of Representatives Armed Services Committee, in considering the fiscal year 1974 military appropriations bill, commented on the high cost of a chaplaincy of more than 3,000 clergymen:

> Considering that many of the military bases in the United States are in or adjacent to cities and towns with religious facilities, the need for such a large chaplain corps, and enlisted assistants, appears questionable. The Committee recommends that the services review its requirements for chaplains and chaplain assistants and report to the Committee.[13]

The Senate committee disagreed, stating that this is not a time to diminish the moral and spiritual support which our nation has made available to its military personnel for two hundred years, and strongly supported the chaplaincy.[14] The Senate-House conference committee supported the Senate position. The fact that a group so knowledgeable about the military as the House committee could make such a suggestion, however, indicates that such sentiment has a good bit of support.

No one, least of all chaplains, would deny that many stateside military people can and should turn to civilian churches for spiritual nurture. Most chaplains have no desire to "compete" with local churches. Neither the denominations that sent them into the armed forces, nor military people themselves, want such competition. Chaplains recognize that the local pastor, who confronts military men and women from a stance of relative permanence, can offer a kind of normal and stable church experience which chaplains themselves, because they are part of the institutional environment and its mobility, cannot provide. Denominational relationships and resources, community involvement, and parish church stewardship structures can provide a far more full and complete church life than can a military chapel. Chaplains, therefore, as much as they enjoy facing from the pulpit a full chapel, nevertheless generally encourage military people to become fully and responsibly involved in local churches of their own denomination whenever possible. They cooperate with local churches and work with them as much as possible. If this were not the case, far more chaplains than the three thousand now on active duty would be required to meet the religious needs of the military community.

For a number of reasons, however, it is desirable to keep chaplains at stateside bases even when there are plenty of churches in the area. Basically, chaplains with troops on military garrison duty in the United States must be there for the same reason the troops themselves must be there. We do not keep combat troops at Fort Hood, Texas, because we expect a Russian or Chinese attack on Texas, but because they must be available somewhere, trained and ready, *in case* they are needed anywhere for combat.

Second, although local churches can and do provide opportunities for worship and religious community for large numbers of military people and families, and stateside chapel programs serve only a minority of the active churchmen in this way, there remain the extensive counseling ministry and other forms of service to the whole institution which are performed by chaplains throughout the week. Even if the surrounding civilian ministers had the time to fill these needs—which clearly they do not—it is doubtful that they would be able to.

Third, although the chapel program is a relatively minor part of the total ministry of chaplains at stateside bases surrounded by civilian churches, it still meets a particular need. Realistically, it must be recognized that the military is the kind of society that encourages its members to allow the "total mobile environment" we examined earlier to become a substitute for the stability others may find in the civilian community structures. Whether or not such a situation is fully desirable is beside the point; it exists. The stateside-based chaplain cannot, therefore, limit himself to a supplementary ministry to transients, prisoners, and duty personnel unable to involve themselves in off-base churches. He must provide as full a ministry as possible to those who, because of the system, feel more at home and can be better served within the total environment which provides them with security.

Fourth, the kind of cooperative and ecumenical church life a military chapel offers does have something to contribute to the cause of religion.

Although it is no substitute for the denominational churches which offer a fuller church life, it adds a unique and worthwhile dimension to the life of the religious community.

One final element is the health of the chaplaincy itself. Even if churches in the civilian communities surrounding military bases were able to provide all the needed ministries and services, it is neither humane nor practical to expect that all chaplains would spend all their time at sea, in combat, or in overseas areas. Rotation from sea to shore duty, and from overseas hardship tours of duty to stateside assignments is as necessary to the family life and emotional health of chaplains as for all other human beings serving in the armed forces.

But while the chaplain ministries to military people ashore and within the United States are necessary, there is also a great need for expanded and enhanced civilian ministries. The special mission and opportunity open to churches near military bases has received little attention or encouragement from denominational or ecumenical church structures. In 1968 the Chaplains Advisory Council of the Presbyterian Church, U. S. (sometimes known as the Southern Presbyterian Church) conducted a study of the work of such churches. The study was undertaken in recognition of a special responsibility:

> Because of a climate permitting year-round military exercises and operations, a disproportionate number of American military bases are located in the area of our General Assembly. The southeast has the heaviest concentration of military personnel of any area of the country with the exception of southern California. This means, in effect, that hundreds of thousands of young adults, whose relationship to the church is one of the greatest enigmas and challenges of our times, come into our region each year from all over the nation. By geographical accident, then, our church has a special obligation to our society to examine our responsibilities to this specialized segment of the population.[15]

The study found little evidence of special efforts to meet this responsibility. A questionaire was distributed to churches ministering to military personnel and families through Presbytery executives, since no list of such churches was in existence. Findings were summarized as follows:

> Few of the churches are making a "special effort" to reach or serve military personnel and their families. Those that are making a special effort, with few exceptions, are "recruiting" ("come and swell our numbers") rather than "serving," if such a distinction can be made. Where a special effort is being made, it is generally directed toward families (14 churches) rather than the young single service-

man. Only seven churches (generally the same ones making a special effort toward families) indicated any effort of this kind. The family effort generally takes the form of visitation. One church has a full-time military visitor (salary paid by Presbytery); three churches have systems whereby military families visit military families; one church has a visitation committee on the Base; two churches have had Vacation Church Schools in military housing areas (one a trailer park for military families); one church has a committee to assist uprooted military families. The "special effort" to reach single servicemen generally takes the form of providing a special Sunday School class for them. Two churches take polaroid pictures of visiting servicemen (one sends to family); one church provides a bus from the Base to the church; one participates in a downtown USO; one sponsors a Sunday evening discussion group for servicemen in a restaurant. There was a general sense of concern on the part of the responding churches. There were several requests for suggestions as to how this ministry can be improved, and several expressions of thanks for focusing attention on the need through sending the questionaire. Some answers to questions on "special effort" were worded in such a way as to indicate a belief that the right way to minister to servicemen is simply to "be the church," without singling out servicemen in any way. This, of course, is a valid attitude which implies no lack of concern.[16]

One striking fact revealed by the study was the amount of lay leadership provided by active duty military personnel in the responding churches. Sixty-two active duty military men were listed by the questionaire as currently serving as elders or deacons. There were indications that the actual number was larger. The questionaire provided space for only three names; several churches, after listing three or four names, added "and several others," or words to that effect. Of the thirty-five churches showing five percent or more service constituency, only five failed to list at least one military man in a position of leadership (one of the five noted that it was most unusual for it to have no military elder or deacon). The general reaction of the responding pastors was that cooperation with chaplains was good. Twenty respondents made distinctly laudatory remarks about chaplains. Six made negative remarks. The remainder made such comments as "relations are good" or left the question blank.

There is every indication that far more can be done by churches in the vicinity of military bases to extend their ministries to military personnel and families, and particularly to single young adults, than is now being done. If the churches are interested in a pluralistic approach to military ministry, as the United Presbyterian task force suggested, this is an excellent place to begin. By the establishment of structures for coordination, encouragement, and support, such ministries could be greatly expanded and enhanced with a minimal expenditure of funds. There is evidence, as noted above, that such an effort would be a two-way street, with a substantial military contribution to church leadership.

There is also an urgent need for ministries to off-duty servicemen and women in downtown and "liberty" areas, which the churches are in a position to provide. The World War II USO model appears to be in trouble. Such USO's and Armed Forces YMCA's as remain in operation are generally struggling, often because they are located in once-popular areas of changing urban communities which are no longer frequented by servicemen. Many are only marginally supported by United Funds because of changing priorities on the part of such funds. But the need still exists. Experimental downtown ministries such as the one in Newport, R. I., mentioned earlier in this book have been promising. Christian Servicemen's Centers operated by evangelical lay movements, such as the Navigators, are flourishing. If the churches are interested in a pluralistic approach to military ministry, this is another wide-open avenue. Far more can be done by civilian ministries supplementing the efforts of chaplains than has been done in the past.

Chaplain Support Structures

A second area in which churches can participate more actively in ministry to the armed forces is in the provision of stronger support and supervision structures for the chaplaincy. In earlier sections of this book dealing with the historical development of the chaplaincy, we noted that the churches as institutions were not involved at all in the development of the chaplaincy in the first hundred years of its existence, that they have assumed an active role only since the First World War, that in the ensuing period their efforts have been somewhat limited, and that only now are they beginning to realize fully the implications of institutional duality. In the chapter on religious pluralism we noted that they have been severely handicapped in dealing with the armed forces by the fragmentation of their efforts.

If the full potential of institutional duality is to be realized and the churches are to exercise their rightful role in connection with their chaplains, the greatest need, perhaps, is for a common structure through which they can speak to the government with a united voice. The legal profession and the medical and health services professions deal with the government from positions of considerable strength. In matters such as military law and health care standards, the positions of the American Bar Association or the American Medical Association carry enormous weight.

The consensual professional opinion of medical or legal officers within the services carries great weight in itself, because of the implication that the consensual professional opinion of the nation, in a matter within professional cognizance, would support it.

No one, however, speaks for the collective interests of the American churches; those interests are too diverse. When the American Baptist Church, in connection with the court-martial of one of its chaplains, threatened non-endorsement or withdrawal of chaplains in its dispute with the Navy, it caused not a ripple. The American Baptist Church is a major Protestant denomination, but its constituency is less than five percent of the American public. The military viewed the prospect of a chaplaincy without American Baptists with some equanimity.

The high point of church-government cooperation in connection with the chaplaincy came at the time of the First World War, when the newly-formed General Committee on Army and Navy Chaplains was *perceived* as representative of American religion in general. Actually it was a good bit less representative than it seemed. It represented only Protestantism, of course. But at that time the myth of a Protestant America was still current, and Roman Catholicism and Judaism were regarded as relatively unimportant in the religious scene. The appointment of the first Roman Catholic and Jewish chaplains were still relatively recent events. The General Committee did not even represent all of Protestantism, but those portions it did not represent were less visible, less organized, and less vocal than they have since become. The screening, quota-establishing, and endorsement power given to it by the armed forces made it necessary for those Protestant churches desiring to provide chaplains to work through it. Because it seemed to be, and was treated as if it were, representative of American religion, it was able to enter into a genuine partnership with government in sponsoring chaplain ministries.

At the time of the Second World War, the General Commission on Chaplains and Armed Forces Personnel (successor to the General Committee) still retained some of its prestige, at least as a common voice for Protestantism. It joined with the Roman Catholic Military Ordinariate and the Jewish Welfare Board in dealing with Congress in connection with legislation affecting chaplains, particularly the establishment of the offices of the Chiefs of Chaplains and provision for the selection of general and flag officers to head the chaplaincies. The military would have liked to deal once again with the General Commission for all Protestant chaplaincy endorsements, but this time major denominations insisted on endorsing separately. In the postwar period, as more and more denominations established their own chaplaincy bureaucracies and as denominations which had never been members became increasingly vocal, fragmentation increased.

There is little hope that the churches can assume the level of responsibility for chaplain ministries which their status as ordained church representatives in the armed forces would warrant, unless they can find a way of establishing a structure for common discussion and action. The General Commission could probably provide the framework for such a structure if the desire were present, but it would have to cease to exist as a Protestant organization in order to do so.

For the most part, the General Commission has gone out of business as an endorsing agency (since all the major denominations now endorse directly), although it still appears to see itself as concerned primarily with endorsements. Most chaplaincy agents of the churches, indeed, continue to see themselves primarily as "endorsing officials."

The General Commission continues to publish *The Chaplain*, the only existing professional journal (aside from an Army house organ, the *Military Chaplains' Review*), which is essentially for the military chaplaincies. Its most important remaining function, probably, is that of serving as a common forum for discussion of chaplaincy matters for the member churches (and to some extent, since the Roman Catholic Military Ordinariate, the Jewish Welfare Board, and some non-member Protestant denominations send observers to some of its meetings, for all churches).

For the General Commission to be reconstituted as a forum representing all chaplaincy-sponsoring churches, it would probably be necessary for it to take the following steps:

1. Give up the endorsing function completely, leaving this to the individual denominations. (Another cooperative endorsing agency for small denominations could be established if necessary).

2. Turn *The Chaplain* into a non-denominational journal. It has for some time come close to such a stance, but has still retained some Protestant orientation. A completely non-denominational professional journal for chaplains is entirely possible, as the chaplaincies themselves have demonstrated with the *Military Chaplains' Review* published by the Army Chaplain Corps and *Chaplain Corps Professional Papers* of the Navy.

3. Sacrifice its own identity, staff, and Protestant relationship, turning its assets and remaining functions over to the successor agency.

4. Prepare, in cooperation with the Roman Catholic Military Ordinariate, the Jewish Welfare Board, and non-member Protestant denominations sponsoring chaplaincies, a plan for a successor agency. Such an agency would have to adopt a completely non-theological and religiously non-partisan stance. It would be pluralistic rather than

ecumenical. It could perform its function only if it were equally open and acceptable to all religious denominations, including those that do not consider themselves involved in the ecumenical movement. Its goal would be to serve as a forum for discussion and channel of communication with the government on matters related to the chaplaincy, representing the full range of America's religious pluralism.

It might not be possible for such an agency to be an "agency" in the organizational sense at all. Perhaps a continuing "Conference on Chaplains and Armed Forces Personnel," meeting semi-annually or quarterly on a regular basis, with some form of proportional representation from all those churches providing chaplains, would be as far as the churches would be willing to go on such an inclusive basis.

We noted earlier than the denominational endorsing officials who have met periodically in the past at the invitation of the Chiefs of Chaplains began in 1974 some tentative movement in the direction of autonomy. The group itself arranged a meeting and extended an invitation to the Chiefs of Chaplains. It is intended that this practice will be continued, with one meeting each year hosted by the Chiefs of Chaplains (Armed Forces Chaplains Board) and another by the endorsing agents. A beginning has thus been made. If it is to develop into a continuing Conference on Chaplains and Armed Forces Personnel to meet the coordination need being described here, however, some continuing administrative structure, to carry out its mandates and to represent it in dealing with the government, must be developed. The General Commission on Chaplains, reconstituted as a far more broadly representative group, would seem to offer the best hope.

Coordination of Military Policy on Chaplains

Such a conference or agency, providing a unified voice for the churches, would point up the parallel need for the three military services to deal with the churches in a unified way. It would be in a position to insist on greater coordination and commonality of military policy. At present the three services have agreed on certain basic standards for chaplaincy appointments, but they apply them in different ways. An applicant who is rejected by one of the services may apply to, and is sometimes accepted by, another. There is duplication of effort between the various services, and between the services and the churches, in processing and examining the qualifications of applicants for appointment.

For the services to turn the selection and appointment of chaplains entirely over to the churches, as the United Church of Christ task force proposed, is not a realistic expectation. The military has as legitimate an interest in the process as the churches have. At present, however, as that report pointed out, the military assumes most of the responsibility. A full partnership, in which the legitimate interests of both institutions are represented and the responsibility shared, would be possible under a unified approach.

Policies and procedures of the three services toward the churches and chaplains differ in many other ways. One notable area is determination of the number of chaplains needed. Historically the Navy has provided far fewer chaplains in proportion to the number of military personnel to be served than the other services. There are differing approaches to chaplain supervision, different promotion systems, and differing policies on terms of service, integration into the regular forces, and releases from active duty. Some of these differences are, of course, the result of basic differences between the services themselves, and as such they will and should be allowed to continue. Many will be eliminated by new legislation which is expected to put into effect a unified Department of Defense Personnel Management System.

Historically, however, the needs and requirements of military chaplaincy as such have never been addressed in an integrated way, by either Congress or the armed forces. Legislation and policy affecting chaplains have always come about as a minor (an unimportant) part of a larger military need or decision. Chaplaincy policy has always been a subsidiary aspect of larger policy. The churches alone, by coordinated action, can ensure that military chaplaincy is treated by the government as a subject in its own right.

A Single Chaplaincy?

It might be asked whether the chaplaincies of the three services should be replaced by a single military chaplaincy, serving all services. Certainly military chaplaincy is one professional specialty within the ministry. As we have seen throughout this book, most statements about chaplains and most of the factors in the analysis of their ministry, apply to all three services. Without exception the denominations deal with the military chaplaincy as a single category of ministry, and there would be advantages from their perspective if the chaplaincy were really a single entity.

We have devoted much attention in this book, however, to the characteristics of military services as total institutions, to the desirability of insider ministries by clergymen who are full members of the institutions, and to the enormous advantage in ministry which comes from fully sharing the life of the institution. In Canada the services themselves have been unified, and a unified chaplaincy is fully part of such an institution. As long as our services remain separate, however, insider ministries require separate chaplaincies in each service. More would be lost than gained by the removal of service identity.

Far more unification of policy and procedures than now exists would be possible, however. The three chaplaincies, while retaining full identity with their respective services, could achieve a far higher level of professional coordination. The present channel of coordination is the Armed Forces Chaplains Board, consisting of the three Chiefs of Chaplains and three Deputy Chiefs, and reporting to the Assistant Secretary of Defense for Manpower. At present, decisions depend on unanimity between the three services, and any implementation of decisions is up to the individual services. The coordinating authority could readily be strengthened to provide Department of Defense level policy decisions in areas of differences and overlapping responsibilities. An inter-church conference such as the one proposed above, empowered to speak with a single voice for the churches in chaplaincy matters, could reasonably expect and press for a stronger Armed Forces Chaplains Board to speak with an equally undivided voice for the services. A true partnership might then come into being.

Widened Role for the Denominations

A single interchurch conference speaking for the churches in their relationships with the government on chaplaincy matters would not replace the individual denominational agencies in their relationships with their own chaplains. The overall thrust of such a move would be to widen the role of the churches in controlling and supervising the ministry of their chaplains, thus strengthening the denominational agencies as well.

Whenever the position and polity of the individual denominations permits, it is helpful for the churches to deal with their chaplains ecumenically. The three major Lutheran bodies have supervised their chaplains jointly through the Lutheran Council in the U.S.A. In 1973 four Presbyterian denominations took a similar step, and their chaplains are now identified in the military only as "Presbyterian," just as all Lutheran chaplains are identified simply as "Lutheran." Such steps have been welcomed by laymen of these denominations in the armed forces and have worked out well.

Continuing Education

One area in which a much wider role for the churches could readily be filled is that of continuing education. The military chaplaincies have led other branches of the ministerial profession in providing and encouraging a wide range of continuing education opportunities. The Navy's program is illustrative. In addition to the postgraduate education in counseling discussed in an earlier chapter, the Navy has six other subspecialty areas for which postgraduate education is provided. Chaplains are selected annually from among those applying and sent to accredited civilian theological seminaries or universities of their choice for one year of graduate study. One chaplain a year is selected for further Ph.D. studies in one of the areas. The subspecialty areas are: (1) Pastoral/ Homiletical (which "may include concentration in one or more of the following disciplines: Theology, Biblical Studies, Homiletics, Liturgy, Ethics, Church Administration, and Religious Education, with the additional dimension of preparation for the supervision of a team ministry"); (2) Counseling; (3) Clinical Training (for supervisory responsibilities); (4) Professional Training/Interpersonal Communication; (5) Mass Media Religious Communication; (6) Behavioral Science/Sociology of Religion; and (7) Comparative Religion.[17] Upon completion of his graduate work, a chaplain is assigned to a special billet designated for his particular qualification, where one of his responsibilities is serving as a trainer and consultant for other chaplains in the area of his specialty.

A number of shorter continuing education opportunities are provided, in addition to the counseling courses and Clinical Pastoral Education discussed in an earlier chapter. These include annual administrative development courses in a number of locations, occasional seminars to meet such specialized needs as ministry to minorities, or ministry through shipboard closed circuit TV, and an annual series of professional seminars on subjects of interest to the entire corps, so located and arranged that more than half the corps attends each year. The Career Development Institutes of the Air Force chaplaincy follow a similar pattern, focusing on professional skills and the theological disciplines and reaching ninety percent of its chaplains each year. The Navy Chaplains School, in addition to an eight-week basic orientation course for chaplains entering active duty, provides each year a nine-month advanced course for fifteen chaplains in the grade of commander. In addition to supervisory and managerial training, this course provides a general sharpening of ministerial and team leadership skills and a year of updating in theology, ethics, Biblical Studies, worship, and a wide range of other professional disciplines.

The chaplaincy also encourages chaplains to engage in their own off-duty programs of continuing education. Government funds are provided to pay part of the tuition costs. In 1972 a pioneering off-duty

Doctor of Ministry degree program was initiated for Navy chaplains in the Norfolk, Virginia, area. Provided by McCormick Theological Seminary in cooperation with the seminaries and universities of the Chicago Theological Institute, the study program focuses on the ministry of the chaplain in his own assignment and allows for a course tailored to his own continuing education needs. Future plans include the expansion of the program with the establishment of two other centers, one at Great Lakes, Illinois, and the other at San Diego, California. When in full operation, any Navy chaplain may enroll in the program and continue his off-duty studies at any one of the three centers as he is transferred from one assignment to another.[18]

Both the Army and the Air Force chaplaincies have their own comparable programs of continuing education. In part because their ministries are somewhat cut off from normal church structures, the chaplaincies have made a special effort to ensure that their members remain alert, informed, and in touch with professional developments in the churches.

Except for the basic orientation training for incoming chaplains, practically all continuing education for chaplains is associated with the ecclesiastical rather than the military side of their institutional duality. For this reason, the chaplaincies depend heavily on civilian church educational resources for their programs. Some courses are conducted in civilian educational institutions, but even when they are conducted at chaplains' schools or on military bases (as with the annual professional seminars), professors from theological seminaries and other civilian church leaders are employed as teachers and resource persons. The field of continuing education, then, is one in which it would be possible for the churches to assume a much wider role than they have in the past. If appropriate church-sponsored structures were available, there is little doubt that the chaplaincies would welcome civilian church leadership in establishment of educational policy and would enter into full partnership with the churches in this field.

The Chaplains Schools

In 1971 the Armed Forces Chaplains Board, at the direction of the Secretary of Defense, sponsored a study of the feasibility of consolidating the three chaplains schools operated independently by the three services. A task force, made up of one representative from the staff of each of the chaplains schools and one from each of the three Chaplains Boards,[19] conducted a thorough study. The task force report, signed by five of the six members, concluded that the consolidating of the three schools was feasible, and that it would result not only in a fiscal saving but in better

programs of continuing education for all three chaplaincies. The Armed
Forces Chaplains Board forwarded the report to the Secretary of Defense
with a divided recommendation, the Navy and Air Force recommending
implementation and the Army dissenting. Because of the absence of
unanimity, no action was taken.

In 1973 the House Armed Services Committee, in its action on the
fiscal 1974 budget request, brought up the issue again:

> One training area the Committee has identified which should be
> consolidated is chaplain training programs. The Army, Navy and
> Air Force have each established training schools for chaplains.
> . . . The Committee directs the services to consolidate the various
> chaplain schools and eliminate unnecessary courses.[20]

The Senate committee refused to go along, and the conference committee removed the consolidation requirement. The possibility, however,
remains an open one.

A consolidated chaplains school would provide a ready vehicle for
a much larger church role in continuing education for chaplains. The
Armed Forces Chaplains Board task force report recommended a civilian Board of Visitors, representing churches and theological seminaries,
for such a consolidated school. A considerably more active role would
be possible if a cooperative church structure existed to assume it. This
might include not only a church voice in the selection of the civilian
teachers and resource persons invited to teach and lead continuing education courses, but possibly even permanent civilian faculty members to
represent church interests.

Regardless of whether or not a consolidated chaplains school is
brought to fruition, and whatever structures are utilized, the churches are
in a position to assume as much responsibility as they desire for the
continuing education of their clergy who are serving as chaplains. Such
professional education is quite basically a church responsibility, and the
services have taken initiative only because the churches have failed to do
so.

Church-Chaplain Interaction on Issues and Policy

In several places in this book—particularly in the chapters on civil
religion and on the involvement of chaplains in character education and
human relations programs, we have taken note of the urgent need of
chaplains for guidance and direction from their churches. As representatives of the churches in a secular institution, the accomodations they
make and position they take on these sometimes controversial issues,

become *de facto* church positions in the view of that institution, and sometimes in the view of the public at large.

The need is not for "party line" instructions or authoritarian control of chaplains in these matters. That is not the style with which most American churches operate. By and large, chaplains are responsible churchmen who keep up with current religious thought and developments in the theological disciplines and are capable of making informed judgments. Their history indicates that they have probably been more faithful to the work and witness of their churches than those churches, which have often ignored them, have had a right to expect.

What is needed, rather, is two-way interaction. Seminars and conferences under church sponsorship can bring chaplains into contact with the best minds of the civilian church on issues such as civil religion and non-church-oriented humanitarian ministries, on which they need guidance. Denominational theological commissions or agencies dealing with social concerns could, in some instances, prepare study papers for the assistance of civilian church and chaplains alike. Resolutions and policy statements, prepared specifically for the guidance of chaplains, could be debated and accepted or rejected by church courts and conventions.

The chaplains, for their part, have much to offer the church at large. There are concerns before the whole church to which their experience would bring a special dimension: church-state relations; war, peace, and amnesty issues; civil religion; interracial ministries; ecumenical relationships; young adult concerns. Yet active duty chaplains are seldom invited to participate in church convocations or commissions dealing with these issues, or in the governing structures of their own denominations, to which they could bring needed insights.

It has been my personal good fortune to have been offered a number of such opportunities by my own denomination. These have included membership in a committee charged with responsibility for restructuring the denomination's central agencies and a committee to plan a denomination-wide young adult convention; an opportunity to teach a class on young adults at a conference of civilian churchmen; and invitations to participate in consultations on various non-military issues, as well as presbytery and synod assignments. It has been my observation, first, that my fellow-churchmen generally express surprise that a military chaplain should be participating in such assignments, and second, that few of my fellow-chaplains have been offered similar opportunities.

Not only the chaplains, but the churches as well, would benefit from greatly expanded interaction, which would bring more churchmen into chaplaincy affairs and more chaplains into the affairs of the church at large.

PROFESSIONAL IDENTITY OF CHAPLAINS

One final issue will be addressed in this attempt to pull together the role of the churches and the role of the military in the future of the chaplaincy. Much has been said earlier in this book about the professional identity of chaplains. The issue has often been discussed, both by chaplains and by churchmen, in terms of the chaplain's membership in his two institutions, the church and the military. Is he primarily a clergyman or a military officer? It is to be hoped that this book has made clear the primacy of the church relationship. He is not only primarily but fully a clergyman. His professional identity is established by the church. While he is at the same time fully a military officer, conducting his ministry within the unique military environment, his mission within the military is still determined by the church.

There is another aspect of the identity question, however, which should also be addressed: the identity of the chaplaincy as a specialized ministry within the clergy. Since the beginning of the Second World War more than thirty years ago, there has seldom been a time when the number of chaplains serving in the armed forces was less than three thousand. We noted at the conclusion of the chapter on the shape of military ministry that the churches have in the past tended to think of the chaplaincy as identical with civilian parish ministry, and have failed to take account of its uniqueness as a specialized kind of ministry.

The kind of partnership we have been suggesting between the churches and the military in providing continuing education programs for chaplains may well lead to a rethinking of the whole field of education for chaplains. Seminaries in which specialized departments of chaplaincy studies would give prospective chaplains the same preparation for dealing with the military environment and its structures now given prospective parochial clergymen for dealing with the parish church environment and its structures are long overdue. Such seminaries would certainly be sought out by those whose calling to the ministry and whose vocational goal has from the beginning pointed toward chaplaincy. A considerable body of scholarly work on this branch of ministry now exists, but in the absence of scholarly centers for such research and writing, it is scattered and fragmented. The considerable number of chaplains who each year are sent by the services for graduate study find few institutions offering courses of study designed for their needs. They must improvise and make do with courses intended for other fields of ministry.

The churches might also rethink their requirement that a chaplaincy candidate spend two, three, or four years in a civilian parish before endorsement can be granted him. Prior to and during World War II, seminary graduates in most churches were allowed to go directly into the chaplaincy for which they had been preparing. Gradually in the postwar period, however, most denominations established such parish-experience requirements.

One unfortunate result of the requirement has been an overall increase in the average age of chaplains. With the educational requirement establishing a relatively mature age for entry into the ministerial profession to begin with, the addition of two to four years in a civilian parish, followed sometimes by an additional wait for a denominational quota or an opening in the chosen service, makes young chaplains extremely rare. The result is that one of the churches' young adult ministries is effectively barred to clergymen who are themselves young adults. One of the most physically demanding of all ministries—with shipboard duty, highline transfers, and life in the field with troops—is effectively barred to clergymen in their period of greatest physical vigor.

Another result has been to blunt the motivational drive of all but the most determined chaplaincy candidates. They are required to take a detour into parish ministry, and then must uproot their families and change vocational directions after spending enough time to become acclimated to parish ministry. The reverse side of the same coin is the encouraging of chaplaincy applications from those who have not been happy with or who have "failed" in their initial parish church experiences.

If the parish experience requirement is based on a desire to root the chaplain more firmly in his own denomination before allowing him to enter an ecumenical ministry as a representative of his church, this is undoubtedly justifiable from the denominational perspective, but ought to be so labeled. To justify it on the grounds of ensuring maturity is specious; civilian parishes should not be required to absorb all ministerial immaturity—the services might as well accept their share. There is no substitute for experience, but a young chaplain might just as well make his initial mistakes on the military as on a civilian congregation.

We have examined in some detail in this book the nature of military ministry—the unique setting in which it takes place, the characteristics of the persons with whom it takes place and the kind of life they lead, the shape of the ministry that results, its special problems and its special challenges. It will become a more effective ministry if the churches recognize its uniqueness and encourage the development of its own professional identity within the ministerial profession.

Since the height of the Vietnamese War, as we have noted before, the number of men and women in the armed forces has decreased from more than three million to approximately two million. What is striking, however, is not the one million reduction, but the two million left—the fact that two million men and women in uniform is normality for our times. No American under forty can remember a period when it was otherwise. The kind of society in which two million people in the armed forces is normal should and does rest uneasily on the conscience of the church. But there it is. And there the church is, too, and there it has been, in a significant way, for more than thirty years.

In the last thirty years, more than three thousand clergymen in uniform at any given time has also been normality. That represents a sizeable portion of the clergy. For the foreseeable future a continued American role as a world power, and therefore continued large military forces, are expected by all of us. The churches work and pray for the time when peace will be so firmly established throughout the world that armed forces are unnecessary. They may deplore deeply the fact that these are still times, despite the spirit of détente, in which our nation feels that it must maintain such a military establishment. But that is our present reality. As long as substantial numbers of America's finest young adults spend part of their youth in the military and many Americans pursue military careers, the ministries of the church must follow them. The chaplains are the representatives of the churches in this important endeavor. The interest, support, and concern of the churches will make them authentic and effective representatives.

Notes

CHAPTER 1

1. Harvey G. Cox, Jr., ed., *Military Chaplains, From a Religious Military to a Military Religion* (New York: American Report Press, 1972).

2. George H. Williams, "The Chaplaincy in the Armed Forces of the United States of America in Historical and Ecclesiastical Perspective," in *Military Chaplains*, pp. 11–57.

3. Dennis C. Kinlaw, "An Analysis of their Work and the Sequential Derivation of Training Objectives for Senior Chaplains" (Doctoral Dissertation, George Washington University, 1973), pp. 40–48; Also, Alexander B. Aronis, "A Summary of Research Literature on the Military Chaplain," *The Chaplain*, 29:2 (Summer, 1972), pp. 6–16.

4. Waldo W. Burchard, "The Role of the Military Chaplain," (Doctoral Dissertation, University of California at Berkeley, 1953).

5. Waldo W. Burchard, "Role Conflicts of Military Chaplains," *Religion, Society and the Individual: An Introduction to the Sociology of Religion*, J. Milton Yinger, ed. (New York: The Macmillan Company, 1957), p. 589.

6. "The Position of the United Presbyterian Church in the U.S.A. on the Practice of Having Ministers of our Church Serve as Military Chaplains Paid by the State," (Washington: Department of Chaplains and Service Personnel, United Presbyterian Church, 1965); Kermit D. Johnson, "A Study of Various Role Expectations for the U. S. Army Chaplain," (Unpublished research paper presented to the faculty of the U. S. Army Command and General Staff College, Fort Leavenworth, Kansas, 1969); Leonard Ahrnsbrak, "Role Conflicts among Navy Chaplains in Light of American Civil Religion," (Unpublished term paper, submitted to Samuel W. Blizzard, Princeton Theological Seminary, Princeton, N. J., 1971); Alexander B. Aronis, "A Comparative Study of the Opinions of Navy Chaplains and their Commanding Officers on Role Expectations, Deficiencies, and Preferred In-Service Education for Navy Chaplains," (Doctoral Dissertation, The American University, 1971).

7. Gordon C. Zahn, *The Military Chaplaincy: A Study of Role Tension in the Royal Air Force* (Toronto, Canada: University of Toronto Press, 1969).

8. *Ibid.*, p. 241 and pp. 232–34.

9. The term "Chaplain Corps," used throughout this book to denote the total group of chaplains in a particular service, is a Navy term. The Army chaplaincy is known technically as the "Chaplains Branch." The Air Force term is "Chaplains Service."

10. A. P. Stokes, *Church and State in the United States*, Vol. I (New York: Harper and Brothers, 1950), p. 269.

11. J. T. Headley, *Chaplains and Clergy of the Revolution* (New York: Charles Scribner, 1864), p. 58.

12. Williams, p. 19.

13. J. C. Fitzpatrick, ed., *The Writings of George Washington from the Original Manuscript Sources*, Vol. V (Washington: U. S. Government Printing Office, 1932), pp. 244–45.

14. Williams, pp. 16–23.

15. Clifford M. Drury, *The History of the Chaplain Corps, United States Navy*, Vol. I (Washing-

ton: Bureau of Naval Personnel, 1949), p. 63. Most of the remainder of this historical sketch is drawn either from Drury or from the Williams essay already cited.

16. Navy Records Collection III: May, 1853:208; quoted by Drury, p. 75.

17. Williams, p. 49.

18. Drury, p. 144.

19. *Ibid.*, p. 167.

20. *Field Manual* No. 16–5 of 26 December 1967, Section 2–8.

21. U. S. Navy *Chaplains Manual,* OPNAVINST 1730, 1, Section 1202. The original draft of this manual was written by the author.

22. *Ministries to Military Personnel,* Report of a United Church task force to the Ninth General Synod, St. Louis, Missouri, June 22–26, 1973, (Philadelphia: United Church Press, 1973), p. 5.

23. *Ministries,* pp. 61–62.

24. *Ibid.*, pp. 63–64.

25. *Ibid.*, pp. 60–61.

26. *Ibid.*, p. 82.

27. *Ibid.*, p. 87.

28. *Ibid.*, p. 91.

29. The Episcopal study was authorized by the Executive Council in 1974, in response to a Resolution passed by the House of Bishops at the 1973 General Convention. A task force, made up of persons nominated by the Episcopal Peace Fellowship and the Office of the Bishop for the Armed Forces, began work in December 1974. The 1972 Convention of the Disciples of Christ defeated a proposal that the Convention declare itself a "peace church" and withdraw all support from the chaplaincy. An *ad hoc* study (not mandated by the denomination) was undertaken by the Chaplaincy Commission of the church. The United Methodist Church in its 1972 General Conference mandated a study of all Specialized Ministries and Appointments, including not only ministry to military personnel but all other non-parish ministries, for report to the 1976 General Conference.

30. Aronis, "A Comparative Study," pp. 82–90.

CHAPTER 2

1. The introductory section of this chapter is reprinted, with revisions by the author, from Richard G. Hutcheson, Jr., "The Chaplain and the Structures of the Military Society," *Church, State and Chaplaincy,* A. R. Appelquist, ed. (Washington: General Commission on Chaplains, 1969), pp. 57–69.

2. Erving Goffman, "On the Characteristics of Total Institutions," *Asylums* (Garden City, N. Y.: Doubleday and Company, Anchor Books, 1961), pp. 3–124.

3. *Ibid.*, pp. 116–117.

4. *Ibid.*, pp. 14–43.

5. *Ibid.*, pp. 45–46.

6. These are Navy and Marine Corps terms for the process by which non-judicial punishment is meted out for minor offenses, under the Uniform Code of Military Justice.

7. John W. Brinsfield, "A Summer in Newport: Summary Paper No. One," (Mimeographed report, 26 July 1967). The author of this report is now an active duty Army chaplain.

CHAPTER 3

1. Richard G. Hutcheson, Jr., "An Examination of the Value System Reflected by the Sensitivity and Encounter Group Movement in Adult Education, 1950–1970" (Doctoral Dissertation, The American University, Washington, D. C., 1971).

2. Cyril N. Parkinson, *Parkinson's Law* (Boston: Houghton-Mifflin Co., 1957).

3. Lawrence J. Peter and Raymond Hull, *The Peter Principle* (New York: William Morrow and Co., 1969).

4. Charles Perrow, *Organizational Analysis: A Sociological View* (Belmont, California: Brooks/Cole Publishing Co., 1970), pp. 50–91, contains an excellent discussion of non-bureaucratic models and the bureaucratizing tendency.

5. James D. Anderson, *To Come Alive! A New Proposal for Revitalizing the Local Church* (New York: Harper and Row, 1973). Although current organizational studies focus on local churches as volunteer organizations, it might be noted that certain church hierarchies and national-level organizations are themselves bureaucracies following the classic pattern. The other major source of Weber's observations (besides the Prussian Army) was the Roman Catholic Church of his day.

6. Max Weber, *The Theory of Social and Economic Organization,* trans. A. M. Henderson and Talcott Parsons; Talcott Parsons, ed. (New York: Oxford University Press, 1947), pp. 324–340.

7. This summary of Weber's analysis of the characteristics of bureaucracy is based in part on discussions in Amitai Etzioni, *Modern Organizations* (Englewood Cliffs, N. J.: Prentice-Hall, Inc., 1964), pp. 50–54; and Peter M. Blau and Marshall W. Meyer, *Bureaucracy in Modern Society,* 2nd ed. (New York: Random House, 1971), pp. 18–23. The quotations are from Weber, *Theory of Social and Economic Organization,* pp. 229–230.

8. *Ministries to Military Personnel,* Report of a United Church task force to the Ninth General Synod, St. Louis, Missouri, June 22–26, 1973 (Philadelphia: United Church Press, 1973), p. 81.

9. *Navy Regulations,* 0722.

10. Army Regulation 165–20 (7).

11. *Army Field Manual* 16–5, pp. 7–8.

12. Etzioni, p. 3. His definition is based on that of Talcott Parsons in *Structure and Process in Modern Societies* (Glencoe, Ill.: The Free Press, 1960), p. 17.

13. Emile Durkheim, *The Elementary Forms of Religious Life,* trans. Joseph Swain (New York: The Free Press, 1965), pp. 474–475.

14. Clifford Ingle, *The Military Chaplain as a Counselor* (Kansas City: Central Seminary Press, 1953), p. 16.

15. Martin Siegel, "Being a Chaplain in Today's Military," in *Military Chaplains,* p. 111.

16. Richard Emerson, "Power-Dependence Relations," *American Sociological Review,* vol. 27 (February, 1962), pp. 31–40.

17. James D. Thompson, *Organizations in Action* (New York: McGraw-Hill Book Co., 1967), pp. 30–34.

18. Burton R. Clark, *Adult Education in Transition* (Berkeley, Calif.: University of California Press, 1956); cited in Thompson, p. 31.

19. Such charges are quoted by Jack C. Landau, "Military's Corps of Chaplains under Fire from Church Groups," *Baltimore News American,* July 17, 1973.

20. William A. Gamson, *Power and Discontent* (Homewood, Ill.: The Dorsey Press, 1968).

21. Thompson, p. 33.

CHAPTER 4

1. Navy Records Collection, III: Nov. and Dec. 1871:66; quoted by Clifford M. Drury, *History of the Chaplain Corps*, vol. 1 (Washington: Bureau of Naval Personnel, 1949), pp. 110–111.

2. Drury, *History of the Chaplain Corps*, vol. 2 (Washington: Bureau of Naval Personnel, 1952), pp. 254–255.

3. L. Alexander Harper, "A New Look at the Chaplain's Role," General Commission on Chaplains pamphlet, 1957; reprinted, with revisions by the author, from *Christian Century*, February 13, 1957.

4. CINCLANTFLT INSTRUCTION 1730.3 of 9 May 1973.

5. Drury, v. 1, p. 30.

6. *Ibid.*, pp. 54–55.

7. *Ibid.*, pp. 90–91.

8. *Ibid.*, p. 40.

9. *Ibid.*, p. 149.

10. *Ibid.*, p. 150.

11. Walter Colton, *The Sea and the Sailor* (New York, 1851), quoted in Drury, v. 1, pp. 83–84.

12. The classic military staff organization in an Army or Marine Corps Division consists of G-1 (Personnel), G-2 (Intelligence), G-3 (Operations), and G-4 (Logistics) sections. Comparable staff sections at the regimental level are designated S-1, S-2, S-3, and S-4. The G-5 staff section, added during the Vietnamese War, was designated "Civil Affairs" on Army staffs initially, and later "Civil-Military Operations."

13. John B. Frazier, *The Navy Chaplain's Manual*, 1918, p. 37–38, quoted in Drury, vol. 1, p. 174.

14. Dennis C. Kinlaw, "An Analysis of their Work and the Sequential Derivation of Training Objectives for Senior Naval Chaplains" (Doctoral Dissertation, George Washington University, Washington, D. C., 1973), pp. 162–165.

15. U. S. Navy *Chaplains Manual*, OPNAVIST 1730.1 par. 6401 and 6402.

16. Robert J. Havighurst, *Human Development and Education* (New York: David McKay Co., 1953). A summary of the developmental tasks of early adulthood is found on pp. 257–267.

17. Erik Erikson, *Childhood and Society*, 2nd ed. (New York: W. W. Norton and Co., 1964) and *Young Man Luther* (New York: W. W. Norton and Co., 1958).

18. This discussion of the LEAD program is based largely on Edward J. Hemphill, Jr., "The Laymen's Enrichment and Development (LEAD) Program," *Chaplain Corps Professional Papers*, V (Washington: Chief of Chaplains, 1969), pp. 1–12.

19. Donald B. Harris, *CREDO—The Second Year*, Brochure (San Diego, California: CREDO, 1972), p. 9.

20. Harris, p. 17.

21. CREDO Newsletter, May, 1974, p. 7.

22. This section is reprinted, with revisions by the author, from Richard G. Hutcheson, Jr., "Parish of Transients: Military Mobility and the Chaplain," *The Chaplain*, June, 1968, pp. 26–30.

23. Thomas R. Pocock, "Closed Circuit TV in USS WILLIAM H. STANDLEY (DLG 32)" Unpublished report to Chief of Chaplains, November, 1973.
24. Harper, p. 4.

CHAPTER 5

1. Randolph N. Jonakait, "Is the Military Chaplaincy Constitutional?" in *Military Chaplains*, pp. 129–137.
2. Randolph N. Jonakait, "The Abuses of the Military Chaplaincy," (Mimeographed Report, American Civil Liberties Union, May, 1973).
3. *School District of Abingdon Township, Pa. v. Schemp*, 374 U. S. 203 (1963).
4. *Abingdon v. Schemp*.
5. *Engel v. Vitale*, 370 U. S. 203 (1963).
6. Charles L. Greenwood, "The Constitutionality of the Military Chaplaincy: A Historical Study," *Church and Society* (March-April, 1974), pp. 25–35.
7. *Ministries to Military Personnel*, Report of a United Church Task Force to the Ninth General Synod, St. Louis, Mo., June 22–26, 1973 (Philadelphia: United Church Press, 1973), p. 11.
8. John C. Bennett, *Christians and the State* (New York: Charles Scribner's Sons, 1958), p. 229.
9. John L. Rand, "The Development of the Military Chaplain in Great Britain," *The Chaplain*, 25:3 (May-June, 1968), pp. 10–16.
10. William J. Hughes, "The Military Chaplain in England, 1640–1660," *The Chaplain*, 29:3 (Fall, 1972), pp. 6–25.
11. Ben E. Spurlock, "The Revolutionary Chaplains," *The Chaplain*, 21:6 (December, 1964), pp. 3–7.
12. Eugene F. Klug, "The Chaplaincy in American Public Life," *The Chaplain*, 23:1 (February, 1966), pp. 15–45; reprinted from *Church and State Under God*, Albert G. Huegli, ed. (St. Louis, Mo.: Concordia Publishing House, 1964).
13. Klaus J. Hermann, "Some Considerations on the Constitutionality of the U. S. Military Chaplaincy," *The Chaplain*, 22:3 (June, 1965), pp. 32–47.
14. Hermann, p. 35.
15. Klug, p. 18.
16. Hermann, p. 36.
17. James Madison, *Detached Memoranda*, quoted in Klug, pp. 22–23.
18. Clifford M. Drury, *The History of the Chaplain Corps*, vol. 1 (Washington: Bureau of Naval Personnel, 1949), p. 10.
19. Drury, p. 24.
20. *Ibid.*, p. 43.
21. Drury, p. 43.
22. George H. Williams, "The Chaplaincy in the Armed Forces of the United States of America in Historical and Ecclesiastical Perspective," in *Military Chaplains*, p. 20, quoting from Washington's Order of 9 July 1776 and statement of 1777, in Anson Phelps Stokes, *Church and State in the United States*, 3 vol. (New York: Harper and Row, 1950), v. 1, p. 271 f.
23. Williams, pp. 25–26.
24. Hermann, p. 35.

25. Williams, p. 37.

26. Williams, p. 24.

27. Klug, p. 23.

28. Williams, pp. 27–28.

29. Drury, pp. 67–68.

30. Drury, pp. 68–69.

31. Drury, p. 69.

32. Drury, p. 144.

33. This section is reprinted with revisions by the author, from Richard G. Hutcheson, Jr., "Religious Pluralism and the Navy Chaplaincy," *U. S. Naval Institute Proceedings,* XCVIII, 2/828, February, 1972.

34. Spencer D. McQueen, "A Half-Century in Behalf of the Chaplaincy," *The Chaplain,* 24:3 (May-June, 1967), pp. 4–42; p. 7.

35. Drury, p. 167.

36. McQueen, pp. 8–9.

37. Andrew Jensen with Martin Abramson, *The Trial of Chaplain Jensen* (New York: Arbor House, 1974), gives an account of this widely publicized trial.

CHAPTER 6

1. George H. Williams, "The Chaplaincy in the Armed Forces of the United States of America in Historical and Ecclesiastical Perspective," in *Military Chaplains,* pp. 12–13.

2. Williams, p. 32.

3. Gordon C. Zahn, "Sociological Impressions of the Chaplaincy," in *Military Chaplains,* p. 78.

4. Randolph N. Jonakait, "The Abuses of the Military Chaplaincy," (Mimeographed Report, American Civil Liberties Union, May, 1973), p. 7.

5. Peter Berger and Daniel Pinard, "Military Religion: An Analysis of Educational Materials Disseminated by Chaplains," in *Military Chaplains,* pp. 87–108.

6. Berger and Pinard, p. 91.

7. The research behind this essay leaves something to be desired; the fact that Berger permitted himself to collaborate on the essay (a note reveals that the research was done by Pinard) and that it was included in the book reveals, perhaps, the depth of feeling aroused by the Vietnamese War. While the introduction of the essay advises that "we do not want to burden these pages with the dreary methodological discussions to which sociologists are professionally addicted" (p. 88), a footnote does give some dreary methodological information. It reveals that "we asked soldiers of our acquaintance to send us all the materials they could get from their chaplains; these materials come from *three* posts [emphasis added] in different parts of the country" (p. 158). The only other source mentioned is materials "examined in libraries" (p. 158)—presumably on the assumption that chaplains "disseminate" materials from the same libraries. An examination of all data actually referred to in the essay reveals thirty-eight citations, of which nine are from a single pamphlet. There are citations from six other pamphlets published for servicemen, from six general religious pamphlets not related to servicemen but presumably distributed by chaplains, from two editorials in *The Chaplain* magazine, and from two articles in general circulation magazines. The total sources, then, are thirteen pamphlets from three Army bases, and four magazine articles.

8. Robert N. Bellah, "Civil Religion in America," *Daedalus,* 96:1, Winter 1967, pp. 1–21.

9. John Dewey, *A Common Faith* (New Haven: Yale University Press, 1934).

10. Will Herberg, *Protestant—Catholic—Jew: An Essay in American Religious Sociology,* rev. ed. (Garden City, New York: Anchor Books, 1960), p. 75.

11. Bellah, p. 12.

12. Dewey, p. 27.

13. The General Commission on Chaplains entered actively into the litigation, submitting an *amicus curiae* brief opposing compulsory church attendance.

CHAPTER 7

1. Letter to Governor Dinwiddie of 12 June 1757; John C. Fitzpatrick, ed., *The Writings of George Washington,* 39 vols. (Washington: U. S. Government Printing Office, 1931–44) II, 56; cited by Williams, p. 18.

2. John B. Frazier, *The Navy Chaplain's Manual,* 1918, p. 40, quoted by Drury, *History of the Chaplain Corps,* vol. I, p. 174.

3. BUPERS INSTRUCTION 1730.7, Subject: The Protection of Moral Standards.

4. *Moral Leadership: the Protection of Moral Standards and Character Education* Program (NAVPERS 15890: Washington, D. C.: Bureau of Naval Personnel, 1959), p. 54. Most of the historical material given here is drawn from this publication and from Richard G. Hutcheson, Jr., "An Examination of the Problem of Motivation in Character Education, with Particular Reference to the Character Education Program of the United States Navy and Marine Corps" (Master's thesis, Union Theological Seminary, New York, 1955).

5. *The Navy Chaplain* (NAVPERS 10804: Washington, D. C.: Bureau of Naval Personnel, 1949), p. 42.

6. *U. S. Navy and Marine Corps Character Education Program,* Bureau of Naval Personnel Brochure, 1954, 8th unnumbered page.

7. *Our Moral and Spiritual Growth Here and Now: Guide Lines for Discussion Leaders,* United States Navy and Marine Corps Character Education Series II, (NAVPERS 91962: Washington, D. C.: Bureau of Naval Personnel, 1953).

8. *Because of You:* United States Navy and Marine Corps Character Education Program Series III, for Forces Afloat. (NAVPERS 15874: Washington, D. C.: Chaplains Division, Bureau of Naval Personnel, 1955), p. 5.

9. *Because of You,* p. 22.

10. *My Life in the Far East:* Character Education Presentations Designed for use in U. S. Navy and Marine Corps in the Far East, Series No. 5 (NAVPERS 15881-A: Washington, D. C.: Bureau of Naval Personnel, 1955), p. 3.

11. *This is My Life:* United States Navy and Marine Corps Character Education Program, Series Four (NAVPERS 15884: Washington, D. C.: Bureau of Naval Personnel, 1956), pp. 25–39.

12. *This is My Life,* pp. 59–70.

13. *Moral Leadership* (NAVPERS 15890), pp. 89–90.

14. The term "church-oriented religion" is used in this discussion to distinguish from civil religion those communities of faith to which Americans are committed in their own churches and personal lives. It is an inadequate term, but it is considered preferable to the term "official faiths" (Protestantism, Catholicism, and Judaism) used by Herberg to draw the same distinction, or "Judeo-Christian tradition" used by Ahrnsbrak (see citation below). Bellah draws the same distinction between civil religion and "Christianity."

15. Leonard L. Ahrnsbrak, "Role Conflicts Among Navy Chaplains in Light of American Civil Religion," (Research paper, Princeton Theological Seminary, May 21, 1971).

16. All quotations are from Ahrnsbrak, pp. 20–25.

17. Ahrnsbrak, pp. 46–47.

18. Thesis Theological Cassettes, Chief of Chaplains Continuing Education Tape, "Civil Religion and the Navy Chaplain," vol. 4, no. 2, December, 1973.

19. See J. Milton Yinger, *The Scientific Study of Religion* (New York: The Macmillan Co., 1970), pp. 437–439.

20. Ahrnsbrak, pp. 60–61.

CHAPTER 8

1. The LEAD program was discussed in Chapter 4. Information regarding it comes from Edward J. Hemphill, Jr., "The Laymen's Enrichment and Development (LEAD) Program," *Chaplain Corps Professional Papers*, V (Washington: Chief of Chaplains, 1969), pp. 1–12.

2. Richard G. Hutcheson, Jr., "An Examination of the Value System Reflected by the Sensitivity and Encounter Group Movement in Adult Education, 1950–1970" (Doctoral Dissertation, The American University, Washington, D. C., 1971), pp. 140–195.

3. Warren Newman, "An Overview of Human Factors Training Programs at the U. S. Naval Academy" (Unpublished Report, Annapolis, Md., U. S. Naval Academy, 1972).

4. Second Marine Division Order 1730.5 of 2 January 1973.

5. George C. Wilson, "Midshipmen Study Morality," *Washington Post*, May 18,1975.

6. Army Regulation 600–30 of 19 October 1971, Par. I.2a and I.2b.

7. AR 600–30, I.6c(1).

8. AR 600–30, I.2.

9. "Human Self-Development: Manhood," D. A. Pamphlet No. 165–6–1 of 19 February 1973.

10. CNO/VCNO Action Sheet 214–72 of 14 April 1972; subject: Chaplain Corps Zero Base Study.

11. Alexander B. Aronis, "A Comparative Study of the Opinions of Navy Chaplains and their Commanding Officers on Role Expectations, Deficiencies, and Preferred In-Service Education for Navy Chaplains" (Doctoral Dissertation, The American University, Washington, D. C., 1971), pp. 74, 106–109.

12. "Chaplain Corps Zero Base Study" (Unpublished Study, Chief of Chaplains, Bureau of Naval Personnel, 1972), pp. 13–14. Most of the preceding discussion of role definition is taken from this study, from a portion written by the author.

13. CINCLANTFLT INSTRUCTION 1730.3 of 9 May 1973.

CHAPTER 9

1. This section, with some modifications, comes from an article by the author, "Should the Military Chaplaincy be Civilianized?" originally published in *Christian Century*, 90:39, October 31, 1973, 1072–1076.

2. *Ministries to Military Personnel:* Report of a United Church task force to the Ninth General Synod, St. Louis, Mo., June 22–26, 1973 (Philadelphia: United Church Press, 1973).

3. Randolph N. Jonakait, "The Abuses of the Military Chaplaincy," (Mimeographed Report, American Civil Liberties Union, New York, May, 1973).

4. Robert McAfee Brown, "Military Chaplaincy as Ministry," in *Military Chaplains*, pp. 139–147.

5. "Armed Forces Chaplains: All Civilians?" *The Chaplain*, 29:1, 1972, pp. 1–86.

6. Lester Kinsolving, "Inside Religion: Military Chaplains Targeted," *Norfolk Virginian-Pilot*, Dec. 23, 1973.

7. Ben E. Spurlock, "The Revolutionary Chaplains," *The Chaplain*, 21:6, December, 1964, p. 6.

8. Eugene F. Klug, "The Chaplaincy in American Public Life," *The Chaplain*, 23:1, February, 1966, quoting from Report No. 124, House of Representatives, 31st Congress, 1st session, Vol. 1, No. 583.

9. "The Position of the United Presbyterian Church in the USA on the Practice of Having Ministers of our Church Serve as Military Chaplains Paid by the State," Adopted by the 177th General Assembly of the United Presbyterian Church in the USA, May 24, 1965. (Pamphlet, Department of Chaplains and Service Personnel, 1965).

10. United States Navy *Chaplains Manual*, Sections 1205 and 3101.

11. "The Position of the United Presbyterian Church."

12. "A Study of the Relationship, Responsibility, and Ministry of the Presbyterian Church, U. S., to Military Personnel" (Mimeographed Report, Chaplains Advisory Council, Board of National Ministries, Atlanta, 1968), p. 20.

13. "Mark-up by the House Appropriations Committee on the DOD FY-74 Appropriations Bill," p. 58.

14. Senate Report No. 93–617, Department of Defense Appropriation Bill, 1974, p. 66.

15. "Study of the Relationship, Responsibility and Ministry of the Presbyterian Church, U. S." pp. 2–3.

16. *Ibid.*, pp. 13–14. Twenty-three presbyteries were contacted, of which 69% (16) responded. Questionaires were sent by presbyteries to 71 churches, of which 70% (50) responded.

17. U. S. Navy *Chaplains Manual*, par. 8404.

18. The author originated and was the local director of this program.

19. The Chaplains' Boards are, in effect, research and development groups. The Army and Air Force chaplaincies have such boards, and the Navy equivalent is its Chaplain Corps Planning Group.

20. "Mark-up by the House Armed Services Committee on the DOD FY-74 Appropriations Bill," pp. 49–50.